Hester Lynch Piozzi

Observations and Reflections Made in the Course of a Journey

Through

France, Italy and Germany

Hester Lynch Piozzi

Observations and Reflections Made in the Course of a Journey Through
France, Italy and Germany

ISBN/EAN: 9783744720458

Printed in Europe, USA, Canada, Australia, Japan

Cover: Foto ©Andreas Hilbeck / pixelio.de

More available books at **www.hansebooks.com**

OBSERVATIONS AND REFLECTIONS

MADE IN THE COURSE OF A

JOURNEY

THROUGH

FRANCE, ITALY, AND GERMANY.

By HESTER LYNCH-PIOZZI.

IN TWO VOLUMES.

VOL. II.

LONDON:

Printed for A. STRAHAN; and T. CADELL in the Strand.

M DCC LXXXIX.

OBSERVATIONS AND REFLECTIONS

MADE IN A JOURNEY THROUGH

France, Italy, and Germany.

NAPLES.

ON the tenth day of this month we arrived early at Naples, for I think it was about two o'clock in the morning; and sure the providence of God preserved us, for never was such weather seen by me since I came into the world; thunder, lightning, storm at sea, rain and wind, contending for mastery, and combining to extinguish the torches bought to light us the last stage: Vesuvius, vomiting fire, and pouring torrents of red hot lava down its sides, was the only object visible; and *that* we saw plainly in the afternoon thirty miles off, where I asked a Franciscan friar, If it was the famous volcano? "Yes," replied he, he, "that's our mountain, which throws up money for us, by calling foreigners to see the extraordinary effects of so surprising a phænomenon." The weather was quiet then, and we had no notion of passing such a horrible night; but an hour after dark, a storm came on, which was really dreadful to endure; or even look upon: the blue lightning, whose colour shewed the nature of the original minerals from which she drew her existence, shone round us in a broad expanse from time to time, and sudden darkness followed in an instant: no object then but the fiery river could be seen, till another flash discovered the waves tossing and breaking, at a height I never saw before.

Nothing sure was ever more sublime or awful than our entrance into Naples at the dead hour we arrived, when not a whisper was to be heard in the streets, and not a glimpse of light was left to guide us, except the small lamp hung now and then at a high window before a favourite image of the Virgin.

My poor maid had by this time nearly lost her wits with terror, and the French valet, crushed with fatigue, and covered with

with rain and sea-spray, had just life enough left to exclaim—" *Ah, Madame! il me semble que nous sommes venus icy exprès pour voir la la fin du monde*.*"

The Ville de Londres inn was full, and could not accommodate our family; but calling up the people of the Crocelle, we obtained a noble apartment, the windows of which look full upon the celebrated bay which washes the wall at our door. Caprea lies opposite the drawing-room or gallery, which is magnificent; and my bed-chamber commands a complete view of the mountain, which I value more, and which called me the first night twenty times away from sleep and supper, though never so in want of both as at that moment surely.

Such were my first impressions of this wonderful metropolis, of which I had been always reading summer descriptions, and had regarded somehow as an Hesperian garden, an earthly paradise, where delicacy and softness subdued every danger, and general sweetness captivated

---

* Lord, Madam! why we came here on purpose sure to see the end of the world.

every sense;—nor have I any reason yet to say it will not still prove so, for though wet, and weary, and hungry, we wanted no fire, and found only inconvenience from that they lighted on our arrival. It was the fashion at Florence to struggle for a Terreno, but here we are all perched up one hundred and forty two steps from the level of the land or sea; large balconies, apparently well secured, give me every enjoyment of a prospect, which no repetition can render tedious: and here we have agreed to stay till Spring, which, I trust, will come out in this country as soon as the new year calls it.

Our eagerness to see sights has been repressed at Naples only by finding every thing a sight; one need not stir out to look for wonders sure, while this amazing mountain continues to exhibit such various scenes of sublimity and beauty at exactly the distance one would chuse to observe it from; a distance which almost admits examination, and certainly excludes immediate fear. When in the silent night, however, one listens to its groaning; while hollow sighs, as of gigantic sorrow,

sorrow, are often heard distinctly in my apartment; nothing can surpass one's sensations of amazement, except the consciousness that custom will abate their keenness: I have not, however, yet learned to lie quiet, when columns of flame, high as the mountain's self, shoot from its crater into the clear atmosphere with a loud and violent noise; nor shall I ever forget the scene it presented one day to my astonished eyes, while a thick cloud, charged heavily with electric matter, passing over, met the fiery explosion by mere chance, and went off in such a manner as effectually baffles all verbal description, and lasted too short a time for a painter to seize the moment, and imitate its very strange effect. Monsieur de Vollaire, however, a native of France, long resident in this city, has obtained, by perpetual observation, a power of representing Vesuvius without that black shadow, which others have thought necessary to increase the contrast, but which greatly takes away all resemblance of its original. Upon reflection it appears to me, that the men most famous at London and Paris for performing tricks with fire have been always Italians in my time, and commonly Neapolitans; no wonder, I should think, Naples would produce prodigious connoisseurs in this way; we have almost perpetual lightning of various colours, according to the soil from whence the vapours are exhaled; sometimes of a pale straw or lemon colour, often white like artificial flame produced by camphor, but oftenest blue, bright as the rays emitted through the coloured liquors set in the window of a chemist's shop in London—and with such thunder!!—" For God's sake, Sir," said I to some of them, " is there no danger of the ships in the harbour here catching fire? why we should all fly up in the air directly, if once these flashes should communicate to the room where any of the vessels keep their powder."—" Gunpowder, Madam!" replies the man, amazed; " why if St. Peter and St. Paul came here with gunpowder on board, we should soon drive them out again: don't you know," aded he, " that every ship discharges her contents at such a place (naming it), and never comes into our port with a grain on board?"

The palaces and churches have no share in one's admiration at Naples, who scorns to depend on man, however mighty, however skilful, for *her* ornaments; while Heaven has bestowed

bestowed on her and her *contorni* all that can excite astonishment, all that can impress awe. We have spent three or four days upon Pozzuoli and its environs; its cavern scooped originally by nature's hand, assisted by the armies of Cocceius Nerva—ever tremendous, ever gloomy grotto!—which leads to the road that shews you Ischia, an old volcano, now an island apparently rent asunder by an earthquake, the division too plain to beg assistance from philosophy: this is commonly called the *Grotto di Posilippo* though; you pass through it to go to every place; not without flambeaux, if you would go safely, and avoid the necessity the poor are under, who, driving their carts through the subterranean passage, cry as they meet each other, to avoid jostling, *alla montagna*, or *alla marina, keep to the rock side,* or *keep to the sea side.* It is at the right hand, awhile before you enter this cavern, that climbing up among a heap of bushes, you find a hollow place, and there go down again—it is the tomb of Virgil; and, for other antiquities, I recollect nothing shewed me when at Rome that gave me as complete an idea how things were really carried on in former days, as does the temple of *Shor Apis* at Pozzuoli, where

the

the area is exactly all it ever was; the ring remains where the victim was fastened to; the priests apartments, lavatories, &c. the drains for carrying the beast's blood away, all yet remains as perfect as it is possible. The end of Caligula's bridge too, but that they say is not his bridge, but a mole built by some succeeding emperor—a madder or a wickeder it could not be—though here Nero bathed, and here he buried his mother Agrippina. Here are the centum camera, the prisons employed by that prince for the cruellest of purposes; and here are his country palaces reserved for the most odious ones: here effeminacy learned to subsist without delicacy or shame, hence honour was excluded by rapacity, and conscience stupefied by constant inebriation: here brainsick folly put nature and common sense upon the rack—Caligula in madness courted the moon to his embraces—and Sylla, satiated with blood, retired, and gave a premature banquet to those worms he had so often fed with the flesh of innocence: here dwelt depravity in various shapes, and here Pandora's chambers left scarcely a *Hope* at the bottom that better times should come:—who can write prose

however

however in such places!—let the impossibility of expressing my thoughts any other way excuse the following

VERSES.

I.

First of Achelous' blood,
Fairest daughter of the flood,
Queen of the Sicilian sea,
Beauteous, bright Parthenope!
Syren sweet, whose magic force
Stops the swiftest in his course;
Wisdom's self, when most severe,
Longs to lend a list'ning ear,
Gently dips the fearful oar,
Trembling eyes the tempting shore,
And sighing quits th' enervate coast,
With only half his virtue lost.

II.

Let thy warm, thy wond'rous clime,
Animate my artless rhyme,
Whilst alternate round me rise
Terror, pleasure, and surprise.—
Here th' astonish'd soul surveys
Dread Vesuvius' awful blaze,
Smoke that to the sky aspires,
Heavy hail of solid fires,

Flames

Flames the fruitful fields o'erflowing,
Ocean with the reflex glowing;
Thunder, whose redoubled sound
Echoes o'er the vaulted ground!—
Such thy glories, such the gloom
That conceals thy secret tomb,
Sov'reign of this enchanted sea,
Where sunk thy charms, Parthenope.

III.

Now by the glimm'ring torch's ray
I tread Pozzuoli's cavern'd way—
Hollow grot! that might beseem
Th' Ætnean cyclop, Polypheme:
And here the bat at noonday 'bides,
And here the houseless beggar hides,
While the holy hermit's voice
Glads me with accustom'd noise.
Now I trace, or trav'llers err,
Modest Maro's sepulchre,
Where nature, sure of his intent,
   Is studious to conceal
That eminence he always meant
   We should not see but feel.
While Sannazarius from the steep
Views, well pleas'd, the fertile deep
Give life to them that seize the scaly fry,
And to their poet—*immortality*.

IV.

Next beauteous Baia's warm remains invite
To Nero's stoves my wond'ring sight;
Where palaces and domes destroy'd
Leave a flat unwholesome void:
Where underneath the cooling wave,
Ordain'd pollution's fav'rite spot to lave,
Now hardly heaves the stifled sigh
Hot, hydropic luxury.
Yet, chas'd by Heav'n's correcting hand,
Tho' various crimes have fled the land;
Tho' brutish vice, tyrannic pow'r,
No longer tread the trembling shore,
   Or taint the ambient air;
By destiny's kind care arrang'd,
Th' inhabitants are scarcely chang'd;
For birds obscene, and beasts of prey,
That seek the night and shun the day,
   Still find a dwelling there.

V.

If then beneath the deep profound
Retires unseen the slipp'ry ground;
   If melted metals pour'd from high
A verdant mountain grows by time,
Where frisking kids can browze and climb,
   And softer scenes supply:
Let us who view the varying scene,
And tread th' instructive paths between,

See

> See famish'd Time his fav'rite sons devour,
> Fix'd for an age—then swallow'd in an hour;
> Let us at least be early wise,
> And forward walk with heav'n-fix'd eyes,
> Each flow'ry isle avoid, each precipice despise;
> Till, spite of pleasure, fear, or pain,
> Eternity's firm coast we gain,
> Whence looking back with alter'd eye,
> These fleeting phantoms we'll descry,
> And find alike the song and theme
> Was but—an empty, airy dream.

When one has exhausted all the ideas presented to the mind by the sight of Monte Nuovo, made in one night by the eruption of Solfa Terra, now sunk into itself and almost extinguished; by the lake Avernus; by the Phlegræan fields, where Jupiter killed the giants, with such thunderbolts as fell about our ears the other night I trust, and buried one of them alive under mount Ætna; when one has seen the Sybil's grott, and the Elysian plains, and every seat of fable and of verse; when one has run about repeating Virgil's verses and Claudian's by turns, and handled the hot sand under the cool waves of Baia; when one has seen Cicero's villa and Diana's temple, and talked about antiquities till one is afraid of one's one's own pedantry, and tired of every one's else; it is almost time to recollect realities of more near interest to such of us as are not ashamed of being Christians, and to remember that it was at Pozzuoli St. Paul arrived after the storms he met with in these seas. The wind is still called here *Sieuroc*, *o sia lo vento Greco*; and their manner of pronouncing it led me to think it might possibly be that called in Scripture *Euro*clydon, abbreviated by that grammatical figure, which lops off the concluding syllables. The old Pastor Patrobas too, who received and entertained the Apostle here, lies interred under the altar of an old church at Pozzuoli, made out of the remains of a temple to Jupiter, whose pillars are in good preservation: I was earnest to see the place at least, as every thing named in the New Testament is of true importance, but one meets few people of the same taste: for Romanists take most delight in venerating traditionary heroes, and Calvinists, perhaps too easily disgusted, desire to venerate no heroes at all.

Some curious inscriptions here, to me not legible, shew how this poor country has been overwhelmed by tyrants, earthquakes, Saracens! not to mention the Goths and Vandals, who however left no traces *but* defolation: while, as the prophet Joel fays, " *The ground was as the garden of Eden before them, and behind them a defolate wildernefs.*

These Mahometan invaders, lefs favage, but not lefs cruel, afforded at leaft an unwilling fhelter in that which is now their capital, for the wretched remains of literature. To their mifty envelopement of fcience, fatigued with ftruggling againft perpetual fuffocation, fucceeded impofture, barbarifm, and credulity; with fuperftition at their head, who still keeps her footing in this country: and infpires fuch veneration for St. Januarius, his name, his blood, his ftatue, &c. that the Neapolitans, who are famous for blafphemous oaths, and a facility of taking the moft facred words into their mouths on every, and I may fay, on *no* occafion, are never heard to repeat *his* name without pulling off their hat, or making fome reverential fign of worfhip at the moment. And I have feen Italians from other ftates greatly fhocked at the groffnefs of thefe their unenlightened neighbours, particularly the half-Indian cuftom of burning

figures

figures upon their fkins with gunpowder: thefe figures, large, and oddly difplayed too, according to the coarfe notions of the wearer.

As the weather is exceedingly warm, and there is little need of clothing for comfort, our Lazaroni have fmall care about appearances, and go with a vaft deal of their perfons uncovered, except by thefe ftrange ornaments. The man who rows you about this lovely bay, has perhaps the angel Raphael, or the blefſed Virgin Mary, delineated on one brawny fun-burnt leg, the faint of the town upon the other: his arms reprefent the Glory, or the feven fpirits of God, or fome ftrange things, while a brafs medal hangs from his neck, expreffive of his favourite martyr: whom they confidently affirm is fo madly venerated by thefe poor uninftructed mortals, that when the mountain burns, or any great difafter threatens them, they beg of our Saviour to fpeak to St. Januarius in their behalf, and intreat him not to refufe them his affiftance. Now though all this was told me by friends of the Romifh perfuafion; and told me too with a juft horror of the fuperftitious folly; I think my remarks and inferences were not agreeable to them, when expreffing my

notion

notion that it was only a relick of the adoration originally paid to Janus in Italy, where the ground yielding up its froſt to the ſoft breath of the new year, is not ill-typified by the liquefaction of the blood; a ceremony which has ſucceeded to various Pagan ones celebrated by Ovid in the firſt book of his Faſti. We know from hiſtory too, that perfumes were offered in *January* always, to ſignify the renovation of *ſweets;* and this was ſo neceſſary, that I think Tacitus tells us Thraſea was firſt impeached for abſence at the time of the new year, when in *Janus*'s preſence, &c. good wiſhes were formed for the Emperor's felicity; and no word of ill omen was to be pronounced.—*Cautum erat apud Romanos ne quod mali ominis verbum calendis* Januariis *efferretur;* ſays Pliny: and the *ſtrenæ*, or new-years gifts, called now by the French " les *etrennes*," and practiſed by Lutherans as well as Romaniſts, is the ſelf-ſame veneration of old *Janus*, if fairly traced up to Tatius King of the Sabines, who ſought a laurel bough plucked from the grove of the goddeſs *Strenia*, or *Strenua*, and preſented it to his favourites on the firſt of *January*, from whence the cuſtom arose;

arose; and Symmachus, in his tenth book, twenty-eighth epistle, mentions it clearly when writing to the Emperors Theodosius and Arcadius—" Strenuarum *usus adolevit auctoritate Tatii regis, qui verbenas felicis arboris ex luco Strenuæ anni.*"

Octavius Cæsar took the name of Augustus on the first of January in Janus's temple, by Plancus's advice, as a lucky day; and I suppose our new-year's ode, sung before the King of England, may be derived from the same source. The old Fathers of the Church declaimed aloud against the custom of new-years gifts, because they considered them as of Pagan original. So much for *Les Etrennes*.

As to *St. Januarius*, there certainly was a martyr of that name at Naples, and to him was transferred much of the veneration originally bestowed on the deity from whom he was probably named. One need not however wander round the world with Banks and Solander, or stare so at the accounts given us in Cook's Voyages of *tattowed Indians*, when Naples will shew one the effects of a like operation, very *very* little better executed, on the broad shoulders of numberless Lazaroni; and of this there is no need to examine books for information, he who runs over the Chiaja may read in large characters the grofs fuperftition of the Napolitani, who have no inclination to lofe their old claffical character for lazinefs—

 Et in otia natam
 Parthenopen;

fays Ovid. I wonder however whether our people would work much furrounded by fimilar circumftances; I fancy not: Englifhmen, poor fellows! muft either work or ftarve; thefe folks want for nothing: a houfe would be an inconvenience to them; they like to fleep out of doors, and it is plain they have fmall care for clothing, as many who poffefs decent habiliments enough, I fpeak of the Lazaroni, throw almoft all off till fome holiday, or time of gala, and fit by the feafide playing at moro with their fingers.

 A Florentine nobleman told me once, that he afked one of thefe fellows to carry his portmanteau for him, and offered him a *carline*, no fmall fum certainly to a Neapolitan, and rather more in proportion than an Englifh fhilling; he had not twenty yards to go with it: " *Are you hungry, Mafter?*" cries the fellow. " *No,*" replied Count Manucci,
         " but

"but what of that?"—"*Why then no more am I:*" was the anfwer, "*and it is too hot weather to carry burthens:*" fo turned about upon the other fide, and lay ftill.

This clafs of people, amounting to a number that terrifies one but to think on, fome fay fixty thoufand fouls, and experience confirms no lefs, give the city an air of gaiety and cheerfulnefs, and one cannot help honeftly rejoicing in. The Strada del Toledo is one continual crowd: nothing can exceed the confufion to a walker, and here are little gigs drawn by one horfe, which, without any bit in his mouth, but a ftring tied round his nofe, tears along with inconceivable rapidity a fmall narrow gilt chair, fet between the two wheels, and no fpring to it, nor any thing elfe which can add to the weight; and this flying car is a kind of *fiacre* you pay fo much for a drive in, I forget the fum.

Horfes are particularly handfome in this town, not fo large as at Milan, but very beautiful and fpirited; the cream-coloured creatures, fuch as draw our king's ftate coach, are a common breed here, and fhine like fattin: here are fome too of a fhining filver white,

white, wonderfully elegant; and the ladies upon the Corſo exhibit a variety ſcarcely credible in the colour of their cattle which draw them: but the coaches, harneſs, trappings, &c. are vaſtly inferior to the Milaneſe, whoſe liveries are often ſplendid; whereas the four or five ill-dreſſed ſtrange-looking fellows that diſgrace the Neapolitan equipages ſeem to be valued only for their number, and have very often much the air of Sir John Falſtaff's recruits.

Yeſterday however ſhewed me what I knew not had exiſted—a ſkew-ball or pye-balled aſs, eminently well-proportioned, coated like a racer in an Engliſh ſtud, ſixteen hands and a half high, his colour bay and white in large patches, and his temper, as the proprietor told me, ſingularly docile and gentle. I have longed perhaps to purchaſe few things in my life more earneſtly than this beautiful and uſeful animal, which I might have had too for two pounds fifteen ſhillings Engliſh, but dared not, leſt like Dogberry I ſhould have been written down for an aſs by my merry country folks, who, I remember, could not let the Queen of England

England herself possess in peace a creature of the same kind, but handsomer still, and from a still hotter climate, called the Zebra.

Apropos to quadrupeds, when Portia, in the Merchant of Venice, enumerates her lovers, she names the Neapolitan prince first; who, she says, does nothing, for his part, but talk of his horse, and makes it his greatest boast that he can shoe him himself. This is almost literally true of a nobleman here; and they really do not throw their pains away; for it is surprising to see what command they have their cattle in, though bits are scarcely used among them.

The coat armour of Naples consists of an unbridled horse; and by what I can make out of their character, they much resemble him;

> Qualis ubi abruptis fugit præsæpia vinclis
> Tandem liber æquus, &c. &c. &c.* ;

generous and gay; headstrong and violent in their disposition; easy to turn, but difficult

---

* Freed from his keepers thus with broken reins
The wanton courser prances o'er the plains.
                                        DRYDEN.

to stop. No authority is respected by them when some strong passion animates them to fury: yet lazily quiet, and unwilling to stir till accident rouses them to terror, or rage urges them forward to incredible exertions of suddenly-bestowed strength. In the eruption of 1779, their fears and superstitions rose to such a height, that they seized the French ambassador upon the bridge, tore him almost out of his carriage as he fled from Portici, and was met by them upon the Ponte della Máddalena, where they threatened him with instant death if he did not get out of his carriage, and prostrating himself before the statue of St. Januarius, which stands there, intreat his protection for the city. All this, however, Monsf. le Comte de Clermont D'Amboise did not comprehend a word of; but taking all the money out of his pocket, threw it down, happily for him, at the feet of the figure, and pacified them at once, gaining time by those means to escape their vengeance.

It was, I think, upon some other occasion that Sir William Hamilton's book relates their unworthy treatment of the venerable Archbishop, who refused them the relicks with which

which they had no doubt of saving the menaced town; but every time Vesuvius burns with danger to the city, they scruple not to insult their Sovereign as he flies from it; throwing large stones after his chariot, guards, &c.; making the insurrection, it is sure to occasion, more perilous, if possible, than the volcano itself. And last night when *La Montagna fu cattiva**, as their expression was, our Laquais de Place observed that it might possibly be because so many hereticks and unbelievers had been up it the day before. "Oh! let us," as King David wisely chose, "fall into the hands of God—not into those of "man."

I wished exceedingly to purchase here the genuine account of Massaniello's far-famed sedition and revolt, more dreadful in a certain way than any of the earthquakes which have at different times shaken this hollow-founded country. But my friends here tell me it was suppressed, and burned by the hands of the common executioner, with many chastisements beside bestowed upon the writer, who tried to escape, but found it more prudent to submit to justice.

---

* When the mountain was in *ill-humour*.

Thomas Agnello was the unluckily-adapted name of the mad fisherman who headed the mob on that truly memorable occasion: but it is not an unusual thing here to cut off the first syllable, and by the figure aphærefis alter the appellation entirely. By that device of dropping the *to*, he has been called Massaniello; and this is one of their methods to render the patois of Naples as unintelligible to us, as if we had never seen Italy till now; and one is above all things tormented with their way of pronouncing names. Here are Don and Donna again at this town as at Milan however, because the King of Spain, or *Ré Cattolico*, as these people always call him, has still much influence; and they seem to think nearly as respectfully of him as of their own immediate sovereign, who is however greatly beloved among them; and so he ought to be, for he is the representative of them all. He rides and rows, and hunts the wild boar, and catches fish in the bay, and sells it in the market, as dear as he can too; but gives away the money they pay him for it, and that directly: so that no suspicion of meanness, or of any thing worse than a little rough

rough merriment can be ever attached to his truly-honeſt, open, undeſigning character.

Stories of monarchs ſeldom give me pleaſure, who ſeldom am perſuaded to give credit to tales told of perſons few people have any acceſs to, and whoſe behaviour towards thoſe few is circumſcribed within the laws of inſipid and dull routine; but this prince lives among his ſubjects with the old Roman idea of a window before his boſom I believe. They know the worſt of him is that he ſhoots at the birds, dances with the girls, eats macaroni, and helps himſelf to it with his fingers, and rows againſt the watermen in the bay, till one of them burſt out o'bleeding at the noſe laſt week, with his uncourtly efforts to outdo the King, who won the trifling wager by this accident: conquered, laughed, and leaped on ſhore amidſt the acclamations of the populace, who huzzaed him home to the palace, from whence he ſent double the ſum he had won to the waterman's wife and children, with other tokens of kindneſs. Mean time, while he reſolves to be happy himſelf, he is equally determined to make no man miſerable.

When

When the Emperor and the Grand Duke talked to him of their new projects for reformation in the church, he told them he faw little advantage they brought into *their* ftates by thefe new-fangled notions; that when he was at Florence and Milan, the deuce a Neapolitan could he find in either, while his capital was crowded with refugees from thence; that in fhort they might do *their* way, but he would do his; that he had not now an enemy in the world, public or private; and that he would not make himfelf any for the fake of propagating doctrines he did not underftand, and would not take the trouble to ftudy: that he fhould fay his prayers as he ufed to do, and had no doubt of their being heard, while he only begged bleffings on his beloved people. So if thefe wife brothers-in-law would learn of him to enjoy life, inftead of fhortening it by unneceffary cares, he invited them to fee him the next morning play a great match at tennis.

The truth is, the jolly Neapolitans lead a coarfe life, but it is an unoppreffed one. Never fure was there in any town a greater fhew of abundance: no fettled market in any given place, I think, but every third fhop full of what the French call so properly *ammunition de Bouche*, while whole boars, kids and small calves dangle from a sort of neat scaffolding, all with their skins on, and make a pretty appearance. Poulterers hang up their animals in the feathers too, not lay them on boards plucked, as at London or Venice.

The Strada del Toledo is at least as long as Oxford Road, and straight as Bond-street, very wide too, the houses all of stone, and at least eight stories high. Over the shops live people of fashion I am told, but the persons of particularly high quality have their palaces in other parts of the town; which town at last is not a large one, but full as an egg: and Mr. Clarke, the antiquarian, who resides here always, informed me that the late distresses in Calabria had driven many families to Naples this year, beside single wanderers innumerable; which wonderfully increased the daily throng one sees passing and repassing. To hear the Lazaroni shout and bawl about the streets night and day, one would really fancy one's self in a semi-barbarous nation; and a Milanese officer, who has lived long among them, protested that the manners of the great corresponded in every respect with
the

the idea given of them by the little. His account of female conduct, and that even in the very high ranks, was such as reminded me of Queen Oberea's sincerity, when Sir Joseph Banks joked her about Otoroo. It is however observable, and surely very praiseworthy, that if the Italians are not ashamed of their crimes, neither are they ashamed of their contrition, I saw this very morning an odd scene at church, which, though new to *me*, appeared, perhaps from its frequent repetition, to strike no one but myself.

A lady with a long white dress, and veiled, came in her carriage, which waited for her at the door, with her own arms upon it, and three servants better dressed than is common here, followed and put a lighted taper in her hand. *En cet etât*, as the French say, she moved slowly up the church, looking like Jane Shore in the last act, but not so feeble; and being arrived at the steps of the high altar, threw herself quite upon her face before it, remaining prostrate there at least five minutes, in the face of the whole congregation, who, equally to my amazement, neither stared nor sneered, neither laughed nor lamented,

mented, but minded their own private devotions—no mafs was faying—till the lady rofe, kiffed the fteps, and bathed them with her tears, mingled with fobs of no affected or hypocritical penitence I am fure. Retiring afterwards to her own feat, where fhe waited with others the commencement of the facred office, having extinguifhed her candle, and apparently lighted her heart; I felt mine quite penetrated by her behaviour, and fancied her like our firft parent defcribed by Milton in the fame manner:

> To confefs
> Humbly her faults, and pardon beg; with tears
> Watering the ground, and with her fighs the air
> Frequenting, fent from heart contrite, in fign
> Of forrow unfeign'd, and humiliation meek.

Let not this ftory, however, miflead any one to think that more general decorum or true devotion can be found in churches of the Romifh perfuafion than in ours—quite the reverfe. This burft of penitential piety was in itfelf an indecorous thing; but it is the nature and genius of the people not to mind small matters. Dogs are suffered to run about and dirty the churches all the time divine service is performing; while the crying of babies, and the most indecent methods taken by the women to pacify them, give one still juster offence. There is no treading for spittle and nastiness of one sort or another, in all the churches of Italy, whose inhabitants allow the filthiness of Naples, but endeavour to justify the disorders of other cities; though I do believe nothing ever equalled the Chiesa de Cavalieri at Pisa, in any Christian land. Santa Giustina at Padua, the Redentore at Venice, St Peter's at Rome, and some of the least frequented churches at Milan, are exceptions; they are kept very clean, and do not, by the scandalous neglect of those appointed to keep them, disgrace the beauty of their buildings.

Here has, however, been a dreadful accident which puts such slight considerations out of one's head. A Friar has killed a woman in the church just by the Crocelle inn, for having refused him favours he suspected she had granted to another. No step is taken though towards punishing the murderer, because

cauſe he is *religioſo, è di più cavaliere.* What a miracle that more ſuch outrages are not daily committed in a country where profeſſion of ſanctity, and real high birth, are protections from law and juſtice! Surely nothing but perfect ſobriety and great goodneſs of diſpoſition can be alleged as a reaſon why worſe is not done every day. I ſaid ſo to a gentleman juſt now, who aſſured me the criminal would not eſcape very ſevere caſtigation; and that perhaps the convent would inflict ſuch ſeverities upon that gentleman as would amply ſupply the want of activity in the exertion of civil power.

It is a ſtupid thing not to mention the common dreſs of the ordinary women here, which ladies likewiſe adopt, if they venture out on foot, deſiring not to be known. Two black ſilk petticoats then ſerve entirely to conceal their whole figure; as when both are tied round their waiſt, one is ſuddenly turned up, and as they pull it quick over their heads, a looſe trimming of narrow black gauze drops over the face, while a hook and eye faſtens all cloſe under the chin, and gives them an air not unlike our country wenches, who throw

throw the gown tail over their heads, to protect them from a summer's shower. The holiday dresses mean time of the peasants round Naples, are very rich and cumbersome. One often sees a great coarse raw-boned fellow on a Sunday, panting for heat under a thick blue velvet coat comically enough; the females in a scarlet cloth petticoat, with a broad gold lace at the bottom, a jacket open before, but charged with heavy ornaments, and the head not unbecomingly dressed with an embroidered handkerchief from Turkey, exactly as one sees them represented here in prints, which they sell dear enough, God knows; and ask, as I am informed by the purchasers, not twice or thrice, but four or five times more than at last they take, as indeed for every thing one buys here: One portrait is better, however, than a thousand words, when single figures are to be delineated; but of the Grotta del Cane, description gives a completer idea than drawing. Both are perhaps nearly unnecessary indeed, when speaking of a place so often and so accurately described. What surprised me most among the ceremonies of this extraordinary place was, that the pent up vapour

vapour shut in an excavation of the rock, should, upon opening the door, gradually move forwards a few yards, but not rise up above a foot from the surface, nor, by what I could observe, ever dissipate in air; I think we left it hovering over the favourite spot, when the poor cur's nose had been forcibly held in it for a minute or two, but he took care after his recovery to keep a very judicious distance. Sporting with animal life is always highly offensive; and the fellow's account that his dog was used to the operation, and had already gone through it eight times, that it did him no harm, &c. I considered as words used merely to quiet our impatience of the experiment, which is infinitely more amusing when tried upon a lighted flambeau, extinguishing it most completely in a moment. What connection there is between flame and vitality, those who know more of the matter than I do, must expound. Certain it is, that many sorts of vapour are equally fatal to both; and where fermentation is either going forward, or has lately been, people accustomed to such matters always try with a candle whether the cask is approachable by man or not;

and I once saw a terrifying accident arise in a great brewhouse, from the headstrong stupidity of a workman who would go down into a vat, the contents of which had lately been drawn off, without sending his proper præcursor the candle, to enquire if all was safe. The consequence was half expected by his companions, who hearing him drop off the steps, and fall flat to the bottom, began instantly hooking him up again, but there were no signs of life; some ran for their master, others for a surgeon, but we were nearest at hand, and recollecting what one had read of the recovery of dogs at Naples, by tossing them suddenly into the lake Agnano, we made the men carry their patient to the cooler, and plunging him over head and ears, restored his life, exactly in the manner of the Grotta del Cane experiment, which succeeded so completely in this fellow's case, I remember, that waking after the temporary suspension, we had much ado to impress so insensible a mortal with a due sense of the danger his rashness had incurred.

But it is time to tell of Herculaneum, Pompeia, and Portici; of a theatre, the scene of gaiety

gaiety and pleasure, overwhelmed by torrents of liquid fire! the inhabitants of a whole town surprised by immediate and unavoidable destruction! Where that very town indeed was built with the lava produced by former eruptions, one would think it scarce possible that such calamities could be totally unexpected;—but no matter, life must go on, though we all know death is coming;—so the bread was baking in their ovens, the meat was smoking on their dishes, some of their wine already decanted for use, the rest in large jars *(amphora)*, now petrified with their contents inside, and fixed to the walls of the cellars in which they stand. —How dreadful are the thoughts which such a sight suggests! how *very* horrible the certainty, that such a scene may be all acted over again to-morrow; and that we, who to-day are spectators, may become spectacles to travellers of a succeeding century, who mistaking our bones for those of the Neapolitans, may carry some of them to their native country back again perhaps; as it came into my head that a French gentleman was doing, when I saw him put a human bone into his pocket this morning, and told him I hoped he had got the jaw of a Gaulish officer, instead of a Roman soldier, for future reflections to energize upon. Of all single objects offered here to one's contemplation, none are more striking than a woman's foot, the *print* of her foot I mean, taken apparently in the very act of running from the river of melted minerals that surrounded her, and which now serves as an intaglio to commemorate the misery it caused. Another melancholy proof of what needs no confirmation, is the impression of a sick female, known to be so from the *stole* she wore, a drapery peculiar to the sex; her bed, converted into a substance like plaster of Paris, still retains the form and covering of her who perished quietly upon it, without ever making even an effort to escape.

That one of these towns is crushed, or rather buried, under loads of heavy lava, and is therefore difficult to disentangle, all have heard; that Pompeia is only lightly covered with pumice-stones and ashes, is new to nobody; it is in the power, as a Venetian gentleman said angrily, of an English hen and chickens to scratch it open in a week, though these lazy Neapolitans will leave it not half dislodged,

dislodged, before a new eruption swallows all again.

Our visit to Portici was more than equally provoking in the same way; to see deposited there all the antiques which are so curious in themselves, so *very* valuable when considered as specimens of ancient art, and of the mode of living practised in ancient Rome, kept at a place where I do sincerely believe they will be again overwhelmed and confounded among the king of Naples's furniture, to the great torture of future antiquarians, and to the disgrace of present insensibility.

The *triclinia* and *stibadia* used at supper by the old Romans prove the verses which our critics have been working at so long, to have been at least well explained by them, and do infinite honour to those who, without the advantage of seeing how the utensils were constructed, knew perfectly well their way of carrying on life, from their acquaintance with a language long since *dead*, and I am sure *buried* under a heap of rubbish heavier and more difficult to remove than all the lava heaped on Herculaneum; but it is a source of perpetual wonder, and let me add perpetual pleasure too, to know that Cicero, and Virgil, and Horace, if alive, would find their writings as well understood, ay and as perfectly tasted, by the scholars of Paris and London, as they had ever been by their own old literary acquaintance.

The sight of the *curule* chair was charming, and one thought of old Papyrius, his long white beard, and ivory stick with which he reproved the insolence of a Gaulish soldier, who, when Brennus entered the city, seeing all those venerable senators sitting in a row, took them for inanimate figures, and stroked Papyrius's beard, to feel whether he was alive or no. The *curule* chair was so called from *currus* a chariot, and this we examined had holes bored in it, where it had been fixed to the car: I do think there is just such a one in the British Musæum, but that did not much engage my attention, so great is the influence of locality upon the mind. The way in which they decypher the old MSS. here likewise is pretty and curious, and requires infinite patience, which as far as they have gone has not been well repaid; the operation *laboriosius est quam Sibyllæ folia colligere**, to use the words of Politian, whose

---

* More laborious than gathering up the Sibyls leaves.

right

right name I learned at Florence to be *Meſſer Angelo di Monte Pulciano.*

May not, however, a more important conſequence than any yet mentioned be found deducible from what we have ſeen this day? for if *Jeſus Chriſt* condeſcended to uſe the Roman, or commonly adopted cuſtom of ſupping on a *triclinium* (as it is plain he did by the recumbent poſture of St. John), when eating the Paſſover for the laſt time with his diſciples at Jeruſalem; that ſect of Chriſtians called Romaniſts ought ſure to be the *laſt*, not *firſt*, to exclude from ſalvation all ſuch of their brethren as do not receive the Lord's Supper preciſely in *their way*; when nothing can be clearer, from our bleſſed Saviour's example, than that he thought old forms, if laudable, not neceſſary or eſſential to the well-performing a devotional rite; ſeeing that to eat the Paſſover according to original inſtitution, thoſe who communicated were bound to take it *ſtanding*, and with a ſtaff in their hands beſide as expreſſive of more haſte.

The Chriſtmas ſeaſon here at Naples is very pleaſingly obſerved; the Italians are peculiarly ingenious in adorning their ſhops I think, and ſetting

setting out their wares; every grocer, fruiterer, &c. now mingles orange, and lemon, and myrtle leaves, among the goods exposed at his door, as we do greens in the churches of England, but with infinitely more taste; and this device produces a very fine effect upon the whole, as one drives along *la Strada del Toledo*, which all morning looks showy from these decorations, and all evening splendid from the profusion of torches, flambeaux, &c. that shine with less regularity indeed, but with more lustre and greater appearance of expensive gaiety, than our neat, clean, steady London lamps. Some odd, pretty, moveable coffeehouses too, or lemonade-shops, set on wheels, and adorned, according to the possessor's taste, with gilding, painting, &c. and covered with ices, orgeats, and other refreshments, as in emulation each of the other, and in a strange variety of shapes and forms too, exquisitely well imagined for the most part,—help forward the finery of Naples exceedingly: I have counted thirty of these *galante* shops on each side the street, which, with their necessary illuminations, make a brilliant figure by candle-light, till twelve o'clock, when all the show is over, and every body put out their lights and quietly

quietly lie down to reſt. Till that hour, however, few things can exceed the tumultuous merriment of Naples, while *volantes*, or running footmen, dreſſed like tumblers before a ſhow, precede all carriages of diſtinction, and endeavour to keep the people from being run over; yet whilſt they are liſtening to Policinello's jokes, or to ſome ſuch ſtreet orator as Dr. Moore deſcribes with equal truth and humour, they often get cruſhed and killed; yet, as Pope ſays,

> See ſome ſtrange comfort ev'ry ſtate attend:—

The *Lazaroni* who has his child run over by the coach of a man of quality, has a regular claim upon him for no leſs than twelve *carlines* (about five ſhillings Engliſh); if it is his wife that meets with the accident, he gets two *ducats*, live or die; and for the maſter of the family (houſe he has none) three is the regular compenſation; and no words paſs here about *trifles*. Truth is, human life is lower rated in all parts of Italy than with us; they think nothing of an individual, but ſee him periſh (excepting by the hand of juſtice) as a cat or dog. A young man fell from our carriage at Milan one evening; he was not a

ſervant

servant of ours, but a friend which, after we were gone home, the coachman had picked up to go with him to the fireworks which were exhibited that night near the *Corso:* there was a crowd and an *embarras,* and the fellow tumbled off and died upon the spot, and nobody even spoke, or I believe *thought* about the matter, except one woman, who supposed that he had neglected to cross himself when he got up behind.

The works of art here at Naples are neither very numerous nor very excellent: I have seen the vaunted present of porcelain intended for the king of England, in return for some cannon presented by him to this court; and think it more entertaining in its design than admirable as a manufacture. Every dish and plate, however, being the portrait as one may say of some famous Etruscan vase, or other antique, dug out of the ruins of these newly-discovered cities, with an account of its supposed story engraved neatly round the figure, makes it interesting and elegant, and worthy enough of one prince to accept, and another to bestow.

There is a work of art, however, peculiar to this city, and attempted in no other; on which

which surprising sums of money are lavished by many of the inhabitants, who connect or associate to this amusement ideas of piety and devotion: the thing when finished is called a *presepio*, and is composed in honour of this sacred season, after which all is taken to pieces, and arranged after a different manner next year. In many houses a room, in some a whole suite of apartments, in others the terrace upon the house-top, is dedicated to this very uncommon show; consisting of a miniature representation in sycamore wood, properly coloured, of the house at Bethlehem, with the blessed Virgin, St. Joseph, and our Saviour in the manger, with attendant angels, &c. as in pictures of the nativity; the figures are about six inches high, and dressed with the most exact propriety. This however, though the principal thing intended to attract spectators' notice, is kept back, so that sometimes I scarcely saw it at all; while a general and excellent landscape, with figures of men at work, women dressing dinner, a long road in real gravel, with rocks, hills, rivers, cattle, camels, every thing that can be imagined, fill the other rooms, so happily disposed

posed too for the most part, the light introduced so artfully, the perspective kept so surprisingly!—one wonders and cries out, it is certainly but a baby-house at best; yet managed by people whose heads naturally turned towards architecture and design, give them power thus to defy a traveller not to feel delighted with the general effect; while if every single figure is not capitally executed, and nicely expressed beside, the proprietor is truly miserable, and will cut a new cow, or vary the horse's attitude, against next Christmas *coûte qui coûte:* and perhaps I should not have said so much about the matter, if there had not been shewn me within this last week, *presepios* which have cost their possessors fifteen hundred or two thousand English pounds; and, rather than relinquish or sell them, many families have gone to ruin: I have wrote the sums down in letters, not figures, for fear of the possibility of a mistake. One of these playthings had the journey of the three kings represented in it, and the presents were all of real gold and silver finely worked; nothing could be better or more livelily finished.—" But, Sir," said I, " why do you dress up one of the Wise Men

with

with a turban and *crescent*, six hundred years before the birth of Mahomet, who first put that mark in the forehead of his followers? The eastern Magi were not *Turks;* this is a breach of *costume.*" My gentleman paused, and thanked me; said he would enquire if there was nothing heretical in the objection; and if all was right, it should be changed next year without fail.

A young lady here of English parents, just ten years old, asked me, very pertinently, " Why this pretty sight was called a *Presepio?*" but said she suddenly, answering herself, " I suppose it is because it is *preceptive:*" such a mistake was more valuable than knowledge, and gave me great esteem of her understanding; the little girl's name was Zaffory.

The King's *menagerie* is neither rich in animals, nor particularly well kept: I wonder a man of his character and disposition should not delight in possessing a very fine one. The bears however were as tame as lapdogs; there was a wolf too, larger than ever I saw a wolf, and an elephant that played a hundred tricks at the command of his keeper,

keeper, little lefs a beaft than he; but as Pope fays, after Horace,

> Let bear or elephant be e'er fo white,
> The people fure, the people are the fight.

Let us then tell about the two affemblies, *o fia converfazioni*, where one goes in fearch of amufement as to the rooms of Bath or Tunbridge exactly; only that one of thefe places is devoted to the *nobiltà*, the other is called *de' buoni amici;* and fuch is the ftate of fubordination in this country, that though the great people may come among the little ones, and be fure of the groffeft adulation, a merchant's wife, fhining in diamonds, being obliged to ftand up reverentially before the chair of a countefs, who does her the honour to fpeak to her; the poor *amici* are totally excluded from the fubfcription of the nobles, nor dare even to return the falutation of a fuperior, fhould a good-natured perfon of that rank be tempted, from frequently feeing them at the rooms, to give them a kind nod in the ftreet or elfewhere. All this feems comical enough to us, and I had much ado to look grave, while a beautiful and well-educated

educated wife of a rich banker here, confeſſed herſelf not fit company for an ignorant mean-looking woman of quality. But though ſuch unintelligible doctrines make one for a moment aſhamed both of one's ſex and ſpecies, that lady's knowledge of various languages, her numerous accompliſhments in a thouſand methods of paſſing time away with innocent elegance, and a ſort of ſtudied addreſs never obſerved in Italy before, gave me infinite delight in her ſociety, and daily increaſed my ſuſpicion that ſhe was a foreigner, till nearer intimacy diſcovered her a German Lutheran, with a ſingular head of thick blonde hair, ſo unlike thoſe I ſee around me. We grew daily better acquainted, and ſhe ſhewed me—but not indignantly at all—ſome ladies from the higher aſſembly ſitting among *theſe*, very low dreſſed indeed, a knotting-bag and counters in their lap, to ſhew their contempt of the company; while ſuch as ſpoke to them ſtood before their ſeat, like children before a governeſs in England, as long as the converſation laſted.

I inquired if the men confined their addreſſes wholly to their own rank? She ſaid, beauty often broke the barrier, and when
a pretty

a pretty woman of the second rank got a *cavalier servente* of the first, much happiness and much distinction was the consequence: but alas! he will not even *try* to push her up among the people of fashion, and when he meets any is sure to look ashamed of his mistress; so that her felicity can consist only in triumphing over equals, for to rival a superior is here an impossibility.

Our Duke and Dutchess of Cumberland have made all Naples adore them though, by going richly dressed, and behaving with infinite courtesy and good-humour, at an assembly or ball given in the *lower rooms*, as the English comically call them. A young Palermitan prince applauded them for it exceedingly; so I took the liberty to express my wonder. "Oh," replied he, " we are not ignorant how much English manners differ from our own: I have already, though but just eighteen years old, as sovereign of my own state, under the King of both Sicilies, condemned a man to death *because he was a rascal*, but the law and the people govern in England I know." My desire of hearing about Sicily, which we could not contrive to visit, made me happy to cultivate Prince Venti-

Ventimiglia's acquaintance; he was very ſtudious, very learned of his age, and uncommonly clever: told me of the antiquities his iſland had to boaſt, with great intelligence, and a ſurpriſing knowledge of ancient hiſtory.

We wiſhed to have made a party to go in the ſame company to Pæſtum, but my cowardice kept me at home, ſo bad was the account of the roads and accommodation; though Abate Bianconi of Milan, for whom I have ſo much eſteem, bid me remember to look at the buildings there attentively; adding, that they were better worth our obſervation than all the boaſted antiquities at Rome; " as they had ſeen (ſaid he) the original foundation of her empire, and outlived its decay; that they had ſeen her ſecond birth too, and power under ſome of her pontiffs over all Europe about ſix or ſeven centuries ago; and that they would now probably remain till all *that* was likewiſe aboliſhed, with only ſlight traces left behind to ſhew that *fuimus*, &c."

How mortifying it is to go home and never ſee this Pæſtum! Prince Ventimiglia went there with Mr. Cox; he profeſſes his intention ſoon to viſit England, concerning the manners and cuſtoms of which he is very inquiſitive, and not ill-verſed in the language; but books drop oddly into people's hands: This gentleman commended Ambroſe Philips's Paſtorals, and I remember the Florentines ſeemed ſtrangely impreſſed with the merit of the other Philips as a poet. Bonducci has tranſlated his Cyder, and calls him *emulous of Milton*, in good time! but it is difficult to diſtinguiſh jeſt from earneſt in a foreign language.

I will not, if I can help it, loſe ſight of our Sicilian however, till I have made him tell me ſomething about Dionyſius's Ear, about the eruptions of Ætna, and the *Caſtagno a cento cavalli*, which, he proteſts, is not magnified by Brydone.

It is wonderfully mortifying to think how little information after all can be obtained of any thing new or any thing ſtrange, though ſo far from one's own country. What I picked up moſt curious and diverting from our converſation, was his expreſſion of ſurpriſe, when at our houſe one day he read a letter from his mother, telling him that ſuch a lady, naming her, remained ſtill unmarried, and even unbetrothed, though now paſt ten years

years old. "She will," said I, "perhaps break through old customs, and chuse for herself, as she is an orphan, and has no one whom she need consult."—"Impossible, Madam!" was the reply.—"But tell me, Prince, for information's sake, if such a lady, this girl for example, should venture to assert the rights of humanity, and make a choice somewhat unusual, *what would come of it?*"—" Why nothing in the world would come of it," answered he; " the lass would be immediately at liberty again, for no man so circumstanced could be permitted to leave the country *alive* you know, nor would her folly benefit his family at all, as her estate would be immediately adjudged to the next heir. No person of inferior rank in our country would therefore, unless absolutely mad, set his life to hazard for the sake of a frolic, the event of which is so well known beforehand;—less still, because, if *love* be in the case, all *personal attachment* may be fully gratified, only let her but be once legally married to a man every way her equal." Could one help recollecting Fielding's song in the Virgin unmasked? who says,

> For now I've found out that as Michaelmas day
>   Is still the forerunner of Lammas;
> So wedding another is just the right way
>   To get at my dear Mr. Thomas.

I will mention another talk I had with a Sicilian lady. We met at the house of the Swedish minister, Monsieur André, uncle to the lamented officer who perished in our sovereign's service in America; and while the rest of the company were entertaining themselves with cards and music, I began laughing in myself at hearing the gentleman and lady who sat next *me*, called by others *Don Raphael* and *Donna Camilla*, because those two names bring Gil Blas into one's head. Their agreeable and interesting conversation however soon gave my mind a more serious turn when discoursing on the liberal premiums now offered by the King of Naples to those who are willing to rebuild and repeople Messina. Donna Camilla politely introduced me to a very sick but pleasing-looking lady, who she said was going to return thither: at which *she*, starting, cried, " Oh God forbid, my dear friend !" in an accent that made me think she had already suffered something from the concus-

concuffions that overwhelmed that city in the year 1783. Her inviting manner, her foft and interefting eyes, whofe languid glances feemed to fhew beauty funk in forrow, and fpirit oppreffed by calamity, engaged my utmoft attention, while Don Raphael preffed her to indulge the foreigner's curiofity with fome particulars of the diftreffes fhe had fhared. Her own feelings were all fhe could relate fhe faid—and thofe confufedly. " You fee that girl there," pointing to a child about feven or eight years old, who ftood liftening to the harpfichord: " fhe efcaped! I cannot, for my foul, guefs how, for we were not together at the time."—" Where were *you*, madam, at the moment of the fatal accident?"--" Who? *me?*" and her eyes lighted up with recollected terror: " I was in the nurfery with my maid, employed in taking ftains out of fome Bruffels lace upon a brazier; two babies, neither of them four years old, playing in the room. The eldeft boy, dear lad! had juft left us, and was in his father's country-houfe. The day grew *fo* dark all on a fudden, and the brazier—Oh, Lord Jefus! I felt the brazier flide from me,

and saw it run down the long room on its three legs. The maid screamed, and I shut my eyes and knelt at a chair. We thought all over; but my husband came, and snatching me up, cried, *run, run.*—I know not how nor where, but all amongst falling houses it was, and people shrieked so, and there was *such* a noise! My poor son! he was fifteen years old; he tried to hold me fast in the crowd. I remember kissing *him:* Dear lad, dear lad! I said. I could speak *just then:* but the throng at the gate! Oh that gate! Thousands at once! ay, thousands! thousands at once: and my poor old confessor too! I knew him: I threw my arms about his aged neck. *Padre mio!* said I— *Padre mio!* Down he dropt, a great stone struck his shoulder; I saw it coming, and my boy pulled me: he saved my life, dear, dear lad! But the crash of the gate, the screams of the people, the heat—Oh such a heat! I felt no more on't though; I saw no more on't; I waked in bed, this girl by me, and her father giving me cordials. We were on shipboard, they told me, coming to Naples to my brother's house here; and do you think I'll ever go back *there* again? No, no; that's a
curst

curst place; I lost my son in it. *Never, never will I see it more!* All my friends try to persuade me, but the sight of it would do my business. If my poor boy were alive indeed! but *he!* ah, poor dear lad! he loved his mother; he held *me* fast—No, no, I'll never see that place again: God has cursed it *now;* I am sure he has."

A narrative so melancholy, so tender, and so true, could not fail of its effect. I ran for refuge to the harpsichord, where a lady was singing divinely. I could not listen though: *her* grateful sweetness who told the dismal story, followed me thither: she had seen my ill-suppressed tears, and followed to embrace me. The tale she had told saddened my heart, and the news we heard returning to the Crocelle did not contribute to lighten its weight, while an amiable young Englishman, who had long lain ill there, was now breathing his last, far from his friends, his country, or their customs; all easily dispensed with, perhaps derided, during the bustle of a journey, and in the madness of superfluous health; but sure to be sighed after, when life's last twilight shuts in precipitately closer and closer round

round a man, and leaves him only the nearer objects to repose and dwell on.

Such was Captain ———'s situation! he had none but a foreign servant with him. We thought it might sooth him to hear " *Can I do any thing for you, Sir?* in an English voice: so I sent my maid: he had no commands he said; he could not eat the jelly she had made him; he wished some clergyman could be found that he might speak to: such a one was vainly enquired for, till it was discovered that ill-health had driven Mr. Mentze to Naples, who kindly administered the last consolation a Christian can receive; and heard the next day, when confined himself to bed, of his countryman's being properly thrust by the banker into the *Buco Protestante;* so they contemptuously call a dirty garden one drives by in this town, where not less than a hundred people, small and great, from our island, annually resort, leaving fifty or sixty thousand pounds behind them at a moderate computation; though if their bodies are obliged to take *perpetual* apartments here, no better place has been hitherto provided for them than this kitchen ground; on which
grow

grow cabbages, cauliflowers, &c. fold to their country folks for double price I trow, the remaining part of the feafon.

Well! well! if the Neapolitans do bury Chriftians like dogs, they make fome fingular compenfations we will confefs, by nurfing dogs like Chriftians. A very veracious man informed me yefter morning, that his poor wife was half broken-hearted at hearing fuch a Countefs's dog was run over; " for," faid he, " having fuckled the pretty creature herfelf, fhe loved it like one of her children." I bid him repeat the circumftance, that no miftake might be made: he did fo; but feeing me look fhocked, or afhamed, or fomething he did not like,—" Why, madam," faid the fellow, " it is a common thing enough for ordinary men's wives to fuckle the lapdogs of ladies of quality:" adding, that they were paid for their milk, and he faw no harm in gratifying one's *fuperiors*. As I was difpofed to fee nothing *but* harm in difputing with fuch a competitor, our conference finifhed foon; but the fact is certain.

Indeed few things can be foolifher than to debate the propriety of cuftoms one is not

bound

bound to obferve or comply with. If you diflike them, the remedy is eafy; turn yours and your horfes heads the other way.

20th January 1786.

Here are the moft excellent, the moft incomparable fifh I ever eat; red mullets, large as our maycril, and of fingularly high flavour; befides the calamaro, or ink-fifh, a dainty worthy of imperial luxury; almond and even apple trees in bloffom, to delight thofe who can be paid for coarfe manners and confined notions by the beauties of a brilliant climate. Here are all the hedges in blow as you drive towards Pozzuoli, and a fnow of white May-flowers cluftering round Virgil's tomb. So ftrong was the fun's heat this morning, even before eleven o'clock, that I carried an umbrella to defend me from his rays, as we fauntered about the walks, which are fpacious and elegant, laid out much in the ftyle of St. James's Park, but with the fea on one fide of you, the broad ftreet, called Chiaja, on the other.

other. What trees are planted there however, either do not grow up so as to afford shade, or else they cut them, and trim them about to make them in pretty shapes forsooth, as we did in England half a century ago.

Be this as it will, the vaunted view from the castle of St. Elmo, though much more deeply *interesting*, is in consequence of this defect less *naturally* pleasing than the prospect from Lomellino's villa near Genoa, or Lord Clifford's park, called King's Weston, in Somersetshire; those two places being, in point of mere situation, possessed of beauties hitherto unrivalled by any thing I have seen. Nor does the steady regularity of this Mediterranean sea make me inclined to prefer it to our more capricious or rather active channel. Sea views have at best too little variety, and when the flux and reflux of the tide are taken away from one, there remains only rough and smooth: whereas the hope which its ebb and flow keep constantly renovating, serves to animate, and a little change the course of one's ideas, just as its swelling and sinking is of use, to purify in some degree, and keep the whole from stagnation.

I made

I made inquiry after the old ſtory of Nicola Peſce, told by Kircher, and ſweetly brought back to all our memories by Goldſmith, who, as Dr. Johnſon ſaid of him, touched nothing that he did not likewiſe adorn; but I could gain no addition to what we have already heard. That there was ſuch a man is certain, who, though become nearly amphibious by living conſtantly in the water, only coming ſometimes on ſhore for ſleep and refreſhment, ſuffered avarice to be his ruin, leaping voluntarily into the Gulph of Charybdis to fetch out a gold cup thrown in thither to tempt him—what could a gold cup have done one would wonder for Nicola Peſce?—yet knowing the dangers of the place, he braved them all it ſeems for this bright reward; and was ſuppoſed to be devoured by one of the polypus fiſh, who, ſticking cloſe to the rocks, extend their arms for prey. When I expreſſed my indignation that he ſhould ſo periſh; " He forgot perhaps," ſaid one preſent, " to recommend himſelf to Santo Gennaro."

The caſtle on this hill, called the Caſtel St. Elmo, would be much my comfort did I fix at Naples; for here are eight thouſand ſoldiers

conſtantly

constantly kept, to secure the city from sudden insurrection; his majesty most wisely trusting their command only to Spanish or German officers, or some few gentlemen from the northern states of Italy, that no personal tenderness for any in the town below may intervene, if occasion for sudden severity should arise. We went to-day and saw their garrison, comfortably and even elegantly kept; and I was wicked enough to rejoice that the soldiers were never, but with the very utmost difficulty, permitted to go among the townsmen for a moment.

To-morrow we mount the Volcano, whose present peaceful disposition has tempted us to inspect it more nearly. Though it appears little less than presumption thus to profane with eyes of examination the favourite alembic of nature, while the great work of projection is carrying on; guarded as all its secret caverns are too with every contradiction; snow and flame! solid bodies heated into liquefaction, and rolling gently down one of its sides; while fluids congeal and harden into ice on the other; nothing can exceed the curiosity of its appearance, now the lava is less rapid,

and

and stiffens as it flows; stiffens too in ridges very surprisingly, and gains an odd aspect, not unlike the pasteboard waves representing sea at a theatre, but black, because this year's eruption has been mingled with coal. The connoisseurs here know the different degrees, dates, and shades of lava to a perfection that amazes one; and Sir William Hamilton's courage, learning, and perfect skill in these matters, is more people's theme here than the Volcano itself. Bartolomeo, the Cyclop of Vesuvius as he is called, studies its effects and operations too with much attention and philosophical exactness, relating the adventures he has had with our minister on the mountain to every Englishman that goes up, with great success. The way one climbs is by tying a broad sash with long ends round this Bartolomeo, letting him walk before one, and holding it fast. As far as the Hermitage there is no great difficulty, and to that place some chuse to ride an ass, but I thought walking safer; and there you are sure of welcome and refreshment from the poor good old man, who sets up a little cross wherever the fire has stopt near his cell; shews you the place with a sort of polite
solemnity

solemnity that impresses, spreads his scanty provisions before you kindly, and tells the past and present state of the eruption accurately, inviting you to partake of

> His rushy couch, his frugal fare,
> His blessing and repose.   GOLDSMITH.

This Hermit is a Frenchman. *J'ai dansé dans mon lit tans de fois**, said he: the expression was not sublime when speaking of an earthquake, to be sure; I looked among his books, however, and found Bruyere. "Would not the Duc de Rochefoucault have done better?" said I. "Did I never see you before, Madam?" said he; "yes, sure I have, and dressed you too, when I was a hair-dresser in London, and lived with Monsf. Martinant, and I dressed pretty Miss Wynne too in the same street. *Vit'elle encore? Vit'elle encore* †? Ah I am old now," continued he; "I remember when black pins first came up." This was charming, and in such an unexpected way, I could hardly prevail upon myself ever to leave the spot; but Mrs. Greatheed having been quite to the cra-

* I have danced in my bed so often this year.
† Is she yet alive? Is she yet alive?

ter's

ter's edge with her only fon, a baby of four years old; fhame rather than inclination urged me forward; I afked the little boy what he had feen; I faw the chimney, replied he, and it was on fire, but I liked the elephant better.

That the fituation of the crater changed in this laft eruption is of little confequence; it will change and change again I fuppofe. The wonder is, that nobody gets killed by venturing fo near, while red-hot ftones are flying about them fo. The Bifhop of Derry did very near get his arm broke; and the Italians are always recounting the exploits of thefe rafh Britons who look into the crater, and carry their wives and children up to the top; while we are, with equal juftice, amazed at the courageous Neapolitans, who build little fnug villages and dwell with as much confidence at the foot of Vefuvius, as our people do in Paddington or Hornfey. When I enquired of an inhabitant of thefe houfes how fhe managed, and whether fhe was not frighted when the Volcano raged, left it fhould carry away her pretty little habitation: " Let it go," faid fhe, " we don't mind now if it goes to-

to-morrow, so as we can make it answer by raising our vines, oranges, &c. against it for three years, our fortune is made before the fourth arrives; and then if the red river comes we can always run away, *scappar via*, ourselves, and hang the property. We only desire three years use of the mountain as a hot wall or forcing-house, and then we are above the world, thanks be to God and St. Januarius," who always comes in for a large share of their veneration; and this morning having heard that the Neapolitans still present each other with a cake upon New-year's day, I began to hug my favourite hypothesis closer, recollecting the old ceremony of the wheaten cake seasoned with salt, and called *Janualis* in the Heathen days. All this however must still end in mere conjecture; for though the weather here favours one's idea of Janus, who loosened the furrow and liquefied the frost, to which the melting our martyr's blood might, without much straining of the matter, be made to allude; yet it must be recollected after all, that the miracle is not performed in this month but that of May, and that St. Januarius did certainly exist and give his life as

VOL. II. F testimony

testimony to the truth of our religion, in the third century. Can one wonder, however, if corruptions and mistakes should have crept in since? And would it not have been equal to a miracle had no tares sprung up in the field of religion, when our Saviour himself informs us that there is an enemy ever watching his opportunity to plant them?

These dear people too at Rome and Naples do live so in the very hulk of ship-wrecked or rather foundered Paganism, have their habitation so at the very bottom of the cask, can it fail to retain the scent when the lees are scarce yet dried up, clean or evaporated? That an odd jumble of past and present days, past and present ideas of dignity, events, and even manner of portioning out their time, still confuse their heads, may be observed in every conversation with them; and when a few weeks ago we revisited, in company of some newly-arrived English friends, the old baths of Baiæ, Locrine lake, &c. Tobias, who rowed us over, bid us observe the Appian way under the water, where indeed it appears quite clearly, even to the tracks of wheels on its old pavement made of very large stones; and seeing me perhaps

haps particularly attentive, "Yes, Madam," said he, "I do assure you, that *Don* Horace and *Don* Virgil, of whom we hear such a deal, used to come from Rome to their country-seats here in a day, over this very road, which is now overflowed as you see it, by repeated earthquakes, but which was then so good and so unbroken, that if they rose early in the morning they could easily gallop hither against the *Ave Maria.*"

It was very observable in our second visit paid to the Stuffe San Germano, that they had increased prodigiously in heat since mount Vesuvius had ceased throwing out fire, though at least fourteen miles from it, and a vast portion of the sea between them; it vexed me to have no thermometer again, but by what one's immediate feelings could inform us, there were many degrees of difference. I could not now bear my hand on any part of them for a moment. The same luckless dog was again produced, and again restored to life, like the lady in Dryden's Fables, who is condemned to be hunted, killed, recovered, and set on foot again for the amusement of her tormentors; a story borrowed from the Italian.

Solfaterra burned my fingers as I plucked an incruftation off, which allured me by the beauty of its colours, and roared with more violence than when I was there before. This horrible volcano is by no means extinguifhed yet, but feems pregnant with wonders, principally combuftible, and likely to break with one at every ftep, all the earth round it being hollow as a drum, and I fhould think of no great thicknefs neither; fo plainly does one hear the fighings underneath, which fome of the country people imagine to be tortured fpirits howling with agony.

It is fuppofed that Lake Agnano, where the dog is flung in, if the dewy grafs do not fuffice to recover him, with its humidity and frefhnefs, as it often does; is but another crater of another volcano, long ago felf-deftroyed by fcorpion-like fuicide; and it is like enough it may be fo. There are not wanting however thofe that think, or fay at leaft, how a fubterraneous or fubaqueous city remains even now under that lake, but lies too deep for infpection.

Sia come fia *, as the Italians exprefs themfelves, thefe environs are beyond all power

* Be it as it may.

of comprehension, much more beyond all effort of words to describe; and as Sannazarius says of Venice, so I am sure it may be said of this place, " That man built Rome, but God created Naples:" for surely, surely he has honoured no other spot with such an accumulation of his wonders: nor can any thing more completely bring the description of the devoted cities mentioned in Genesis before one's eyes, than these concealed fires, which there I trust burst up unexpectedly, and, attended by such lightning as only hot countries can exhibit, devoured all at once, nor spared the too incredulous inquirer, who turned her head back with contempt of expected judgments, but entangling her feet in the pursuing stream of lava, fixed her fast, a monument of bituminous salt.

Though surrounded by such terrifying objects, the Neapolitans are not, I think, disposed to cowardly, though easily persuaded to devotional superstitions; they are not afraid of spectres or supernatural apparitions, but sleep contentedly and soundly in small rooms, made for the ancient dead, and now actually in the occupation of old Roman bodies, the catacombs belonging to whom are still very impressive to the fancy; and I have known many an English gentleman, who would not endure to have his courage impeached by *living wight*, whose imagination would notwithstanding have disturbed his slumbers not a little, had he been obliged to pass one night where these poor women sleep securely, wishing only for that money which travellers are not unwilling to bestow; and perhaps a walk among these hollow caves of death, these sad repositories of what was once animated by valour and illuminated by science, strike one much more than all the urns and lachrymatories of Portici.

How judicious is Mr. Addison's remark, " That *Sisté Viator!* which has a striking effect among the Roman tombs placed by the road side, loses all its power over the mind when placed in the body of a church:" I think he might have said the same, had he lived to see funereal urns used as decorations of hackney-coach pannels, and *Caput Bovis* over the doors in New Tavistock-street.

It is worth recollecting however, that the Dictator Sylla is supposed to be the first man of consequence who ordered his body to be burned at Rome, as till then, burial was apparently

parently the fashion: his death, occasioned by the *morbus pedicularis*, made his interment difficult, and what necessity suggested to be done for him, grew up into a custom, and the sycophants of power, ever hasty to follow their superiors, now shewed their zeal even in *post obit* imitation. But while I am writing, more modern and less tyrannic claimants for respect agreeably disturb one's meditations on the cruelty and oppression used by these wicked possessors of immortal though ill-gotten fame.

The Queen of Naples is delivered, and we are all to make merry: the *Castello d' Uovo*, just under our windows, is to be illuminated: and from the Carthusian convent on the hill, to my poor solitary old acquaintance the hermit and hair-dresser, who inhabits a cleft in mount Vesuvius, all resolve to be happy, and to rejoice in the felicity of a prince that loves them.——— Shouting, and candles, and torches, and coloured lamps, and Polinchinello above all the rest, did their best to drive forward the general joy, and make known the birth of the royal baby for many miles round the capital; and there was a splendid opera the next night, in this finest of all fine theatres, though that of Milan pleases me better; as I prefer the elegant curtains which festoon it over the boxes there, to our heavy gilt ornaments here at Naples; and their boasted looking-glasses, never cleaned, have no effect as I perceive towards helping forward the enchantment. A *festa di ballo*, or masquerade, given here however, was exceedingly gay, and the dresses surprisingly rich: our party, a very large one, all Italians, retired at one in the morning to quite the finest supper of its size I ever saw. Fish of various sorts, incomparable in their kinds, composed eight dishes of the first course; we had thirty-eight set on the table in that course, forty-nine in the second, with wines and dessert truly magnificent, for all which Mr. Piozzi protested to me that we paid only three shillings and six-pence a head English money; but for the truth of that he must answer: we sate down twenty-two persons to supper, and I observed there were numbers of these parties made in different taverns, or apartments adjoining to the theatre, whither after refreshment we returned, and danced till daylight.

The

The theatre is a vaſt building, even when not inhabited or ſet off by lights and company: all of ſtone too, like that of Milan; but particularly defended from fire by St. Anthony, who has an altar and chapel erected to his honour, and ſhowily decorated at the door; and on Sunday night, January the twenty-ſecond, there were fireworks exhibited in honour of himſelf and his *pig*, which was placed on the top, and illuminated with no ſmall ingenuity: the fire catching hold of his tail firſt—*con riſpetto*—as ſaid our Cicerone. But *il Rè Lear è le ſue tre Figlie* are advertiſed, and I am ſick to-night and cannot go.

Oh what a time have I choſe out, &c.
To wear a kerchief—would I were not ſick!

My loſs however is ſomewhat compenſated; for though I could not ſee our own Shakeſpear's play acted at Naples, I went ſome days after to one of the charming theatres this town is entertained by every evening, and ſaw a play which ſtruck me exceedingly: the plot was ſimply this—An Engliſhman appears, dreſſed preciſely as a Quaker, his hat on his head, his

his hands in his pockets, and with a very pensive air says he will take that pistol, producing one, and shoot himself; "for," says he, " the politics go wrong at home now, and I hate the ministerial party, so England does not please me; I tried France, but the people there laughed so about nothing, and sung so much out of tune, I could not bear France; so I went over to Holland; those Dutch dogs are so covetous and hard-hearted, they think of nothing but their money; I could not endure a place where one heard no sound in the whole country but frogs croaking and ducats chinking. *Maladetti!* so I went to Spain, where I narrowly escaped a sun-stroke for the sake of seeing those idle beggarly dons, that if they do condescend to cobble a man's shoe, think they must do it with a sword by their side. I came here to Naples therefore, but ne'er a woman will afford one a chase, all are too easily caught to divert *me*, who like something in prospect; and though it is so fine a country, one can get no fox-hunting, only running after a wild pig. Yes, yes, I *must* shoot myself, the world is so *very* dull I am tired on't."—He then

then coolly prepares matters for the operation, when a young woman burſts into his apartment, bewails her fate a moment, and then faints away. Our countryman lays by his piſtol, brings the lady to life, and having heard part of her ſtory, ſets her in a place of ſafety. More confuſion follows; a gentleman enters ſtorming with rage at a treacherous friend he hints at, and a falſe miſtreſs; the Engliſhman gravely advifes him to ſhoot himſelf: " No, no," replies the warm Italian, " I will ſhoot *them* though, if I can catch them; but want of money hinders me from proſecuting the ſearch." *That* however is now inſtantly ſupplied by the generous Briton, who enters into their affairs, detects and puniſhes the rogue who had betrayed them all, ſettles the marriage and reconciliation of his new friends, adds himſelf ſomething to the good girl's fortune, and concludes the piece with ſaying that he has altered his intentions, and will think no more of ſhooting himſelf, while life may in all countries be rendered pleaſant to him who will employ it in the ſervice of his fellow-creatures; and finiſhes with theſe words, that *ſuch are the ſentiments of an Engliſhman.*

Were

Were this pretty story in the hands of one of our elegant dramatic writers, how charming an entertainment would it make us! Mr. Andrews shall have it certainly, for though very flattering in its intentions towards our countrymen, and the *ground-plot*, as a *surveyor* would call it, well imagined; the play itself was scarcely written I believe, and very little esteemed by the Italians; who made excuses for its grossness, and said that their theatre was at a very low ebb; and so I believe it is. Yet their genius is restless, and for ever fermenting; and although, like their volcano, of which every individual has a spark, it naturally throws out of its mouth more rubbish than marble; like that too, from some occasional eruptions we may gather gems stuck fast among substances of an inferior nature, which want only disentangling, and a new polish, to make them valued, even beyond those that reward the toil of an expecting miner.

The word gems reminds one of *Capo di Monte*, where the king's *cameos* are taken care of, and where the medallist may find perpetual entertainment; for I do believe nothing can exceed the riches of this collection; though it requires

requires good eyes, great experience, and long study, to examine their merits with accurate skill, and praise them with intelligent rapture: of these three requisites I boast none, so cannot enjoy this regale as much as many others; but I have a mortal aversion to those who encumber the general progress of science by reciprocating contempt upon its various branches: the politician however, who weighs the interests of contending powers, or endeavours at the happiness of regulating some particular state; who studies to prevent the encroachments of prerogative, or impede advances to anarchy; hears with faint approbation, at best, of the discoveries made in the moon by modern astronomers—discoveries of a country where he can obtain no power, and settle no system of government—discoveries too, which can only be procured by peeping through glasses which few can purchase, at a place which no man can desire to approach. While the musical composer equally laments the fate of the fossilist, who literally buries his talent in the ground, and equally dead to all the charms of taste, the transports of true expression, and the delights of harmony, rises with the sun only to shun his beams,

and

and seek in the dripping caverns of the earth the effects of his diminished influence. The medallist has had much of this scorn to contend with; yet he that makes it his study to register great events, is perhaps next to him who has contributed to their birth: and this palace displays a degree of riches *en ce genre*, difficult to conceive.

I was, however, better entertained by admiring the incomparable Schidonis, which are to be found only here: he was a scholar, or rather an imitator, of Correggio; and what he has done seems more the result of genius animated by observation, than of profound thought or minute nicety; he painted such ragged folks as he found upon the *Chiaja;* yet his pictures differ no less from the Dutch school, than do those which flow from the majestic pencil of the demi-divine Caracci and their followers, and for the same reason; their minds reflected dignity and grace, his eyes looked upon forms finely proportioned, though covered with tatters, or perhaps scarcely covered at all; no smugness, no plumpness, no *vulgar* character, ever crossed the fancy of Schidone; for a *Lazaroni* at Naples, like a sailor at Portsmouth, is no mean character,

character, though he is a coarfe one; it is in the low Parifian, and the true-bred London blackguard, we muft look for innate bafeneſs, and near approaches to brutality; nor are the Hollanders wanting in originals I truſt, when one has feen fo many copies of the human form from their hands, divefted of foul as I may fay, and, like Prior's Emma when ſhe reſolves to ramble with her outlawed lover,

> And mingle with the people's wretched lee—
> Oh line extreme of human infamy!—
> Left by her look or colour be expreſt
> The mark of aught high-born, or ever better dreſt.

Here is a beautiful performance too of the Venetian ſchool—a refurrection of Lazarus, by Leandro Baſſano, eſteemed the beſt performance of that family, and full of merit—the merit of *character* I mean; while Mary's eyes are wholly employed, and her mind apparently engroſſed by the Saviour's benignity, and almighty power; Martha thinks merely on the preſent exertion of them, and only watches the deliverance of her beloved brother from the tomb: the reſtored Lazarus too—an apparent corpſe, re-awakened ſuddenly to a thouſand ſenſations at once, wonder, gratitude, and affectionate delight!

delight!—How can one coldly sit to hear the connoisseurs *admire the folds of the drapery?* Lanfranc's St. Michael too is a very noble picture; and though his angel is infinitely less angelic than that of Guido, his devil is a less ordinary and vulgar devil than that of his fellow-student, which somewhat too much resembles the common peeping satyr in a landscape; whereas Lanfranc's Lucifer seems embued with more intellectual vices—rage, revenge, and ambition.

But I am called from my observations and reflexions, to see what the Neapolitans call *il trionfo di Policinello,* a person for whom they profess peculiar value. Harlequin and Brighella here scarcely share the fondness of an audience, while at Venice, Milan, &c. much pleasantry is always cast into *their* characters.

The triumph was a pageant of prodigious size, set on four broad wheels like our waggons, but larger; it consisted of a pyramid of men, twenty-eight in number, placed with wonderful ingenuity all of one size, something like what one has seen exhibited at Sadler's Wells, the Royal Circus, &c.; dressed in one uniform,

uniform, viz. the white habit and puce-coloured mask of *caro* Policinello; difpofed too with that fkill which tumblers alone can either difplay or defcribe; a fingle figure, ftill in the fame drefs, crowning the whole, and forming a point at the top, by ftanding fixed on the fhoulders of his companions, and playing merrily on the fiddle; while twelve oxen of a beautiful white colour, and trapped with many fhining ornaments, drew the whole flowly over the city, amidft the acclamations of innumerable fpectators, that followed and applauded the performance with fhouts.

What I have learned from this fhow, and many others of the fame kind, is of no greater value than the derivation of *his name* who is fo much the favourite of Naples: but from the mafk he appears in, cut and coloured fo as exactly to refemble a *flea*, with hook nofe and wrinkles, like the body of that animal; his employment too, being ever ready to hop, and fkip, and jump about, with affectation of uncommon elafticity, giving his neighbours a fly pinch from time to time: all thefe circumftances, added to the very intimate acquaintance and connection all the Neapolitans have with this, the leaft offenfive of all the innumerable infects that infest them; and, last of all, *his name*, which, corrupt it how we please, was originally *Pulicinello*; leaves me persuaded that the appellation is merely *little flea*.

' A drive to Caserta, the king's great palace, not yet quite finished, carries me away from this important study, and leaves me little time to enjoy the praises due to a discovery of so much consequence.

The drive perhaps pleased us better than the palace, which is a prodigious mass of building indeed, and to my eye appears to cover more space than proud Versailles itself; court within court, and quadrangle within quadrangle; it is an enormous bulk to be sure—not pile—for it is not high in proportion to the surrounding objects somehow; and being composed all of brick, presents ideas rather of squat solidity, than of princely magnificence. Ostentation is expected always to strike, as elegance is known to charm, the beholder; and space seldom fails in its immediate effect upon the mind; but here the *valley* (I might say *hole*) this house is set in, looks too little for it; and offends one in the same manner as the more beautiful

beautiful buildings do at Buxton, where from every hill one expects to tumble down upon the new Crescent below. The stair-case is such, however, as I am persuaded no other palace can shew; vastly wider than any the French king can boast, and infinitely more precious with regard to the marbles which compose its sides. The immensity of it, however, though it enhances the value, does not do much honour to the taste of him who contrived it. No apartments can answer the expectations raised by such an approach; and in fact the chapel alone is worthy an ascent so fit for a triumphal procession, instead of a pair of stairs. That chapel is I confess of exquisite beauty and elegance; and there is a picture, by Mengs, of the blessed Virgin Mary's presentation when a girl, that is really *paitrie des graces;* it scarcely can be admired or commended enough, and one can scarcely prevail on one's self ever to quit it. Her marriage, a picture on the other side, is not so happily imagined; but it seems as if the painter thought that joke too good to part with, that there never was a particularly excellent picture of a wedding; and that Poussin himself

himself failed, when having represented all the six other sacraments so admirably, that of marriage has been found fault with by the connoisseurs of every succeeding generation.

Well! if the palace at Caserta must be deemed more heavy than handsome, I fear the gardens must likewise be avowed to be laid out in a manner one would rather term savage than natural: all artifice is banished however: the king of Naples scorns petty tricks for the amusement of petty minds;—he turns a whole river down his cascade,—*a real one;* and if its formation is not of the first rate for assuming an appearance of nature, it has the merit of being sincerely that which others only pretend to be: while I am told that his architects are now employed in connecting the great stones awkwardly disposed in two rows down each side the torrent, with the very rocks and mountains among which the spring rises; if they effect this, their cascade will, so far as ever I have read or heard, be single in its kind.

Van Vittelli's aqueduct is a prodigiously beautiful, magnificent, and what is more, a useful performance: having the finest models of antiquity, he is said to have surpassed them all.

all. Why such superb and expensive methods should be still used to conduct water up and down Italy, any more than other nations, or why they are not equally necessary in France and England, nobody informs me. Madame de Bocages enquired long ago, when she was taken to see the fountain Trevi at Rome, why they had no water at Paris but the Seine? I think the question so natural, that one wishes to repeat it; and one great reason, little urged by others, incites me to look with envy on the delicious and almost innumerable gushes of water that cool the air of Naples and of Rome, and pour their pellucid tides through almost every street of those luxurious cities: *it is this*, that I consider them as a preservative against that dreadfullest of all maladies, canine madness; a distemper which, notwithstanding the excessive heat, has here scarcely a name. Sure it is the plenty of drink the dogs meet at every turn, that must be the sole cause of a blessing so desirable.

My stay has been always much shorter than I wished it, in every great town of Italy; but *here!* where numberless wonders strike the sense without fatiguing it, I do feel double pleasure;

pleasure; and among all the new ideas I have acquired since England lessened to my sight upon the sea, those gained at Naples will be the last to quit me. The works of art may be found great and lovely, but the drunken Faun and the dying Gladiator will fade from one's remembrance, and leave the glow of Solfaterra and the gloom of Posilippo indelibly impressed. Vesuvius too! that terrified me so when first we drove into this amazing town, what future images can ever obliterate the thrilling sensations it at first occasioned? Surely the sight of old friends after a tedious absence can alone supply the vacancy that a mind must feel which quits such sublime, such animated scenery, and experiences a sudden deprivation of delight, finding the bosom all at once unfurnished of what has yielded it for three swiftly-flown months, perpetual change of undecaying pleasures.

To-morrow I shall take my last look at the Bay, and driving forward, hope at night to lodge at Terracina.

JOURNEY from NAPLES to ROME.

The morning of the day we left our fair Parthenope was paſſed in recollecting her various charms: every one who leaves her carries off the ſame ſenſations. I have aſked ſeveral inhabitants of other Italian States what they liked beſt in Italy except home; it was Naples always, dear delightful Naples! When I ſay this, I mean always to exclude thoſe whoſe particular purſuits lead them to cities which contain the prize they preſs for. Engliſh people when unprejudiced expreſs the like preference. Attachments formed by love or friendſhip, though they give charms to every place, cannot be admitted as a reaſon for commending any one above the reſt. A traveller without candour it is vain to read; one might as well hope to get a juſt view of nature by looking through a coloured glaſs, as to gain a true account of foreign countries, by turning over pages dictated by prejudice.

With the nobility of Naples I had no acquaintance, and can of courſe ſay nothing of their manners. Thoſe of the middling people ſeem to be behind-hand with their neighbours; it is so odd that they should never yet have arrived at calling their money by other names than those of the weights, an *ounce* and a *grain*; the coins however are not ugly.

The evening of the day we left this surprising city was spent out of its king's dominions, at Terracina, which now affords one of the best inns in Italy; it is kept by a Frenchman, whose price, though high, is regulated, whose behaviour is agreeable, and whose suppers and beds are delightful. Near the spot where his house now stands, there was in ancient Pagan days a temple, erected to the memory of the beardless Jupiter called Anxurus, of which Pausanias, and I believe Scaliger too, take notice; though the medal of Pansa is *imago barbata, sed intonsa*, they tell me; and Statius extends himself in describing the innocence of Jupiter and Juno's conversation and connection in their early youth. Both of them had statues of particular magnificence venerated with very peculiar ceremonies, erected for them in this town, however, *ut Anxur fuit quæ nunc Terracinæ sunt* *. The tenth Thebaid too speaks much *de templo*

---

* Which was once Anxur, and now is Terracina.

sacro et Junoni puellæ, Jovis Axuro *; and who knows after all whether these odd circumstances might not be the original reason of Anxur's grammatical peculiarity, well known to all from the line in old *Propria que maribus*,

. ` Et genus Anxur quod dat utrumque?

This place was founded and colonised by Æmilius Mamercus and Lucius Plautus, Anno Mundi 3725 I think; they took the town of Priverna, and sent each three hundred citizens to settle this new city, where Jupiter Anxurus was worshipped, as Virgil among so many other writers bears testimony:

Circeumque jugum, quèis Jupiter Anxuris arvis Præsidet †. 7th ÆNEID.

Æmilius Mamercus was a very pious consul, and when he served before with Genutius his colleague, made himself famous for driving the nail into Minerva's temple to stop the progress of the plague; he was therefore likely

* The temple sacred to the maiden Juno and unrazored Jove.
† And the steep hills of Circe stretch around,
Where fair Feronia boasts her stately grove,
And Anxur glories in her guardian Jove. PITT.

enough

enough to encourage this superstitious worship of the beardless Jupiter.

Some books of geography, very old ones, had given me reason to make enquiry after a poisonous fountain in the rocks near Terracina. My enquiries were not vain. The fountain still exists, and whoever drinks it dies; though Martial says,

> Sive salutiferis candidus Anxur acquis *.

The place is now cruelly unwholesome however; so much so, that our French landlord protests he is obliged to leave it all the summer months, at least the very hot season, and retire with his family to Molo di Gaeta. He told us with rational delight enough of a visit the Pope had made to those places some few years ago; and that he had been heard to say to some of his attendants how there was no *mal aria* at all thereabouts in past days: an observation which had much amazed them. It was equally their wonder how his Holiness went o'walking about with a book in his hand or pocket, repeating verses by the seaside. One of them had asked the name of the book, but nobody could remember it. " Was it *Virgil?*" said one of our company. " Eh mon

---

* White Anxur's salutary waters roll.

Dieu,

Dieu, Madame, vous l'avez divinée *," replied the man. But, O dear (thought I), how would thefe poor people have ftared, if their amiable fovereign, enlightened and elegant as his mind is, had happened to talk more in their prefence of what he had been reading on the fea fhore, *Virgil* or *Homer*; had he chanced to mention that *Molo di Gaeta* was in ancient times the feat of the Leftrygones, and inhabited by canibals, men who eat one another! and furely it is fcarcely lefs comical than curious, to recollect how Ulyffes expreffes his fenfations on firft landing juft by this now lovely and highly-cultivated fpot, when he pathetically exclaims,

———Upon what coaft,
On what *new* region is Ulyffes toft?
Poffeft by wild barbarians fierce in arms,
Or men whofe bofoms tender pity warms?
Pope's Odyssey.

Poor Cicero might indeed have afked the queftion feven or eight centuries after, in days falfely faid to be civilized to a ftate of perfection; when his moft inhuman murder near this town, completed the meafure of their crimes; who to their country's fate added that of its philofopher, its orator, its acknowledged father

* Why, Madam, you have hit on it fure enough.

and

and preserver.—Cruel, ungrateful Rome! ever crimson with the blood of its own best citizens—theatre of civil discord and proscriptions, unheard of in any history but her's; who, next to Jerusalem in sins, has been next in sufferings too; though twice so highly favoured by Heaven—from the dreadful moment when all her power was at once crushed by barbarism, and even her language rendered *dead* among mankind—to the present hour, when even her second splendours, like the last gleams of an *aurora borealis*, fade gradually from the view, and sink almost imperceptibly into decay. Nor can the exemplary virtues and admirable conduct of *this*, and of her four last princes, redeem her from ruin long threatened to her past tyrannical offences; any more than could the merits of Marcus Aurelius and Antoninus Pius compensate for the crimes of Tiberius, Caligula, and Nero.—Let the death of Cicero, which inspired this rhapsody, contribute to excuse it; and let me turn my eyes to the bewitching spot—

Where Circe dwelt, the daughter of the day.

That such enchantresses should inhabit such regions could have been scarce a wonder in
Homer's

Homer's time I trow; the fame country ftill retains the fame power of producing fingers, to whom our Englifh may with propriety enough cry out;

———Hail, *foreign* wonder!
Whom certes our rough fhades did never breed.
MILTON.

That fhe fhould be the offspring of Phœbus too, in a place where the fun's rays have fo much power, was a well-imagined fable one may *feel;* and her inftructions to Ulyffes for his fucceeding voyage, juft, apt, and proper: enjoining him a prayer to Crateis the mother of Scylla, to pacify her rapacious daughter's fury, is the leaft intelligible of all Circe's advice, to me. But when I faw the nafty trick they had at Naples, of fpreading out the ox-hides to dry upon the fea fhore, as one drives to Portici; the Sicilian herds, mentioned in the Odyffey, and their crawling fkins, came into my head in a moment.

We have left thefe fcenes of fabulous wonder and real pleafure however; left the warm veftiges of claffic ftory, and places which have produced the nobleft efforts of the human mind; places which have ferved as no ignoble themes for truly immortal fong; all
quitted

quitted now! all left for recollection to mufe on, and for fancy to combine: but thefe eyes I fear will never more furvey them. Well! no matter—

> When like the bafelefs fabric of a vifion,
> The cloud-capt tow'rs, the gorgeous palaces,
> The folemn temples, the great globe itfelf,
> Yea all which it inherit, fhall diffolve;
> And like fome unfubftantial pageant faded
> Leave not a wreck behind.

R O M E.

WE are come here juft in time to fee the three laft days of the carnival, and very droll it is to walk or drive, and fee the people run about the ftreets, all in fome gay difguife or other, and mafked, and patched, and painted to make fport. The Corfo is now quite a fcene of diftraction; the coachmen on the boxes pretending to be drunk, and throwing fugar-plumbs at the women, which it grows hard to find out in the crowd and confufion, as the evening, which fhuts in early, is the feftive hour: and there is fome little hazard in parading the ftreets, left an accident might happen;

pen; though a temporary rail and *trottoir* are erected, to keep the carriages off. Our high joke, however, seems to consist in the men putting on girls clothes: a woman is somewhat a rarity at Rome, and strangely superfluous as it should appear by the extraordinary substitutes found for them on the stage: it is more than wonderful to see great strong fellows dancing the women's parts in these fashionable dramas, pastoral and heroic ballets as they call them. *Soprano* singers did not so surprise me with their feminine appearance in the Opera; but these clumsy *figurantes*! all stout, coarse-looking men, kicking about in hooped petticoats, were to me irresistibly ridiculous: the gentlemen with me however, both Italians and English, were too much disgusted to laugh, while *la premiere danseuse* acted the coquet beauty, or distracted mother, with a black beard which no art could subdue, and destroyed every illusion of the pantomime at a glance. All this struck nobody but us foreigners after all; tumultuous and often *tender* applauses from the pit convinced us of *their heart-felt* approbation! and in the parterre sat gentlemen much celebrated at Rome for their taste and refinement.

As

As their exhibition did not please our party, notwithstanding its singularity, we went but once to the theatre, except when a Festa di Ballo was advertised to begin at eleven o'clock one night, but detained the company waiting on its stairs for two hours at least beyond the time: for my own part I was better amused *outside* the doors, than *in*. Masquerades can of themselves give very little pleasure except when they are new things. What was most my delight and wonder to observe, was the sight of perhaps two hundred people of different ranks, all in my mind strangely ill-treated by a nobleman; who having a private supper in the room, prevented their entrance who paid for admission; all mortified, all crowded together in an inconvenient place; all suffering much from heat, and more from disappointment; yet all in perfect good humour with each other, and with the gentleman who detained in longing and ardent, but not impatiently-expressed expectation, such a number of *Romans:* who, as I could not avoid remarking, certainly deserve to rule over all the world once more, if, as we often read in history, *command* is to be best learned from the practice of *obedience*.

The mafquerade was carried on when we had once begun it, with more tafte and elegance here, than either at Naples or Milan; fo it was at Florence, I remember; more dreffes of contrivance and fancy being produced. We had a very pretty device laft night, of a man who pretended to carry ftatues about as if for fale: the gentlemen and ladies who perfonated the figures were incomparable from the choice of attitudes, and fkill in colouring; but *il carnovale è morto*, as the women of quality told us laft night from their coaches, in which they carried little tranfparent lanthorns of a round form, red, blue, green, &c. to help forward the fhine; and thefe they throw at each other as they did fugar plums in the other towns; while the millions of fmall thin bougie candles held in every hand, and ftuck up at every balcony, make the *Strada del Popolo* as light as day, and produce a wonderfully pretty effect, gay, natural, and pleafing.

The unftudied hilarity of Italians is very rejoicing to the heart, from one's confcioufnefs that it is the refult of cheerfulnefs really felt; not a mere incentive to happinefs hoped for. The death of Carnovale, who was carried to his grave with fo many candles fuddenly extinguifhed at twelve o'clock laſt night, has reſtored us to a tranquil poſſeſſion of ourſelves, and to an opportunity of examining the beauties of nature and art that ſurround one.

St. Peter's church is inconteſtably the firſt object in this city, ſo crowded with ſingle figures: That this church ſhould be built in the form of a Latin croſs inſtead of a Greek one may be wrong for ought I know; that columns would have done better than piers inſide, I do not think; but that whatever has been done by man might have been done better, if that is all the critics want, I readily allow. This church is, after all their objections, nearer to perfect than any other building in the world; and when Michael Angelo, looking at the Pantheon, ſaid, " Is this the beſt our vaunted anceſtors could do? If ſo, I will ſhew the advancement of the art, in ſuſpending a dome of equal ſize to this up in the air." He made a glorious boaſt, and was perhaps the only perſon ever exiſting who could have performed his promiſe.

The figures of angels, or rather cherubims, eight feet high, which ſupport the vaſes holding holy water, as they are made after the form of babies, do perfectly and cloſely repreſent infants of eighteen or twenty months old;

old; nor till one comes quite clofe to them indeed, is it poffible to difcern that they are coloffal. This is brought by fome as a proof of the exact proportions kept, and of the prodigious fpace occupied, by the area of this immenfe edifice; and urged by others, as a peculiarity of the *human* body to deceive fo at a diftance, moft unjuftly: for one is furprifed exactly in the fame manner by the doves, which ornament the church in various parts of it. *They* likewife appear of the natural fize, and completely within one's reach upon entering the door, but foon as approached, recede to a confiderable height, and prove their magnitude nicely proportioned to that of the angels and other decorations.

The canopied altar, and its appurtenances, are likewife all coloffal I think, when they tell me of four hundred and fifty thoufand pounds weight of bronze brought from the Pantheon, and ufed to form the wreathed pillars which fupport, and the torfes that adorn it. Yet airy lightnefs and exquifite elegance are the characteriftics of the fabric, not gloomy greatnefs, or heavy folidity. How immenfe then muft be the fpace it ftands stands on! four hundred and sixty-seven of my steps carried me from the door to the end. Warwick castle would be contained in its middle *aisle*. Here are one hundred and twenty silver lamps, each larger than I could lift, constantly burning round the altar; and one never sees either them, or the light they dispense, till forced upon the observation of them, so completely are they lost in the general grandeur of the whole. In short, with a profusion of wealth that astonishes, and of splendour that dazzles, as soon as you enter on an examination of its secondary parts, every man's *first* impression at entering St. Peter's church, must be surprise at seeing it so clear of superfluous ornament. This is the true character of innate excellence, the *simplex munditiis*, or *freedom from decoration*; the noble simplicity to which no embellishment can add dignity, but seems a mere appendage. Getting on the top of this stupendous edifice, is however the readiest way to fill one's mind with a deserving notion of its extent, capacity, and beauty; nor is any operation easier, so happily contrived is the ascent. Contrivance here is an ill-chosen word too, so luminous so convenient is the walk,

walk, so spacious the galleries beside, that all idea of danger is removed, when you perceive that even round the undefended cornice, our king's state coach might be most safely driven.

The monuments, although incomparable, scarcely obtain a share of your admiration for the first ten times of your surveying the place; Guglielmo della Porta's famous figure, supporting that dedicated to the memory of Paul the Third, was found so happy an imitation of female beauty by some madman here however, that it is said he was inflamed with a Pigmalion-like passion for it, of which the Pontiff hearing, commanded the statue to be draped. The steps at almost the end of this church we have all heard were porphyry, and so they are; how many hundred feet long I have now forgotten :—no matter; what I have not forgotten is, that I thought as I looked at them—why so they *should* be porphyry—and that was all. While the vases and cisterns of the same beautiful substance at Villa Borghese attracted my wonder; and Clement X.'s urn at St. John de Lateran, appeared to me an urn fitter for the ashes of an Egyptian monarch, Busiris or Sesostris,

than

than for a Christian priest or sovereign, since universal dominion has been abolished. Nothing, however, *can* look very grand in St. Peter's church; and though I saw the general benediction given (I hope partook it) upon Easter day, my constant impression was, that the people were below the place; no pomp, no glare, no dove and glory on the chair of state, but what looked too little for the area that contained them. Sublimity disdains to catch the vulgar eye, she elevates the soul; nor can long-drawn processions, or splendid ceremonies, suffice to content those travellers who seek for images that never tarnish, and for truths that never can decay. Pius Sextus, in his morning dress, paying his private devotions at the altar, without any pageantry, and with very few attendants, struck me more a thousand and a thousand times, than when arrayed in gold, in colours, and diamonds, he was carried to the front of a balcony big enough to have contained the conclave; and there, shaded by two white fans, which, though really enormous, looked no larger than that a girl carries in her pocket, pronounced words which on account of the height they came from were difficult to hear.

All

All this is known and felt by the managers of these theatrical exhibitions so certainly, that they judiciously confine great part of them to the *Capella Sestini,* which being large enough to impress the mind with its solemnity, and not spacious enough for the priests, congregation, and all, to be lost in it, is well adapted for those various functions that really make Rome a scene of perpetual gala during the holy week; which an English friend here protested to me he had never spent with so little devotion in his life before. The *miserere* has, however, a strong power over one's mind—the absence of all instrumental music, the steadiness of so many human voices, the gloom of the place, the picture of Michael Angelo's last judgment covering its walls, united with the mourning dress of the spectators—is altogether calculated with great ingenuity to give a sudden stroke to the imagination, and kindle that temporary blaze of devotion it is wisely enough intended to excite: but even this has much of its effect destroyed, from the admission of too many people: crowd and bustle, and struggle for places, leave no room for any ideas to range themselves,

themselves, and least of all, serious ones: nor would the opening of our sacred music in Westminster Abbey, when nine hundred performers join to celebrate *Messiah*'s praises, make that impression which it does upon the mind, were not the king, and court, and all the audience, as still as death, when the first note is taken.

The ceremony of washing the pilgrims feet is a pleasing one: it is seen in high perfection here at Rome; where all that the pope personally performs is done with infinite grace, and with an air of mingled majesty and sweetness, difficult to hit, but singularly becoming in him, who is both priest of God, and sovereign of his people.

But how, said Cyrus, shall I make men think me more excellent than themselves? *By being really so*, replies Xenophon, putting his words into the mouth of Cambyses. Pius Sextus takes no deeper method I believe, yet all acknowledge his superiour merit: No prince can less affect state, nor no clergyman can less adopt hypocritical behaviour. The Pope powders his hair like any other of the Cardinals, and is, it seems, the first who has ever done so. When he takes the air it is in

a faa fashionable carriage, with a few, a very few guards on horseback, and is by no means desirous of making himself a shew. Now and then an old woman begs his blessing as he passes; but I almost remember the time when our bishops of Bangor and St. Asaph were followed by the country people in North Wales full as much or more, and with just the same feelings. One man in particular we used to talk of, who came from a distant part of our mountainous province, with much expence in proportion to his abilities, poor fellow, and terrible fatigue; he was a tenant of my father's, who asked him how he ventured to undertake so troublesome a journey? It was to get my good Lord's blessing, replied the farmer, *I hope it will cure my rheumatism.* Kissing the slipper at Rome will probably, in a hundred years more, be a thing to be thus faintly recollected by a few very old people; and it is strange to me it should have lasted so long. No man better knows than the present learned and pious successor of St. Peter, that St. Peter himself would permit no act of adoration to his own person; and that he severely reproved Cornelius for kneeling to him, charging him to rise and stand upon his feet, adding

ing these remarkable words, *seeing I also am a man* *. Surely it will at last be found out among them that such a ceremony is inconsistent with the Pope's character as a Christian priest, however it may suit state matters to continue it in the character of a sovereign. The road he is now making on every side his capital to facilitate foreigners approach, the money he has laid out on the conveniencies of the Vatican, the desire he feels of reforming a police much in want of reformation, joined to an immaculate character for private virtue and an elegant taste for the fine arts, must make every one wish for a long continuance of his health and dignity; though the wits and jokers, when they see his arms up, as they are often placed in galleries, &c. about the palace, and consist of a zephyr blowing on a flower, a pair of eagle's wings, and a few stars, have invented this Epigram, to say that when the Emperor has got his eagle back, the King of France his fleurs de lys, and the stars are gone to heaven, Braschi will have nothing left him but the *wind*:

 Redde aquilam Cæsari, Francorum lilia regi,
 Sydera redde polo, cætera Brasche tibi.

---

* Surge, et ego ipse homo sum.   VULGATE.

These

These verses were given me by an agreeable Benedictine Friar, member of a convent belonging to St. Paul's *fuor delle mura*; he was a learned man, a native of Ragusa, had been particularly intimate with Wortley Montague, whose variety of acquirements had impressed him exceedingly.

He shewed us the curiosities of his church, the finest in Rome next to St. Peter's, and had silver gates; but the plating is worn off and only the brass remains. There is an old Egyptian candlestick above five feet high preserved here, and many other singularities adorn the church. The Pillars are 136 in number, all marble, and each consisting of one unjoined and undivided piece; 40 of these are fluted, and two which did belong to a temple of Mars are seven feet and a half each in diameter. Here is likewise the place where Nero ran for refuge to the house of his freed-man, and in the cloister a stone, with this inscription on it,

Hoc specus accepit post aurea tecta Neronem*.

Here is an altar supported by four pillars of red porphyry, and here are the pictures of all the popes; St. Peter first, and our present Braf-

---

* This hiding-hole received Nero after his golden house.

chi laſt. It has given much occaſion for chat that there ſhould now be no room left to hang a ſucceſſor's portrait, and that he who now occupies the chair is painted in powdered hair and a white head-dreſs, ſuch as he wears every day, to the great affliction of his courtiers, who recommended the uſual ſtate diadem; but " No, no," ſaid he, " there have been *red cap Popes* enough, mine ſhall be only white, and *white it is*.

This beautiful edifice was built by the Emperor Theodoſius, and there is an old picture at the top, of our Saviour giving the benediction in the form that all the Greek prieſts give it now. Apropos, there have been many ſects of Oriental Chriſtians dropt into the Church of Rome within theſe late years; a very venerable old Armenian ſays Greek maſs regularly in St. Peter's church every day before one particular altar; his long black dreſs and white beard attracted much of my notice; he ſaw it did, and now whenever we meet in the ſtreet by chance he kindly ſtands ſtill to bleſs me. But the Syriac or Maronites have a church to themſelves juſt by the *Bocca della Verita*; and extremely curious we thought it to ſee their ceremonies upon Palm Sunday, when their aged patriarch, not

leſs

less than ninety-three years old, and richly attired with an inconvenient weight of drapery, and a mitre shaped like that of Aaron in our Bibles exactly, was supported by two olive coloured orientals, while he pronounced a benediction on the tree that stood near the altar, and was at least ten feet high. The attendant clergy, habited after their own eastern taste, and very superbly, had broad phylacteries bound on their foreheads after the fashion of the Jews, and carried long strips of parchment up and down the church, with the law written on them in Syriac characters, while they formed themselves into a procession and led their truly reverend principal back to his place. An exhibition so striking, with the view of many monuments round the walls, sacred to the memory of such, and such a bishop of Damascus, gave so strong an impression of Asiatic manners to the mind, that one felt glad to find Europe round one at going out again. One of the treasures much renowned in it we have seen to-day, the transfiguration painted by Rafaelle; it was the *first* thing the Emperor *did* visit when he came to Rome, and so a Franciscan Friar who shews it, told us. He saw a gentleman walk into church it seems, and leaving his friends

at

at dinner, went out to converſe with him. "*Pull aſide the curtain, Sir,*" ſaid the ſtranger, "*for I am in haſte to ſee this maſter-piece of your immortal Raphael.*" I was as willing to be in a hurry as *he*, ſays the Friar, and obſerved how fortunate it was for us that it could not be moved, otherwiſe we had loſt it long ago; for, Sir, ſaid I, they would have carried it away from poor *Monte Citoria* to ſome finer *temple* long ago; though, let me tell you, this is an elegant Doric building too, and one of Bramante's beſt works, much admired by the Engliſh in particular. I hope, if it pleaſe God now that I ſhould live but a very little longer, I may have the honour of ſhewing it *the Emperor*. " Is he expected?" enquired the gentleman. "Every day, Sir," replies the Friar. " And *well now*," cries the foreigner, " what ſort of a man do you expect to ſee? Why, Sir, you ſeem a traveller, did *you* ever ſee him?" quoth the Franciſcan. " Yes, ſure, my good friend, very often indeed, he is as plain a man as myſelf, has good intentions, and an honeſt heart; and I think you would like him if you knew him, becauſe he puts nobody out of their way."

This

This dialogue, natural and simple, had taken such hold of our good *religieux*'s fancy, that not a word would he say about the picture, while his imagination was so full of the prince, and of his own amazement at the salutation of his companions, when returning to the refectory;—" Why, Gaetano," cried they, "thou haſt been converſing with *Cæſar*:"—I too liked the tale, becauſe it was artleſs, and becauſe it was true. But the picture ſurpaſſes all praiſe; the woman kneeling on the foreground, her back to the ſpectators, ſeems a repetition of the figure in Raphael's famous picture of the Vatican on fire, that is ſhewn in the chambers called particularly by his name; where the perſonifications of Juſtice and Meekneſs, engraved by Strange, ſeize one's attention very forcibly: it is obſervable, that the firſt is every body's favourite in the painting, the laſt in the engraving.

Raphael's Bible, as one of the long galleries is comically called by the connoiſſeurs, breaks one's neck to look at it. The ſtories, beginning with Adam and Eve, are painted in ſmall compartments; the colouring as vivid now as if it were done laſt week; and the
arabeſques

arabefques fo gay and pretty, they are very often reprefented on fans; and we have fine engravings in England of all, yet, though exquifitely done, they give one fomehow a falfe notion of the whole: fo did Piranefi's prints too, though invaluable, when confidered by themfelves as proofs of the artift's merit. His judicious manner, however, of keeping all coarfe objects from interfering with the grand ones, though it mightily increafes the dignity, and adds to the fpirit of his performance, is apt to lead him who wifhes for information, into a ftyle of thinking that will at laft produce difappointment as to general appearances, which here at Rome is really difproportionate to the aftonifhing productions of art contained within its walls.

But I muft leave this glorious Vatican, with the perpetual regret of having feen fcarcely any thing of its invaluable library, except the prodigious fize and judicious ornaments of it: neither book nor MS. could I prevail on the librarian to fhew me, except fome love-letters from Henry the Eighth of England to Anne Boleyn, which he faid were moft likely to intereft *me:* they were very grofs and indecent ones to be fure; fo I felt offended, and

went

went away, in a very ill humour, to see Castle St. Angelo; where the emperor Adrian intended perpetually to repose; but the urn containing his ashes is now kept in a garden belonging to one of the courts in the palace, near the Apollo and other Greek statues of peculiar excellence. From his tomb too, some of the pillars of St. Paul's were taken, and this splendid mausolæum converted into a sort of citadel, where Sixtus Quintus deposited three millions of gold, it is said; and Alexander the Sixth retired to shield himself from Charles the Eighth of France, who entered Rome by torch-light in 1494, and forced the Pope to give him what the French historians call *l'investiture du royaume de Naples;* after which he took Capua, and made his conquering entry into Naples the February following, 1495; Ferdinand, son of Alphonso, flying before him. This Pope was the father of the famous Cæsar Borgia; and it was on this occasion, I believe, that the French wits made the well-known distich on his notorious avarice and rapacity:

Vendit Alexander claves, altaria, Christum,
    Vendere jure potest, emerat ille prius*.

---

* Our Alexander sells keys, altars, heaven;
When law and right are sold, he'll buy:—that's even.

This Castle St. Angelo went once, I believe, under the name of the Ælian Bridge, when the emperor Adrian first fixed his mind on making a monument for himself there. The soldiers of Belisarius are said to have destroyed numberless statues which then adorned it, by their odd manner of defending the place from the Gothic assaulters. It is now a sort of tower for the confinement of state prisoners; and decorated with many well-painted, but ill-kept pictures of Polydore and Julio Romano.

The fire-works exhibited here on Easter-day are the completest things of their kind in the world; three thousand rockets, all sent up into the air at once, make a wonderful burst indeed, and serve as a pretty imitation of Vesuvius: the lighting up of the building too on a sudden with fire-pots, had a new and beautiful effect; we all liked the entertainment vastly.

I looked here for what some French *recueil*, *Menagiana* if I remember rightly, had taught me to expect; this was some brass cannon belonging to Christina queen of Sweden, who had caused them to be cast, and added an engraving

engraving on them with these remarkable words;

Habet sua fulmina Juno*.

No such thing, however, could be found or heard of. Indeed a search after truth requires such patience, such penetration, and such learning, that it is no wonder she is so seldom got a glimpse of; whoever is diligently desirous to find her, is so perplexed by ignorance, so retarded by caution, so confounded by different explications of the same thing recurring at every turn, so sickened with silly credulity on the one hand, and so offended with pertness and pyrrhonism on the other, that it is fairly rendered impossible for one to keep clear of prejudices, while the steady resolution to do so becomes itself a prejudice.—But with regard to little follies, it is better to laugh at than lament them.

We were shewn one morning lately the spot where it is supposed St. Paul suffered decapitation; and our *Cicerone* pointed out to us three fountains, about the warmth of Buxton, Matlock, or Bristol water, which were said to have burst from the ground at the moment of his martyrization. A Dutch gen-

* Juno too has her thunder.

tleman in company, and a steady Calvinist, loudly ridiculed the tradition, called it an idle tale, and triumphantly expressed his *certain conviction*, that such an event *could not possibly* have ever taken place. To this assertion no reply was made; and as we drove home all together, the conversation having taken a wide range and a different turn, he related in the course of it a long Rousseau-like tale of a lady he once knew, who having the strongest possible attachment to one lover, married another upon principles of filial obedience, still retaining inviolate her passion for the object of her choice, who, adorned with every excellence and every grace, continued a correspondence with her across the Atlantic ocean; having instantly changed his hemisphere, not to give the husband disturbance; who on his part admired their letters, many of which were written in *his* praise, who had so cruelly interrupted their felicity. Seeing some marks of disbelief in my countenance, he begun observing, in an altered tone of voice, that *common* and *vulgar* minds might hold such events to be out of possibility, and such sentiments to be out of nature, but it was only because they were *above* the *comprehension* and beyond the

the reach of people educated in large and corrupt capitals, Paris, Rome, or London, to think true. Now was not some share of good breeding (best learned in great capitals perhaps) necessary to prevent one from retorting upon such an orator—that it was more likely nature should have been permitted to deviate in favour of Paul the apostle of Jesus Christ, than of a fat inhabitant of North Zealand, no way distinguished from the mass of mankind?

But we have been called to pass some moments on the Cælian hill; and see the *Chiesa di San Gregorio*, interesting above all others to travellers who delight in the vestiges of Pagan Rome: as, having been built upon a Patrician's house, it still to a great degree retains the form of one; while to the scholar who is pleased with anecdotes of ecclesiastical history, the days recur when the stone chair they shew us, contented the meek and venerable bishop of Rome who sate in it, while his gentle spirit sought the welfare of every Christian, and refused to persecute even the benighted and unbelieving Jews; opposing only the arms of piety and prayer, to the few enemies his transcendent excellence had raised him.

him. His picture here is considered as a master-piece of Annibale Caracci; and it is strange to think that the trial-pieces, as they are called, should be erroneously treated of in the Carpenteriana: when speaking of the contention between the two scholars, to decide which the master sent for an old woman, Monsieur de Carpentier tells us the dispute lay between Domenichino and Albano—a gross mistake; as it was Guido, not Albano, who ventured to paint something in rivalry with Domenichino, relative to St. Andrew and his martyrdom; and these trial-pieces produced from her the same preference given by every spectator who has seen them since: for when Caracci (unwilling to offend either of his scholars, as both were men of the highest rank and talents) enquired of *her* what *she* thought of Guido's performance?—" Indeed," replied the old woman, " I have never yet looked at it, so fully has my mind been occupied by the powers shewn in that of Domenichino."

The *vecchia* is here at Rome the common phrase when speaking of your only female servant, a person not unlike an Oxford or Cambridge bed-maker in appearance; and much amazed

amazed was I two days ago at the anfwer of *our vecchia*, when curiofity prompted me to afk her age:—" *O, Madam, I am a very aged woman,*" was the reply, " *and have two grandchildren married; I am forty-two years old*, poveretta me!" I told an Italian gentleman who dined with us what Caterina had faid, and begged him to afk the *laquais de place*, who waited on us at table, a fimilar queftion. He appeared a large, well-looking, fturdy fellow, about thirty-eight years old; but faid he was fcarce twenty-two; that he had been married fix years, and had five children. How old was your wife when you met?—" Thirteen, Sir," anfwered Carlo: fo all is kept even at leaft; for if they end life fooner than in colder climates, they begin it earlier it is plain.

Yet fuch things feem ftrange to *us;* fo do a thoufand which occur in thefe warm countries in the commoneft life. Brick floors, for example, with hangings of a dirty printed cotton, affording no bad fhelter for fpiders, bugs, &c.; a table in the fame room, encrufted with *verd antique*, very fine and worthy of Wilton houfe; with fome exceeding good copies

copies of the finest pictures here at Rome; form the furniture of our present lodging: and now we have got the little casement windows clean to look at it, I pass whole hours admiring, even in the copy, our glorious descent from the cross, by Daniel de Volterra; which to say truth loses less than many a great performance of the same kind, because its merits consist in composition and design; and as sentiment, not style, is translatable, so grouping and putting figures finely together can be easier transmitted by a copy, than the meaner excellencies of colouring and finishing. Homer and Cervantes may be enjoyed by those who never learned their language, at least to a great degree; while a true taste of Gray's Odes or Martial's Epigrams has been hitherto found exceedingly difficult to communicate. It would, however, be cruel to deny the merit of colouring to Daniel de Volterra's descent from the cross, only because being painted in fresco it has suffered so terribly by time and want of care, but it is now kept covered, and they remove the curtain when any body desires to contemplate its various beauties.

The

The church of Santa Maria Maggiore has been too long unspoken of, rich as it is with the first gold torn from the unfortunate aborigines of America; a present from Ferdinand and Isabella of Spain to the Pope, in return for that permission he had given them to exert and establish their sanguinary sway over those luckless nations. One pillar from the temple of Peace is an ill-adapted ornament to this edifice, built nearly in the form of an ancient *basilica;* and with so expensive a quantity of gilding, that it is said two hundred and fifty thousand pounds were expended on one chapel only, which is at last inferior in fame and beauty to *cappella Corsini;* in riches and magnificence to *cappella Borghese,* where an amethyst frame of immense value surrounds the names, in gold cypher, of our blessed Saviour and his Mother, the ground of which is of transparent jasper, and cannot be matched for elegance or perfection, being at least four feet high (the tablets I mean), and three feet wide. But to this Borghese family, I am well persuaded, it would be a real fatigue to count the wealth which they enjoy.

Villa

Villa Pamphili is a lovely place, or might be made so; but laying out pleasure grounds is not the forte of Italian taste. I never saw one of them, except Lomellino of Genoa, who had higher notions of a garden than what an opera scene affords; and that is merely a range of trees in great pots with gilded handles, and rows of tall cypresses planted one between every two pots, all straight over against each other in long lines; with an octangular marble bason to hold water in the middle, covered for the most part with a thick green scum.

At Villa Pamphili is a picture of Sanctorius, who made the weighing balance spoken of by Addison in the Spectator; it was originally contrived for the Pamphili Pope. And here is an old statue of Clodius profaning the mysteries of the Bona Dea, as we read in the Roman history. And here are camels working in the park like horses: we found them playing about at their leisure when we were at Pisa, and at Milan they were shewed for a show; so little does one state of Italy connect with another. These three cities cannot possibly be much further from each other than London, York, and Exeter; yet the manners differ entirely,

entirely, and what is done in one place is not known at all in the other. It muſt be remembered that they are all ſeparate ſtates.

At the Farneſini palace our amuſements were of a nature very contrary to this; but every place produces amuſement when one is willing to be pleaſed. After looking over the various and ineſtimable productions of art contained there, we came at laſt to the celebrated marriage of Alexander's Roxana; where, ſay ſome of the books of deſcription, the world's greateſt hero is repreſented by Europe's greateſt painter. Some French gentlemen were in our company, and looking ſteadily at the picture for a while, one of them exclaimed, "*A la fin voila ce qui eſt vrayment noble; cet Alexandre là; il paroit effectivement le roy de France même* *."

The Spada palace boaſts Guercino's Dido, ſo diſliked by the critics, who ſay ſhe looks ſpitted; but extremely eſteemed by thoſe that underſtand its merit in other reſpects. There is alſo the very ſtatue kept at this palace, at the feet of which Cæſar fell when he was aſſaſſinated at the capitol: thoſe who ſhew it

* Here's ſomething at laſt that's truly great however! why this Alexander looks fit to be king of France.

never

never fail to relate his care to die gracefully; which was likewise the laſt deſire that occupied Lucretia's mind: Auguſtus too, juſtly conſidering his life as ſcenical, deſired the *plaudits* of his friends at its concluſion: and even Flavius Veſpaſian, a plain man as one ſhould think during a pretty large portion of his exiſtence, wiſhed at laſt to *die like an emperor.* That this ſtatue of Pompey ſhould have been accidentally found with the head lying in one man's ground and the body in another, is curious enough: a rage for appropriation gets the better of all the love of arts; ſo the contending parties (like the ſiſters in David Simple, with their fine-worked carpet) fairly ſevered the ſtatue, and took home each his half; the proprietor of this palace meanwhile purchaſed the two pieces, ſtuck them once more together, and here they are. —Pity but the ſovereign had carried both off for himſelf.—Pius Sextus however is not ſo diſpoſed: he has had a legacy left him within theſe laſt years, to the prejudice of ſome nobleman's heirs; who loudly lamented *their fate*, and *his tyranny* who could take advantage, as they expreſſed it, of their relation's caprice.

price. The Pope did not give it them back, becaufe they behaved fo ill, he faid; but neither did he feize what was left him, by dint of defpotic authority; *he went to law* with the family for it, which I thought a very ftrange thing; *and loft his caufe,* which I thought a ftill ftranger.

We have juft been to fee his gardens; they are poor things enough; and the device of reprefenting Vulcan's cave with the Cyclops, in *water*-works, was more worthy of Ireland than Rome! Monte Cavallo is however a palace of prodigious dignity; the pictures beyond meafure excellent; his collection of china-ware valuable and tafteful, and there are two Mexican jars that can never be equalled.

Villa Albani is the moft dazzling of any place yet however; and the caryatid pillars the fineft things in it, though replete with wonders, and diftracting with objects each worthy a whole day's attention. Here is an antique lift of Euripides's plays in marble, as thofe tell me who can read the Greek infcriptions; I lofe infinite pleafure every day, for want of deeper learning. Pillars not only of

giall'

giall' antique, but of *paglia**, which no house but this possesses, amaze and delight *indocti doctique* though; the Vatican itself cannot shew such: a red marble mask here, three feet and a half in diameter, is unrivalled; they tell you it is worth its own weight in louis d'ors: a canopus in basalt too; and cameos by the thousand.

Mengs should have painted a more elegant Apollo for the centre of such a gallery; but his muses make amends; the Viaggiana says they are all portraits, but I could get nobody to tell me whose. The Abbé Winckelman, who if I recollect aright lost his life by his passion for *virtù*, arranged this stupendous collection, in conjunction with the cardinal, whose taste was by all his contemporaries acknowledged the best in Rome.

We were carried this morning to a cabinet of natural history belonging to another cardinal, but it did not answer the account given of it by our conductors.

What has most struck me here as a real improvement upon social and civil life, was the school of Abate Sylvester, who, upon the

* *Paglia* is a straw-coloured marble, wonderfully beautiful, and extremely rare; found only in some northern tracts of Africa, I am told here.

plan of Monsieur L'Epée at Paris, teaches the deaf and dumb people to speak, read, write, and cast accounts; he likewise teaches them the principles of logic, and instructs them in the sacred mysteries of our holy religion. I am not naturally credulous, nor apt to take payment in words for meanings; much of my *life* has been spent, and all my *youth*, in the tuition of babies; I was of course less likely to be deceived; and I can safely say, that they did appear to have learned all he taught them: that appearance too, if it were no more, is so difficult to obtain, the patience required from the master is so very great, and the good he is doing to mankind so extensive, that I did not like offensively to detect the difference between *knowing* a syllogism, and *appearing* to know it. With regard to morality, the pupils have certainly gained many præcognita. While the capital scholars were shewing off to another party, I addressed a girl who sat working in the window, and perceived that she could explain the meaning of the commandments competently well. To prove the truth, I pretended to pick a gentleman's pocket who stood near me; *peccato!* said the wench distinctly; she was about ten years old perhaps: but a little boy of seven was deservedly the

master's

master's favourite; he really possessed the most intelligent and interesting countenance I ever saw, and when to explain the major, minor, and consequence, he put the two first together into his hat with an air of triumph, we were enchanted with him. Some one to teize him said he had red hair; he instantly led them to a picture of our Saviour which hung in the room, said it was the same colour of his, and ought to be respected.

Surely it is little to the credit of us English, that this worthy Abbé Sylvester should have a stipend from government; that Monsieur L'Epée de Paris should be encouraged in the same good work; that Mr. Braidwood's Scotch pupils should justly engage every one's notice—while *we sleep!* A friend in company seeing me fret at this, asked me if I, or any one else, had ever seen or heard of a person really qualified for the common duties of society by any of these professors;—" That a deaf and dumb man should understand how to discourse about the hypostatic union," added he, " I will not desire; but was there ever known in Paris, Edinburgh, or Rome, a deaf and dumb shoemaker, carpenter, or taylor? Or did ever any watchmaker, fishmonger, or wheelwright, ever keep and willingly

ingly employ a deaf and dumb journeyman?"—Nobody replied; and we went on our way to see what was easier decided upon and understood—the tomb of Raphael at the Pantheon.

Among the many tours that have been written, a musical tour, an astronomical tour, &c. I wonder we have never had a sepulchral tour, making the tombs of famous men its object of attention. That Raphael, Caracci, with many more people of eminence, sleep at the Pantheon, is however but a secondary consideration; few can think of the monuments in this church, till they have often contemplated its architecture, which is so finely proportioned that on first entering you think it smaller than it really is: the pillars are enormous, the shafts all of one piece, the composition Egyptian granite; these are the sixteen which support the portico built by Agrippa; whose car, adorned with trophies and drawn by brazen horses, once decorated the pediment, where the holes formed by the cramps which fastened it are still visible. Genseric changed the gate, and connoisseurs know not where he placed that which Agrippa made: the present gate is magnificent, but does not fit the place; much of the brafs plating was removed by Urban the Eighth, and carried to St. Peter's: he was the Barberini pope; and of him the people faid—

 Barbarini faciunt barbara, &c.

He was a poet however, and could make epigrams himfelf; there is a very fine edition of his poems printed at Paris under the title of *Maffei Barberini Poemata;* and fuch was his knowledge of Greek literature, that he was called the Attic bee. The drunken faun afleep at Palazzo Barberini, by fome accounted the firft ftatue in Rome, we owe wholly to his care in its prefervation.

But the Pantheon muft not be quitted till we have mentioned its pavement, where the precious ftones are not difpofed, as in many churches, without tafte or care, apparently by chance; here all is inlaid, fo as to enchant the eye with its elegance, while it dazzles one with its riches: the black porphyry, in fmall fquares, difpofed in compartments, and infcribed as one may call it in pavonazzino perhaps; the red, bounded by ferpentine; the granites, in giall antique,

antique, have an undescribable effect; no Florence table was ever so beautiful: nor can we here regret the caryatid pillars said by Pliny to have graced this temple in his time; while the four prodigious columns, two of Egyptian granite, two of porphyry, still remain, and replace them so very well. Montiosius, who sought for the pillars said by Pliny to have been placed by Diogenes, an Athenian architect, as supporters of this temple, relates however, that in the year 1580 he saw four of them buried in the ground as high as their shoulders: but it does not seem a tale much attended to; though I confess my own desire of digging, as he points out the place so exactly, on the right hand side of the portico. The best modern caryatids are in the old Louvre at Paris, done by Goujon; but those of Villa Albani are true antiques, perfect in beauty, inestimable in value.

The church that now stands where a temple to Bacchus was built, *fuori delle mura*, engaged our attention this morning. Nothing can be fresher than the old decorations in honour of this jocund deity; the figures of men and women

women carrying grapes, oxen drawing barrels, &c. all the progress of a gay and plenteous vintage; a sacrifice at the end. I forget to whom the church is now dedicated, but *it is* a church; and from under it has been dug up a sarcophagus, all of one piece of red porphyry, which represents on its sides a Bacchanalian triumph; the coffin is nine feet long, and the Pope intends removing it to the Vatican, as a companion to that of Scipio Æmilianus, found a few months ago; his name engraven on it, and his bones inside. Before the proper precautions could be taken however, *they* were flung away by mistaken zeal and prejudice; but an Englishman, say they, who loves an unbeliever, got possession of a *tooth:* meantime the ashes of the emperor Adrian, who, as Eusebius tells us, set up the figure of a swine on the gates of Bethlehem, built a temple in honour of Venus, on Mount Calvary; another to Jupiter, upon the hill whence our Saviour ascended into heaven in sight of his disciples;—*his* ashes are kept in a gilt pine-apple, brought from Castle St. Angelo, and preserved among other rarities in the Pope's musæum. So poor Scipio's remains needed not to have been treated worse than

than *his*, as we know not how good a Christian he might have made, had he lived but 150 years later.: we are sure that he was a wise and a warlike man; that he fulfilled the scriptures unwittingly by burning Carthage; and that he protected Polybius, whom he would scarcely suffer out of his sight.

After looking often at the pictures of St. Sebastian, I have now seen his church founded by Constantine: he lies here in white marble, done by Bernini; and here are more marvellous columns.—I am tired of looking out words to express their various merits.

The catacombs attract me more strongly; here, and here alone, can one obtain a just idea of the melancholy lives, and dismal deaths, endured by those who first dared at Rome to profess a religion inoffensive and beneficial to all mankind. San Filippo Neri has his body somewhat distinguished from the rest of these old pious Christians, among whom he lived to a surprising age, making a cave his residence. Relics are now dug up every day from these retreats, and venerated as having once belonged to martyrs murdered for their early attachment to a belief now happily

happily difplayed over one quarter of the world, and making daily progrefs in another not difcovered when thofe heroic mortals died to atteft its truth. There is however great danger of deception in digging out the relics, thefe catacombs having been in Trajan's time made a burial-place for flaves; and fuch it continued to be during the reign of thofe Roman emperors who defpifed rather than perfecuted the new religion in its infancy. The confcioufnefs of this fact fhould cure the paffion many here fhew for relics, the authenticity of which can never be afcertained. Thofe fhewn to the people in St. Peter's church one evening in the holy week, all came from here it feems; and loudly do our Proteftant travellers exclaim at their idolatry who kneel during the expofure; though for my life I cannot fee how the cuftom is *idolatrous*. He who at the moment a dead martyr's robe is fhewn him, begs grace of God to follow that great example, is certainly doing no harm, or in any wife contradicting the rules of our Anglican church, whofe collects for every faint's day exprefs a like fupplication for power to imitate that faint's good example;

if

if once they worship the relics indeed, it were better they were burned; and to say true, they should not be exposed without a sermon explaining their use, lest vulgar minds might be unhappily misled to mistake the real end of their exposure, and profanely substitute the creature for the Creator. Meanwhile no one has a right to ridicule the love of what once belonged to a favourite character, who has ever felt attachment to a dead friend's snuff-box, or desire of possessing Scipio Æmilianus's tooth.

But the best effort to excite temporary devotion, and commemorate sacred seasons, was the illuminated cross upon Good Friday night, depending from the high dome of St. Peter's church; where its effect upon the architecture is strangely powerful, so large are the masses both of light and shade; whilst the sublime images raised in one's mind by its noble simplicity and solitary light, hover before the fancy, and lead recollection round through a thousand gloomy and mysterious passages, with no unsteady pace however, while she follows the rays which beam from the Redeemer's cross. Being obliged indeed to go with company to these solemnities, takes off from their effect, and turns imagination into another channel, disagreeably enough, but it must be so; where there is a thing to be seen every one will go to see it, and that which was intended to produce sensations of gladness, gratitude, or wonder, ends *in being a show.* The consciousness of this fact only kept me from wishing to see the Duomo di Milano, or the cathedral of Canterbury illuminated just so, with lamps placed in rows upon a plain wooden cross; which surely would have, upon those old Gothic structures, an unequalled effect as to the forming of light and shadow.

But let us wish for any thing now rather than a *fine sight.* I am tired with the very word *a sight*; while the Jesuits church here at Rome, with the figure of St. Ignatius all covered with precious stones, with bronze angels by Bernini, and every decoration that money can purchase and industry collect, rather dazzles than delights one, I think.

The Italians seem to find out, I know not why, that it is a good thing the Jesuits are gone; though they steadily endeavour to retain those principles of despotism which it was their

peculiar

peculiar province to infpire and confirm, and whilft all men muft fee that the work of education goes on worfe in other hands. Indeed nothing can be wilder than committing youth to the tuition of monks and nuns, unlefs, like them, they were intended for the cloifter. Young people are but too ready to find fault with their teachers, and thefe are given into the hands of thofe teachers who have a fault *ready found.* Every chriftian, every moral inftruction driven into their tender minds, weakens with the experience that he or fhe who inculcated it was a reclufe; and that they who are to live in the world forfooth, muft have more enlarged notions: whereas, to a Jefuit tutor, no fuch objection could be made; they were themfelves men of the world, their inftitution not only permitted but obliged them to mingle with mankind, to ftudy characters, to attend to the various tranfactions paffing round them, and take an active part. It was indeed this fpirit pufhed too far, which undid and deftroyed their order, fo ufeful to the church of Rome. Connections with various nations they found beft obtained by commerce, and the fweets of commerce once tafted, what body of men has been yet able to relinquifh?

But

But the principles of trade are formed in direct oppofition to that fpirit of fubordination by which alone *their* exiftence could continue; and it is unjuft to charge any fingle event or perfon with the diffolution of a body, incompatible with that ftate of opennefs and freedom to which Europe is haftening. Incorporated focieties too carry, like individuals, the feeds of their own deftruction in their bofoms;

> As man perhaps the moment of his breath
> Receives the lurking principle of death;
> The young difeafe, which muft fubdue at length,
> Grows with his growth, and ftrengthens with his ftrength.

Every warehoufe opened in every part of Europe, every fettlement obtained abroad, facilitated their undoing, by loofening the band which tied them clofe together. Extremes can never keep their diftance from each other, while human affairs trot but in a circle; and furely no ftronger proof of that pofition can be found, than the fight of Quakers in Penfylvania, and Jefuits in Paraguay, who lived with their converted Indian neighbours, alike in harmony, and peace, and love.

We

We have been led to reflections of this fort by a view of girls portioned here at Rome once a year, some for marriage and others for a nunnery; the last set were handsomest and fewest, and the people I converse with say that every day makes almost visible diminution in the number of monks and nuns. I know not, however, whether Italy will go on much the better for having so few convents; some should surely be left, nay some *must* be left in a country where it is not possible for every man to obtain a decent livelihood by labour as in England: no army, no navy, very little commerce possible to the inland states, and very little need of it in any; little study of the law too, where the prince or baron's lips pronounce on the decision of property; what must people do where so few professions are open? Can they *all* be physicians, priests, or shop-keepers, where little physic is taken, and few goods bought? There are already more clergy than can live, and I saw an *abate* with the *petit collet* at Lucca, playing in the orchestra at the opera for eighteen pence pay. Let us be all contented with the benefits received from heaven, and let us learn better than to set up *self*, whether nation or individual, as a stand-
ard

ard to which all others must be reduced; while imitation is at last but meanness, and each may in his own sphere serve God and love his neighbours, while variety renders life more pleasing. *Quod sis esse velis* *, is an admirable maxim, and surely no self-denial is necessary to its practice; while God has kindly given to Italians a bright sky, a penetrating intellect, a genius for the polite and liberal arts, and a soil which produces literally, as well as figuratively, almost spontaneous fruits. He has bestowed on Englishmen a mild and wholesome climate, a spirit of application and improvement, a judicious manner of thinking to increase, and commerce to procure, those few comforts their own island fails to produce. The mind of an Italian is commonly like his country, extensive, warm, and beautiful from the irregular diversification of its ideas; an ardent character, a glowing landscape. That of an Englishman is cultivated, rich, and regularly disposed; a steady character, a delicious landscape.

I must not quit Rome however without a word of Angelica Kauffman, who, though neither English nor Italian, has contrived to

* What you are already, that desire to be for ever.

charm

charm both nations, and shew her superior talents both here and there. Beside her paintings, of which the world has been the judge, her conversation attracts all people of taste to her house, which none can bear to leave without difficulty and regret. But a sight of the Santa Croce palace, with its disgusting *Job*, and the man in armour so visibly horror-striken, puts all painters but Salvator Rosa for a while out of one's head. This master's works are not frequent, though he painted with facility. I suppose he is difficult to imitate or copy, so what we have of him is *original*. There are too many living objects here in Job's condition, not to render walking in the streets extremely disagreeable; and though we are told there are seventeen markets in Rome, I can find none, the *forum boarium* being kept alike in all parts of the city for ought I see; butchers standing at their shop doors, which are not shut nor the shop cleaned even on Sundays, while blood is suffered to run along the kennels in a manner very shocking to humanity. Mr. Greatheed made me remark that the knife they use now, is the same employed by the old Romans in cutting up the

sacrificed

sacrificed victim; and there are in fact ancient figures in many bas-reliefs of this town, which represent the inferior officers, or *popæ*, with a priest's albe reaching from their arms and tucked up tight, with the sacrificing knife fastened to it, exactly as the modern butcher wears his dress. The apron was called *limus*, and there was a purple welt sewed on it in such a manner as to represent a serpent:

Velati limo, et verbenâ tempora vincti*;

which Servius explains at length, but gives no reason for the serpentine form, by some people exalted, particularly Mr. Hogarth, as nearly allied to the perfection of all possible grace. This looks hypothetical, but when the map of both hemispheres displayed before one, shews that the Sun's path forms the same line, called by pre-eminence Ecliptic, we will pardon their predilection in its favour.

But it is time to take leave of this *Roma triumphans*, as she is represented in one statue with a weeping province at her foot, *so* beautiful! it reminded me of Queen Eleanor and fair Rosamond. The Viaggiana sent me to look for many things I should not have found with-

* Girt with the limus, and as to their temples, *they* were crowned with vervain.

out that inftructive guide, particularly the fingular infcription on Gaudentius the actor's tomb, importing that Vefpafian rewarded him with death, but that *Kriftus*, for fo Chrift is fpelt, will reward him with a finer theatre in heaven. He was one of our early martyrs it appears, and an altar to *him* would furely be now more judicioufly placed at a playhoufe door than one to good St. Anthony, under whofe protection the theatre at Naples is built; with no great propriety it muft be confeffed, when that Saint, difgufted by the levities of life, retired to finifh his exiftence, far from the haunts of man, among the horrors of an unfrequented defert. So has it chanced however, that by many fects of Chriftians, the player and his profeffion have been feverely reprobated; Calvinifts forbid them their walls as deftructive to morality, while Romanifts, confidering them as juftly excommunicated, refufe them the common rites of fepulture. Scripture affords no ground for fuch feverity. Dr. Johnfon once told me that St. Paul quoted in his epiftles a comedy of Menander; and I got the librarian at Venice to fhew me the paffage marked as a quotation in one of the old editions: it is then

a fair

a fair inference enough that the apostle could never have prohibited to his followers the sight of plays, when he cited them himself; they were indeed more innocent than any other show of the days he lived in, and if well managed may be always made subservient to the great causes of religion and virtue. The passage cited was this:

Evil communication corrupts good manners.

And now with regard to the present state of morals at Rome, one must not judge from staring stories told one; it is like Heliogabalus's method of computing the number of his citizens from the weight of their cobwebs. It is wonderful to me the people are no worse, where no methods are taken to keep them from being bad.

As to the society, I speak not from myself, for I saw nothing of it; some English liked it, but more complained. Wanting amusement, however, can be no complaint, even without society, in a city so pregnant with wonders, so productive of reflections; and if the Roman nobles are haughty, who can wonder; when one sees doors of agate, and chimney-ney-pieces of amethyst, one can scarcely be surprised at the possessors pride, should they in contempt turn their backs upon a foreigner, whom they are early taught to consider as the Turks consider women, creatures formed for their *use* only, or at best *amusement*, and devoted to certain destruction at the hour of death. With such principles, the hatred and scorn they naturally feel for a protestant will easily swell into superciliousness, or burst out into arrogance, the moment it is unrestrained by the necessity of forms among the rich, and the desire of pillage in the poor.

But I shall be glad *now* to exchange lapis lazuli for violets, and verd antique for green fields. Here are more amethysts about Rome than lilacs; and the laburnum which at this gay season adorns the environs of London, I look for in vain about the Porta del Popolo. The proud purple tulip which decorates the ground hereabouts, opposed to the British harebell, is *Italy* and *England* again; but the *harebell* by cultivation becomes a *hyacinth*, the *tulip* remains where it began. We are now at the 16th of April, yet I know not how or why it is, although the oaks, young, small, and straggling as they are, have the leaves come out all broad and full already, though the fig is bursting out every day and hour, and the mulberry tree, so tardy in our climate, that I have often been unable to see scarcely a bud upon them even in May, is here completely furnished. Apple trees are yet in blossom round this city, and the few elms that can be found, are but just unfolding. Common shrubs continue their wintry appearance, and in the general look of spring little is gained. The hedges now of Kent and Surrey are filled with fragrance I am sure, and primroses in the remoter provinces torment the sportsmen with spoiling the drag on a soft scenting morning; while limes, horse-chesnuts, &c. contribute to produce an effect not so inferior to that fostered by Italian sunshine, as I expected to find it.

Why the first breath of far-distant summer should thus affect the oak and fig, yet leave the elm and apple as with us, the botanists must tell; few advances have been made in vegetation since we left Naples, that is certain; the hedges were as forward near Pozzuoli two full months ago. And here are no China oranges to be bought; no, nor a cherry or strawberry to be seen, while every man of fashion's fashion's table in London is covered with them; and all the shops of Covent-garden and St. James's-street hang out their luxurious temptations of fruit, to prove the proximity of summer, and the advantages of industrious cultivation. Our eating pleased me more at every town than this; where however a man might live very well I believe for sixpence a-day, and lodge for twenty pounds a-year; and whoever has no attachment to religion, friends, or country; no prejudices to plague his neighbours with, and no dislike to take the world as it goes, for six or seven years of his life, may spend them profitably at Rome, if either his business or his pleasure be made out of the works of art; as an income of two, or indeed one hundred pounds *per annum*, will purchase a man more refined delights of that kind here, than as many thousands in England: nor need he want society at the first houses, palaces one ought to call them, as Italians measure no man's merit by the weight of his purse; they know how to reverence even poverty, and soften all its sorrows with an appearance of respect, when they find it unfortunately connected with noble birth. His own country folk's neglect, as they pass through, would indeed

deed be likely enough to disturb his felicity, and lessen the kindness of his Roman friends, who having no idea of a person's being shunned for *any* other *possible reason* except the want of a pedigree, would conclude that *his* must be essentially deficient, and lament their having laid out so many caresses on an impostor.

The air of this city is unwholesome to foreigners, but if they pass the first year, the remainder goes well enough; many English seem very healthy, who are established here without even the smallest intention of returning home to Great Britain, for which place we are setting out to-morrow, 19th April 1786, and quit a town that still retains so many just pretences to be styled the first among the cities of the earth; to which almost as many strangers are now attracted by curiosity, as were dragged thither by violence in the first stage of its dominion, impelled by superstitious zeal in the second. The rage for antiquities now seems to have spread its contagion of connoisseurship over all those people whose predecessors tore down, levelled, and destoyed, or buried under ground their statues, pictures, every work of art;

Poles,

Poles, Russians, Swedes, and Germans innumerable, flock daily hither in this age, to admire with rapture the remains of those very fabrics which their own barbarous ancestors pulled down ten centuries ago; and give for the head of a *Livia*, a *Probus*, or *Gallienus*, what emperors and queens could not then use with any efficacy, for the preservation of their own persons, now grown sacred by rust, and valuable from their difficulty to be decyphered. The English were wont to be the only travellers of Europe, the only dupes too in this way; but desire of distinction is diffused among all the northern nations, and our Romans here have it more in their power, with that prudence to assist them which it is said they do not want, if not to *conquer* their neighbours once again, at least to *ruin* them, by dint of digging up their dead heroes, and calling in the assistance of their old Pagan deities, *now* useful to them in a *new* manner, and ever propitious to this city, although

> Enlighten'd Europe with disdain
> Beholds the reverenc'd heathen train,
> Nor names them more in this her clearer day,
> Unless with fabled force to aid the poet's lay.
> R. MERRY.

From ROME to ANCONA.

In our road hither we paffed through what remains of Veia, once fo efteemed and liked by the Romans, that they had a good mind, after they had driven Brennus back, to change the feat of empire and remove it there; but a belief in augury prevented it, and that event was put off till Conftantine, feduced by beauties of fituation, made the fatal change, and broke the laft thread which had fo long bound tight together the fafces of Roman fway. We did not tafte the *Vinum Veientanum* mentioned by Martial and Horace, but trotted on to Civita Caftellana, where Camillus rejected the bafe offer of the fchoolmafter of Fefcennium; a good picture of his well-judged punifhment is ftill preferved in the Capitol.

The firft night of our journey was fpent at Otricoli, where I heard the cuckoo fing in a fhriller fharper note than he does in England. I had never liftened to him before fince I left my own country, and his fong alone would have

have convinced me I was no longer in it. Porta di Fuga at Spoleta gates, commemorating poor Hannibal's precipitate retreat after the battle of Thrasymene, may perhaps detain us a while upon this Flaminian way; it was not Titus Flaminius though, whose negotiations ruined Hannibal for ever, that gave name to the road, but Caius of the same family; they had been Flamens formerly, and were therefore called Flaminius, when drawn up by accident or merit into notice; the same custom still obtains with us: we have *Dr. Priestley* and *Mr. Parsons*.

Narni Bridge cost us some trouble in clambering, and more in disputing whether it was originally an aqueduct or a bridge—or both. It is a magnificent structure, irregularly built, the arches of majestic height, but all unequal. There was water enough under it when I was there to take off the impropriety apparent to many of turning so large an arch over so small a stream. Yet notwithstanding that the river was much swelled by long continuance of the violent rains which lately so overflowed the city of Rome, assisted by the Tyber, that people went about the streets in boats, notwithstanding

standing the snows tumbled down from the surrounding mountains, must have much increased the quantity, and lowered the colour of the river:—We found it even *now* yellow with brimstone, and well deserving the epithet of *sulphureous Nar*.

The next day's drive carried us forward to Terni, where a severe concussion of the earth suffered only three nights since, kept all the little town in terrible alarm; the houses were deserted, the churches crowded, supplications and processions in every street, and people singing all night to the Virgin under our window.

Well! the next morning we hired horses for our gentlemen; a little cart, not inconvenient at all, for my maid and me; and scrambled over many rocks to view the far-famed waterfall, through a sweet country, pleasingly intersected with hedges and planted with vines; the ground finely undulated, and rising by gradations of hill till the eye loses itself among the lofty Appenines; surly as they seem, and one would think impervious; but against human art and human ambition, the boundary of rocks and roaring seas lift their proud heads in vain. Man renders them

them subservient to his imperial will, and forces them to facilitate, not impede his dominion; while ocean's self supports his ships, and the mountain yields marble to decorate his palace.

This is however no moment and no place to begin a panegyric upon the power of man, and of his skill to subjugate the works of nature, where the people are trembling at its past, and dreading its future effects.

The cascade we came to see is formed by the fall of a whole river, which here abruptly drops into the Nar, from a height so prodigious, and by a course so unbroken, that it is difficult to communicate, so as to receive the idea: for no eye can measure the depth of the precipice, such is the tossing up of foam from its bottom; and the terrible noise heard long before one arrives so stunned and confounded all my wits at once, that many minutes passed before I observed the horror in our conductors, who coming with us, then first perceived how the late earthquake had twisted the torrent out of its proper channel, and thrown it down another neighbouring rock, leaving the original bed black and deserted, as a dismal proof of the concussion's force.

One

One of our English friends who had visited Schaffhausen, made no difficulty to prefer this wonderful cascade to the fall of the Rhine at that place; and what with the fissures made in the ground by recent earthquakes, the sight of propt-up cottages which fright the fancy more than those already fallen, and the roar of dashing waters driven from their destined currents by what the people here emphatically term palpitations of the earth; one feels a thousand sensations of sublimity unexcited by less accidents, and soon obliterated by real danger.

Why the inhabitants will have this tumbling river be *Topino*, I know not; but no suggestions of mine could make them name it Velino, as our travellers uniformly call it: for, say they, *quello è il nome del forgente**;* and in fact Virgil's line,

Sulfureâ Nar, albus acqua fontesque Velini,

says no more.

The mountains after Terni grow steep and difficult; no one who wishes to see the Appenines in perfection must miss this road, yet are they not comparable to the Alps at best, which being more lofty, more craggy, and

* That's the name of the spring.

almost

almost universally terminating in points of granite devoid of horizontal strata, give one a more majestic idea of their original and duration. Spoleto is on the top of one of them, and Porta della Fuga meets one at its gates. Here as our coach broke (and who can wonder?) we have time to talk over old stories, and *look for streams immortaliz'd in song* : for being tied together only with ropes, we cannot hurry through a country most delightful of all others to be detained in.

The little temple to the river god Clitumnus afforded matter of discussion amongst our party, whether this was, or was not the very one mentioned by Pliny : *Adjacet templum priscum et religiosum. Stat Clitumnus ipse amictus ornatusque* *.

Mr. Greatheed was angry with me for admiring spiral columns, as he said pillars were always meant to support something, and spiral lines betrayed weakness. Mr. Chappelow quoted every classic author that had ever mentioned the white cattle ; and I said that so far as they were whiter than other beasts of the same kind, so far were they worse ; for that

* There was an old religious temple hard by, where Clitumnus himself was venerated with suitable dress and ornaments.

whiteness

whiteness in the works of nature shewed feebleness still more than spirals in the works of art perhaps. So chatting on—but on no Flaminian way, we arrived at Foligno; where the people told us that it was the quality of those waters to turn the clothing of many animals white, and accordingly all the fowls looked like those of *Darking*. I had however no taste of their beauty, recollecting that when I kept poultry, some accident poisoned me a very beautiful black hen, the breed of Lord Mansfield at Caen Wood: she recovered her illness; but at the next moulting season, her feathers came as white as the swans. " Let us look," says Mr. Sh———, " if all the women here have got grey hair.

Tolentino and Macerata we will not speak about, while Loretto courts description, and the richest treasures of Europe stand in the most delicious district of it. The number of beggars offended me, because I hold it next to impossibility that they should want in a country so luxuriantly abundant; and their prostrations as they kneel and kiss the ground before you, are more calculated to produce disgust from British travellers, than compassion. Nor can
I think

I think thefe vagabonds diftreffed in earneft at *this* time above all others; when their fovereign provides them with employment on the beautiful new road he is making, and infifts on their being well paid, who are found willing to work. But the town itfelf of Loretto claims my attention; fo clear are its ftreets, fo numerous and cheerful and induftrious are its inhabitants: one would think they had refolved to rob paffengers of the trite remark which the fight of dead wealth always infpires, *that the money might be better beftowed upon the living poor.* For here are very few poor families, and fewer idlers than one expects to fee in a place where not bufinefs but devotion is the leading characteriftic. So quiet too and inoffenfive are the folks here, that fcarcely any robberies or murders, or any but very petty infringements of the law, are ever committed among them. Yet people grieve to fee that wealth collected, which once diffufed would certainly make many happy; and thofe treafures lying dead, which well difperfed might keep thoufands alive. This obfervation, not always made perhaps by thofe who feel it moft, or that would fooneft give

their

their share of it away, if once possessed, is now, from being so often repeated, become neither *bright* nor *new*. We will not however be petulantly hasty to censure those who first began the lamentation, remembering that our blessed Saviour's earliest disciples, and those most immediately about him too, could not forbear grudging to see precious ointment poured upon his feet, whom they themselves confessed to be the Son of God. We should likewise recollect his mild but grave reproof of those men who gave so decided a preference to the poor over his sacred person, so soon to be sacrificed *for them*, and his testimony to the woman's earnest love and zeal expressed by giving him the finest thing she had. Such acceptance as she met with, I suppose prompted the hopes of many who have been distinguished by their rich presents to Loretto; and let not those at least mock or molest them, who have been doing nothing better with their money. Upon examination of the jewels it is curious to observe that the intrinsic value of the presents is manifestly greater, the more ancient they are; but taste succeeds to solidity in every thing, and proofs of that position may

be

be found every ftep one treads. The veftments, all embroidered over with picked pearl, are quite beyond my powers of eftimation. The gold baby given at the birth of Louis Quatorze, of fize and weight equal to the real infant, has had its value often computed; I forget the fum though. A rock of emeralds in their native bed prefented by the Queen of Portugal, though of Occidental growth, is furely ineftimable; and our fanguinary Mary's heart of rubies is highly efteemed. I afked if Charles the Ninth of France had fent any thing; for I thought *their* prefents fhould have been placed together: far, far even from the wooden image of *her* who was a model of meeknefs, and carried in her fpotlefs bofom the Prince of Peace. Many very exquifite pieces of art too have found their way into the Virgin's cabinet; the pearl however is the ftriking rarity, as it exhibits in the manner of a blot on marble, the figure of our bleffed Saviour fitting on a cloud clafped in his mother's arms. Princefs Borghefe fent an elegantly-fet diamond necklace no longer ago than laft Chriftmas-day; it is valued at a thoufand pounds fterling Englifh: but the riches

riches of that family appear to me inexhaustible. Whoever sees it will say, she might have spent the money better; but let them reflect that one may say that of *all* expence almost; and it is not from the state of Loretto these treasures are taken at last: they *bring* money there; and if any person has a right to complain, it must be the subjects of distant princes, who yet would scarcely have divided among *them* the sapphires, &c. they have sent in presents to Loretto.

It was curious to see the devotees drag themselves round the holy house upon their knees; but the Santa Scala at Rome had shewn me the same operation performed with more difficulty; and a written injunction at bottom, less agreeable for Italians to comply with, than any possible prostration; viz. That no one should spit as he went up or down, except in his pocket-handkerchief. The lamps which burn night and day before the black image here at Loretto are of solid gold, and there is such a crowd of them I scarcely could see the figure for my own part; and that one may see still less, the attendant canons throw a veil over one's face going in.

The

The confessionals, where all may be heard in their own language, is not peculiar to this church; I met with it somewhere else, but have forgotten where, though I much esteemed the establishment. It is very entertaining here too, to see inscriptions in twelve different tongues, giving an account of the miraculous removal and arrival here of the *Santa Casa*: I was delighted with the Welch one; and our conductor said there came not unfrequently pilgrims from the vale of Llwydd, who in their turns told the wonders of their *holy well*. In Latin then, and Greek, and Hebrew, Syriac, Phœnician, Arabic, French, Spanish, German, Welch, and Tuscan, may you read a story, once believed of equal credit, and more revered I fear, than even the sacred words of God speaking by the scriptures; but which is now certainly upon the wane. I told a learned ecclesiastic at Rome, that we should return home by the way of Loretto:— " There is no need," said he, " to caution a native of your island against credulity; but pray do not believe that we are ourselves satisfied with the tale you will read there; no man of learning but knows, that Adrian destroyed

ſtroyed every trace and veſtige of Chriſtianity that he could find in the Eaſt; and he was acute, and diligent, and powerful. The empreſs Helena long after him, with piety that equalled even his profaneneſs, could never hear of this holy houſe; how then ſhould it have waited till ſo many long years after Jeſus Chriſt? Truth is, Pope Boniface the VIIIth, who canonized St. Louis, who inſtituted the jubilee, who quarrelled with Philippe le Bel about a new cruſade, and who at laſt fretted himſelf to death, though he had conquered all his enemies, becauſe he feared ſome loſs of power to the church;—deſired to give mankind a new object of attention, and encouraged an old viſionary, in the year 1296, to propagate the tale he half-believed himſelf; how the bleſſed Virgin had appeared to him, and related the ſtory you will read upon the walls, which was then firſt committed to paper. In conſequence of this intelligence, Boniface ſent men into the Eaſt that he could beſt depend upon, and they brought back juſt ſuch particulars as would beſt pleaſe the Pope; and in thoſe days you can ſcarce think how quick the blaze of ſuperſtition caught and communicated itself: no one wished to deny what his neighbour was willing to believe, and what he himself would then have gained no credit by contradicting. Positive evidence of what the house really was, or whence it came, it was in a few years impossible to obtain; nor did Boniface the VIIIth know it himself I suppose, much less the old visionary who first set the matter a-going. Meantime the house itself has *no foundation*, whatever the story may have; it is a very singular house as you may see; it has been venerated by the best and wisest among Christians now for five hundred years: even the Turks (who have the same method of honouring their Prophet with gifts, as we do the Virgin Mary) respect the very name of Loretto:—why then should the place be to any order of thinking beings a just object of insult or mockery?"—Here he ended his discourse, the recollection of which never left me whilst we remained at the place.

What Dr. Moore says of the singing chaplains with *soprano* voices, who say mass at the altars of Loretto, is true enough, and may perhaps have been originally borrowed from the Pagan celebration of the rites of Cybele.

When Christianity was young, and weak, and tender, and unsupported by erudition, dreadful mistakes and errors easily crept in: the heathen converts hearing much of *Mater Dei*, confounded her idea with that of their *Mater Deorum;* and we were shewn, among the rarities of Rome, a *bronze Madonna,* with a tower on her head, exactly as Cybele is represented.

That the jewels are taken out of this treasury and replaced with false stones, is a speech always said over fine things by the vulgar: I have heard the same thing affirmed of the diamonds at St. Denis; and can recollect the common people saying, when our King of England was crowned, that all the real precious stones were locked up, or sold for state expences; while the jewels shewn to *them* were only calculated to dazzle for the day. As there is always infinite falsehood in the world, so there is always wonderful care, however ill applied, to avoid being duped; a terror which hangs heavily over weak minds in particular, and frights them as far from truth on the one side, as credulity tempts them away from it on the other.

But

But we must visit the apothecary's pots, painted by Raphael, and leave Loretto, to proceed along the side of this lovely sea, hearing the pilgrims sing most sweetly as they go along in troops towards the town, with now and then a female voice peculiarly distinguished from the rest: by this means a new image is presented to one's mind; the sight of such figures too half alarm the fancy, and give an air of distance from England, which nothing has hitherto inspired half so strongly. This charming Adriatic gulph beside, though more than delicious to drive by, does not, like the Mediterranean, convey homeish or familiar ideas; one feels that it belongs exclusively to Venice; one knows that ancient Greece is on the opposite shore, and that with a quick sail one should soon see Macedonia; and descending but a little to the southward, visit Athens, Corinth, Sparta, Thebes—seats of philosophy, freedom, virtue; whence models of excellence and patterns of perfection have been drawn for twenty succeeding centuries!

Here are plenty of nightingales, but they do not sing as well as in Hertfordshire: birds gain in colour as you approach the tropic, but they

they lose in song; under the torrid zone I have heard they never sing at all; with us in England the latest leave off by midsummer, when the work of incubation goes forward, and the parental duties begin: the nightingale too chuses the coolest hour; and though I have yet heard her in Italy only early in the mornings, Virgil knew she sung in the night:

Flet noctem, &c.*

To hear birds it is however indispensably necessary that there should be high trees; and except in these parts of Italy, and those about Genoa and Sienna, no timber of any good growth can I find. The *roccolo* too, and other methods taken to catch small birds, which many delight in eating, and more in taking, lessen the quantity of natural music vexatiously enough; while gaudy insects ill supply their place, and sharpen their stings at pleasure when deprived of their greatest enemies. We are here less tormented than usual however, while the prospects are varied so that every look produces a new and beautiful landscape.

* Nightly lamenting, &c.

Ancona

Ancona is a town perfectly agreeable to strangers, from the good humour with which every nation is received, and every religion patiently endured: something of all this the scholars say may be found in the derivation of its name, which being Greek I have nothing to do with. Pliny tells us its original, and says;

A Siculis condita est colonia Ancona*.

That Dalmatia should be opposite, yet to us at present inaccessible, we all regret; I drank sea water however, so did not leave untasted the waves which Lucan speaks of:

Illic Dalmaticis obnoxia fluctibus Ancon †.

The fine turbots did not any of them fall to our share; but here are good fish, and, to say true, every thing eatable as much in perfection as possible: I could never since I arrived at Turin find real cause of complaint—*serious* complaint I mean except at that savage-looking place called Radicofani; and some other petty town in Tuscany, near

---

* The colony of Ancona, founded by Sicilians.
† The beauteous gulph which fair Ancona laves,
 Ancona wash'd by white Dalmatian waves.

Sienna, where I eat too many eggs and grapes, becauſe there was nothing elſe.

Nice accommodations muſt not be looked for, and need not be regretted, where ſo much amuſement during the day gives one good diſpoſition to ſleep found at night: the worſt is, men and women, ſervants and maſters, muſt often meſs together; but if one frets about ſuch things, it is better ſtay at home. The Italians like travelling in England no better than the Engliſh do travelling in Italy; whilſt an exorbitant expence is incurred by the journey, not well repaid to them by the waiters white chitterlins, tambour waiſtcoats, and independent "*No, Sir,*" echoed round a well-furniſhed inn or tavern; which puts them but in the place of Socrates at the fair, who cried out—"*How many things have theſe people gathered together that I do not want!*"— A noble Florentine complained exceedingly to me once of the Engliſh hotels, where he was made to help pay for thoſe good gold watches the fellows who attended him drew from their pockets; ſo he ſet up his quarters comically enough at the waggoners full Moon upon the old bridge at Bath, to be quit of the *ſchiavitù*, as he called it, of living like a gentleman,

tleman, "where," fays he, "I am not known to be one." The truth is, a continental nobleman can have little heart of a country, where, to be treated as a man of fafhion, he muft abfolutely behave as fuch: his rank is afcertained at *home*, and people's deportment to him regulated by long-eftablifhed cuftoms; nor can it be fuppofed flattering to its prejudices, to feel himfelf joftled in the ftreet, or driven againft upon the road by a rich trader, while he is contriving the cheapeft method of going to look over his manufactory. Wealth diffufed makes all men comfortable, and leaves no man fplendid; gives every body two difhes, but nobody two hundred. Objects of fhow are therefore unfrequent in England, and a foreigner who travels through our country in fearch of pofitive fights, will, after much money fpent, go home but poorly entertained:—" There is neither *quarefima*," will he fay, " nor *carnovale* in *any* fenfe of the word, among thofe infipid iflanders."— For he who does not love our government, and tafte our manners which refult from it, can never be delighted in England; while the inhabitants of our nation may always be
amufed

amused in theirs, without any esteem of it at all.

I know not how Ancona produced all these tedious reflexions: it is a trading place, and a sea-port town. Men working in chains upon the new mole did not please me though, and their insensibility shocks one:—" Give a poor thief something, master," says one impudent fellow;—" *Son stato ladro padrone* *;" —with a grin. That such people should be corrupt or coarse however is no wonder; what surprised me most was, that when one of our company spoke of his conduct to a man of the town—" Why, what would you have, Sir ?"—replies the person applied to—" when the poor creature is *castigato*, it is enough sure, no need to make him be melancholy too:"—and added with true Italian good-nature,—" *Siamo tutti peccatori* †."

The mole is a prodigious work indeed; a warm friend to Venice can scarce wish its speedy conclusion, as the useful and necessary parts of the project are already nearly accomplished, and it would be pity to seduce more

---

* I am a light-fingered fellow, Master.
† We are all sinners you know.

commerce away from Venice, which has already lost so much.

The triumphal arch of Trajan, described by every traveller, and justly admired by all; white as his virtue, shining as his character, and durable as his fame; fixed our eyes a long time in admiration, and made us, while we examined the beautiful structure, recollect his incomparable qualities to whom it was dedicated,—" *Inter Cæsares optimus**,"—says one of their old writers: nor could either column or arch be so sure a proof that he was thought so, as the wish breathed at the inauguration of succeeding emperors; *Sis tu felicior Augusto, melior Trajano* †.

If these Ancona men were not proud of themselves, one should hate them; descended as they are from those Syracusans liberated by Timoleon, who freed them first from the tyranny of Dionysius; fostered afterwards by Trajan, as peculiarly worth *his* notice; and patronised in succeeding times by the good Corsini Pope, Clement XII. whose care for them appears by the useful *lazaretto* he built,

---

* The best among the Cæsars.

† Mayst thou be happier than Augustus!—better than Trajan!

" to

"to save," said he, "our best subjects, our subjects of Ancona."

But we are hastening forward as fast as our broken carriage will permit, to Padua, where we shall leave it: thither to arrive, we pass through Senegallia, built by the Gauls, and still retaining the Gaulish name, but now little remarkable. What struck me most was my own crossing the *Rubicon* in my way back to England, and our comfortable return to

BOLOGNA,

AFTER admiring the high forehead and innocent simper of Baroccio's beauties at Pesaro, where the best European silk now comes from; against which the produce of Rimini vainly endeavours to vie. That town was once an Umbrian colony I think, and there is a fine memorial there where *Diocletianus reposuit*, resolving perhaps to end where Julius Cæsar had begun; he died at Salo however in Dalmatia,

Quâ maris Adriaci longas ferit unda Salones.

Ravenna l'Antica tired more than it pleased us; *Fano* is a populous pretty little town; but I know no reason why it was originally dedicated to Fortune. Truth is, we are weary of thefe facred *fanes*, and long to fee once more our amiable friends at Venice and at Milan.

I have miffed San Marino at laft, but receive kind affurances every day that the lofs is fmall; being now little more than a convent feated on a hill, which affords refuge for robbers; and that the prefent Pope meditates its deftruction as a nufance to the neighbouring towns. There never was any coin ftruck there it feems; I thought there had: but the train of reflections excited by even a diftant view of it are curious enough as oppofed to its protectrefs Rome; which, founded by robbers and banditti, ends in being the feat of fanctity and prieftly government; while San Marino, begun by a hermit, and fecluded from all other ftates for the mere purpofes of purer devotion, finifhes by its neceffary removal as a repofitory for affaffins, and a refuge for thofe who break the laws with violence.

Such is this variable and capricious world! and fo dies away my defire to examine this political curiofity; the extinction of which I am half forry for. Privation is ftill a melancholy

lancholy idea, and were one to hear that the race of wasps were extirpated, it would grieve one.

Bologna affords one time for every meditation. No inn upon the Bath road is more elegant than the Pellegrino; and we regretted our broken equipage the less as it drew us slowly through so sweet a country. The medlar blossoms adorn the hedges with their blanche roses; the hawthorn bushes, later here than with us, perfume them; and the roads, little travelled, do not torment one with the dust as in England, where it not only offends the traveller, but takes away some beauty from the country, by giving a brown or whitish look to the shrubs and trees. We shall repose here very comfortably, or at least change our mode of being busy, which refreshes one perhaps more than positive idleness. " But life," says some writer, " is a continual fever;" and sure ours has been completely so for these two years. A charming lady of our country, for whom I have the highest esteem, protests she shall be happy to get back to London if it is only for the relief of sitting still, and resolving to see no more sights: exchanging fasto, fiera, and frittura,

for

for a muffin, a mop, and a morning newspaper: three things equally unknown in Italy, as the other three among us.

With regard to pictures however, *l'Appetit vient en mangeant**, as I experienced completely when traversing the Zampieri palace with eagerness that increased at every step. I once more half-worshipped the works of divine Guercino. Nothing shall prevent my going to his birth-place at Cento, whether in our way or out of it.

We ran about the Specola again, and received a thousand polite attentions from the gentleman who shewed it. The piece of native gold here is much finer than that we saw among the treasures of Loretto, which being *du nouveau continent* is always inferior. " But every thing does," as Monf. de Buffon observes, " degenerate in the West except birds;" and the Brazilian plumage seems to surpass all possibility of further glow. The continent however shews us no specimens preserved half as well as those of Sir Ashton Lever. The marine rarities here at Bologna are very capital; but I saw them to advantage

* Eating increases one's appetite.

now, in company of Mr. Chappelow. We find this city at once hot, and loud, and pious; lefs empty of occupation though than laft time; for here is a new Gonfaloniere chofen in to-day, and the drums beat, and the trumpets found, and fome donations are diftributed about, much in the proportions Tom Davis defcribes Garrick's to have been; fmall pieces of money, and large pieces of cake, with quantities of meat, bread, and birds, borne about the town in proceffion, to make difplay of *his* bounty, who gives all this away at the time he is elected into office. Kids dreffed with ribbon therefore, alive and carried on men's fhoulders fhowily adorned, lambs wafhed white as fnow, and pretty red and white calves hanging their fimple faces out of fine gilt bafkets, paraded the ftreets all day. What ftruck us moft however was an ox, handfomer and of a more filvery coat than I thought an ox's hide capable of being brought to; his horns gold, and a garland of rofes between them. This was beautiful; reminded one of all one had ever read and heard of victims going to facrifice; and put in our heads again the old ftories of Hercules, Euryftheus, &c.

At

At Bologna though, every thing puts people in mind of their *prayers;* so a few good women nothing doubting but when shows were going forward, religious meanings must be near at hand, dropt down on their knees in the street, and recommended themselves, or their dead friends perhaps, to heaven, with fervent and innocent earnestness, while the cattle passed along. An English clergyman in our company, hurt and grieved, yet half-disposed to laugh, cried, *What are these dear creatures muttering about now for, as if their salvation depended upon it?*—It was absurd enough to be sure; but in order to check our tittering disposition, I recollected to him, that I had once heard an ignorant woman in Hertfordshire repeat the absolution herself after the priest, with equally ill-placed fervour: for which he reprimanded her, and afterwards explained to her the grossness of the impropriety. When we have added to our stock of connoisseurship the graceful Sampson, drinking after his victory, by Guido, in this town, we shall quit it, and proceed through empty and deserted Ferrara to

PADUA.

We set out then for Ferrara, in our kind friend's post-chaise; that is, my maid and I did: our good-natured gentlemen creeping slowly after in the broken coach; and how ended this project for insuring safety? Why in the chaise losing its hind wheel, and in our return to the carriage we had quitted. But it is for ever so, I think;—the sick folks live always, and the well ones die.

We took turn therefore and left our friends; but could not forbear a visit to Cento, where I wished much to see what Guercino had done for the ornament of his native place, and was amply repaid my pains by the sight of one picture, which, for its immediate power over the mind, at least over mine, has no equal even in Palazzo Zampieri. It is a scene highly touching. The appearance of our Saviour to his Mother after his resurrection. The dignity, the divinity of the Christ! the terror-checked transport visible in the parent Saint, whose expressive countenance and pathetic attitude

titude difplay fervent adoration, maternal tenderness, and meek humility at once! How often have I faid, *this* is the fineft picture we have feen yet! when looking on the Caraccis and their fchool. I will fay no more, the painter's art can go no further than *this*. My partial preference of Guercino to any thing and to every thing, fhall not however bribe me to fupprefs my grief and indignation at his ftrange method of commemorating his own name over the altar where he was baptifed, which fhocks every proteftant traveller by its profanenefs, while the Romanifts admire his invention, and applaud his piety. Guercino then, fo called becaufe he was the *little one-eyed man*, had a fancy to reprefent his *real* appellation of *John Francis Barbieri* in the church; and took this mode as an ingenious one, painting St. John upon the right hand, St. Francis on the left, as two large full-length figures, and God the Father in the middle with a *long beard* for *Barbieri*.

This is a mixture of Abel Drugger's contrivance in the Alchymift, and the infantine folly of three babies I once knew in England, children of a nobleman, who were feverely whipt by their governefs for playing at Father,

Son, and Holy Ghoſt, ſitting upon three chairs, with ſolemn countenances, in order to impreſs their tender fancies with a repreſentation of what the good governeſs innocently and laudably had told them about the myſterious and incomprehenſible Trinity. Let me add, that the eldeſt of theſe babies was not ſix years old, and the youngeſt but four, when they were caught in the blaſphemous folly. Our Italians ſeem to be got very little further at forty.

Padua appears cleaner and prettier than it did laſt year; but ſo many things contribute to make me love it better, that it is no wonder one is prejudiced in its favour. It was *ſo* difficult to get ſafe hither, the roads being very bad, the people were ſo kind when we were here laſt, and the very inn-keeper and his aſſiſtants ſeemed ſo obligingly rejoiced to ſee us again, that I felt my heart quite expand at entering the Aquila d'oro, where we were ſoon rejoined by Mr. and Mrs. Greatheed, with whom we had parted in the Romagna, when they took the Perugia road, inſtead of returning by Bologna, a place they had ſeen before. Had we come three days ſooner we might have ſeen the tranſit of Mercury from Abate Toaldo's

Toaldo's obfervatory; but our own tranfit took up all our thoughts, and it is a very great mercy that we are come fafe at laft. I think it was as much as four bulls and fix horfes could do to drag us into Rovigo.

> Bologna la Graffa
> Ma Padua la paffa *,

fay the Venetians: and round this town where the heat is indeed prodigious, they get the beft vipers for the Venice treacle, I am told. Here are quantities of curious plants to be feen blooming now in the botanical garden, and our kind profeffor told me I need not languifh fo for horfe chefnuts; for they would all be in flower as we returned up the Brenta from Venice. " They are all in flower *now*, Sir," faid I, " in my own grounds, eight miles from London: but our Englifh oaks are not half fo forward as yours are." He recollected the aphorifm fo much a favourite with our country folks; how a Britifh heart ought not to dilate with the early funfhine of profperity, or droop at the firft blafts of adverfe fortune, as

---

* Though fat Bologna feeds to the fill,
 Our Padua is fatter ftill.

the British oak refuses to put out his leaves at summer's early solicitations, and scorns to drop them at winter's first rude shake.

Well! I have once more walked over St. Antony's church, and examined the bas reliefs that adorn his shrine; but their effect has ceased. Whoever has spent some time in the Musæum Clementinum is callous to the wonders which sculpture can perform.

Has one not read in Ulloa's travels, of a resting-place on the side of a Cordillera among the Andes, where the ascending traveller is regularly observed to put on additional clothing, while he who comes down the mountain feels so hot that he throws his clothes away? So it is with the shrine of St. Antonio di Padua, and one's passion for the sculpture that adorns it: while Santa Giustina's church retains her power over the mind, a power never missed by simplicity, while great effort has often small effect. But we are hastening to Venice, and shall leave our cares and our coach behind; superfluous as they both are, in a city which admits of neither.

VENICE.

Our watery journey was indeed delightful; friendship, music, poetry combined their charms with those of nature to enchant us, and make one think the passage was too short, though longing to embrace our much-regretted sweet companions. The scent of odoriferous plants, the smoothness of the water, the sweetness of the piano forte, which allured to its banks many of the gay inhabitants, who glad of a change in the variety of their amusements, came down to the shores and danced or sang, as we went by, seized every sense at once, and filled me with unaffected pleasure. I longed to see the weeping willow planted along this elegant stream; but the Venetians like to see nothing weep I fancy: yet the Salix Babylonica would have a fine effect here, and spread to a prodigious growth, like those on which the captive Israelites once hung their harps, on the banks of the river Euphrates. " Of all Europe however," Millar says, " it prospers best in pensive Britain;"

> Nor prov'd the blifs that lulls Italia's breaft,
> When red-brow'd evening calmly finks to reft.

Thefe lines, quoted from Merry's Paulina, remind me of the pleafure we enjoyed in reading that glorious poem as we floated down the Brenta. I have certainly read no poetry fince; that would be like looking at Sanfovino's fculpture, after having feen the Apollo, the Venus, and the Flora Farnefe. The view of Venice only made us fhut the book. Lovely Venice! wife in her councils, grave and fteady in her juft authority, fplendid in her palaces, gay in her cafinos, and charming in all.

> Fama tra noi Roma pompofa e fanta,
> Venezia ricca, faggia, e fignorile*,

fays the Italian who celebrates all their towns by adding a well-adapted epithet to each. But Sannazarius, who experienced in return for it more than even Britifh bounty would have beftowed, exalts it in his famous epigram to a decided preference even over Rome itfelf.

---

* Pompous and holy ancient Rome we call,
Venice rich, wife, and lordly over all.

Viderat

Viderat Adriacis Venetam Neptunus in undis
  Stare urbem, et toti ponere jura Mari;
Nunc mihi Tarpeias quantum vis Jupiter, arces
  Objice, et illa tui mœnia Martis ait
Sit Pelago Tibrim præfers, urbem aspice utramque
  Illam homines dices, hanc posuisse Deos.

And now really, if the subject did not bribe me to admiration of them, I should have much ado to think these six lines better worth fifty pounds a piece, the price Sannazarius was paid for them, than many lines I have read; as mythological allusions are always cheaply obtained, and this can hardly be said to run with any peculiar happiness: for if Mars built the Wall, and Jupiter founded the Capitol, how could Neptune justly challenge this last among all people, to look on both, and say, That men built Rome, but the Gods founded Venice. Had he said, that after all their pains, *this* was the manner in which those two cities would in future times strike all impartial observers, it would have been *enough;* and it would have been *true*, and when fiction has done its best,

Le vray seul est aimable *.

---

* Truth alone is pleasing.

Here, however, is the best translation or imitation I can make, of the best praise ever given to this justly celebrated city. Baron Cronthal, the learned librarian of Brera, gave me, when at Milan, the epigram, and persuaded me to try at a translation, but I never could succeed till I had been upon the grand canal.

> When Neptune first with pleasure and surprise,
> Proud from her subject sea saw Venice rise;
> Let Jove, said he, vaunt his fam'd walls no more,
> Tarpeia's rock, or Tyber's fane-full shore;
> While human hands those glittering fabrics frame,
> By touch celestial beauteous Venice came.

It is a sweet place sure enough, and the caged* nightingales who, when men are most silent, answer each other across the canals, increase the enchantments of Venetian moon-light; while the full gondolas skimming over the tide with a lanthorn in their stern, like glow-worms of a dark evening, dashing the cool wave too as they glide along, leave no moments unmarked by peculiarity of pleasure. The Doge's wedding has however been less brilliant this year; his galleys have been sent to fight the Turks and Corsairs, and the splendor at home of course suffers some tem-

---

* Wilt thou have music? hark, Apollo plays,
And twenty *caged* nightingales shall sing.
SHAKESPEARE.

porary diminution; but the corso of boats in the evening must be for ever charming, and the musical parties upon the water delightful. We passed this morning in Pinelli's library, a collection so valuable from the frequence of old editions, particularly the old fourteen hundreds as we call them, that it is supposed they will be purchased by some crowned head; and here are specimens of Aldus's printing too, very curious; but there are too many curiosities,

I'm strangled with the waste fertility,

as Milton says. Pinelli had an excellent taste for pictures likewise, and here at Venice there are paintings to satisfy, nay satiate connoisseurship herself. Tintoret's force of colouring at St. Rocque's, displayed in the crucifixion, can surely be exceeded by no disposition of light and shade; but the Scuola Bolognese has hardened my heart against merit of any other sort, so much more easy to be obtained, than that of character, dignity, and truth. Paul Veronese forgets too seldom his original trade of *orefice*, there is too much gold and silver in his drapery; and though Darius's ladies are judiciously adorned with a great deal of it here at Palazzo Pisani, I would willingly have
abated

abated some brocade, for an addition of expressive majesty in the Alexander. What a striking difference there is too between Guercino's prodigal returned, and a picture at some Venetian palace of the same story treated by Leandro Bassano! yet who can forbear crying out Nature, nature! when in the last named work one sees the faithful spaniel run out to meet and acknowledge his poor young master though in rags, while the cook admiring the uncommon fatness of the calf, seems to anticipate the pleasure of a jolly day: so if the old father does look a little like pantaloon, why one forgives him, for we are not told that the fable had to do with *nobilta*, though Guercino has made *his* master of the house a rich and stately oriental, who meets and consoles, near a column of Grecian architecture, his penitent son, whose half-uncovered form exhibits beauty sunk into decay, and whose graceful expression of shame and sorrow shew the dignity of his original birth, and little expectation of the ill-endured pains his poverty has caused: the elder brother, meantime, glowing with resentment, and turning with apparent scorn away from the sight of a scene so little to the honour of the family. Basta!
as

as the Italians say; when we were at Rome we purchased a fine view of St. Mark's Place Venice; now we are at Venice we have bought a sketch of Guido's Aurora. The Doge's dinner was magnificent, the plate older and I think finer than the Pope's; I forget on what occasion it was given, I mean the feast, but had it been an annual ceremony our kind friends would have shewn it us last year. We must leave them once more, for a long time I fear, but I part with less regret because the heat grows almost insupportable; and either the stench of the small canals, or else the too great abundance of sardelline, a fresh anchovy with which these seas abound, keep me unwell and in perpetual fear of catching a putrid fever, should I indulge in eating once again of so rich but dangerous a dainty. Besides that one may be tired of exertion, and fatigued with festivity, purchased at the price of sleep and quiet.

   Non Hybla non me specifer capit Nilus,
   Nec quæ paludes delicata Pomptinus
   Ex arce clivi spectat uva Sestini.
   Quid concupiscam ? quæris ergo,—*dormire* *.

---

* Not Hybla's sweets, nor Naples devoloons,
  Nor grapes which hide the hill with rich festoons;
  Nor fat Bologna's valley, have I chose;
  What is your wish then ? May I speak ?—*repose*.

To PADUA.

THEN we returned the twelfth of June, and surely it is too difficult to describe the sweet sensations excited by the enjoyment of

Each rural sight, each rural sound;

as the dear banks of the Brenta first saluted our return to *terra firma* from the watery residence of our *bella dominante*. We dined at a lovely villa belonging to an amiable friend upon the margin of the river, where the kind embraces of the Padrona di Casa, added to the fragrance of her garden, and the sweet breath of oxen drawing in her team, revived me once more to the enjoyment of cheerful conversation, by restoring my natural health, and proving beyond a possibility of doubt, that my late disorder was of the putrid kind. We dined in a grotto-like room, and partook the evening refreshments, cake, ice, and lemonade, under a tree by the river side, whilst my own feelings reminded me of the sailors delight described in Anson's voyages when they landed at Juan Fernandez.

Fernandez. Night was best disposed of in the barge, and I observed as we entered Padua early in the morning, how surprisingly quick had been the progress of summer; but in these countries vegetation is so rapid, that every thing makes haste to come and more to go. Scarce have you tasted green peafe or strawberries, before they are out of season; and if you do *not* swallow your pleasures, as Madame la Presidente said, you have a chance to miss of getting any pleasures at all. Here is no mediocrity in any thing, no moderate weather, no middle rank of life, no twilight; whatever is not night is day, and whatever is not love is hatred; and that the English should eat peaches in May, and green peafe in October, sounds to Italian ears as a miracle; they comfort themselves, however, by saying that they *must* be very insipid, while *we* know that fruits forced by strong fire are at least many of them higher in flavour than those produced by sun; the pine-apple particularly, which West Indians confess eats better with us than with them. Figs and cherries, however, defy a hot-house, and grapes raised by art are worth little except for shew; peaches, nectarines, and ananas are the glory of a British gardener, and no country but England can shew such. Our morning, passed at the villa of the senator Quirini, set us on this train of thinking, for every culled excellence adorned it, and brought to my mind Voltaire's description of Pococuranti in Candide, false only in the ostentation, and *there* the character fails; misled by a French idea, that pleasure is nothing without the delight of shewing that you are pleased, like the old adage, or often-quoted passage about learning:

Scire tuum nihil est, nisi te scire hoc sciat alter *.

A Venetian has no such notions; by force of mind and dint of elegance inherent in it, he pleases himself first, and finds every body else delighted of course, nor would quit his own country except for paradise; while an English nobleman clumps his trees, and twists his river, to comply with his neighbour's taste, when perhaps he has none of his own; feels disgusted with all he has done, and runs away to live in Italy.

The evening of this day was spent at the theatre, where I was glad the audience were no better pleased, for the plaudits of an Italian

* . Thy knowledge is nothing till other men know that thou knowest it.

Platea

Platea at an air they like, when one's nerves are weak and the weather very hot, are all but totally infupportable. What then muft thefe poor actors have fuffered, who laboured fo violently to entertain us? A tragedy in rhyme upon the fubject of Julius Sabinus and his wife Epponina was the reprefentation; and wonderfully indeed did the players ftruggle, and bounce, and fprunt, like vigorous patients refifting the influence of a difeafe called opifthotonos, or dry gripes of Jamaica; "Were their jaws once locked we fhould do better," faid Mr. Chappelow. " Che fpacca monti mai!" exclaimed the gentle Padovani. *Spacca monte* means juft our Englifh Drawcanfir, a fellow that fplits mountains with his blufter, a captain *Blowmedown*.

The fair at Padua is a better place for fpending one's time than the theatre; it is built round a pretty area, and I much wonder the middle is not filled by a band of mufic. Our Aftley is expected to fhine here fhortly, and the ladies are in hafte to fee *il bel Inglefe a Cavallo*; but we muft be feduced to ftay no longer among thofe whom I muft ever leave with grateful regret and truly affectionate regard. Our carriage is repaired, and the man says it will now carry us safely round the world if we please; our first stage however will be no farther than to pretty

VERONA.

THE road from Padua hither is a vile one; one can scarcely make twenty miles a-day in any part of the Venetian state. Its senators, accustomed to water carriage, have little care for us who go by land. The Palanzuola way is worse however, and I am glad once more to see sweet Verona.

Petruchio and Catharine might easily have met with all the adventures related by Grumio on their journey thither, but when once arrived she should have been contented. This city is as lovely as ever, more so than it was last April twelvemonth, when the spring was sullen and backward; every hill now glows with the gay produce of summer, and every valley smiles with plenty expected or pleasure possessed. The antiquities however look less respectable

respectable than when I left them; no amphitheatre will do after the Roman Colossæum, and our triumphal arch here looked so pitiful, I wondered what was come to it. So must it always happen to the performances of art, which we compare one against another, and find that as man made the best of them, so some man may in some moment make a better still: but the productions of nature are the works of God; we can only compare them with other things done by the same Almighty Master, whose power is equally discernible in all, from the fly's antennæ to the elephant's proboscis. Bozza's collection gave birth to this last sentence; the farther one goes the more astonishing grows his musæum, the neglect of which is sure no credit to the present age. I find his cabinet much fuller than I left it, and adorned with many new specimens from the southern seas, besides flying-fish innumerable, beautifully preserved, and one predaceous creature caught in the very act of gorging his prey, a proof of their destruction being instant as that of the dwellers in Pompeia, who had their dinners dished when the eruption overwhelmed them.

We took leave of our learned friends here with concern, but hope to see them again, and tread the stucco floors so prettily mottled and variegated, they look like the cold mock turtle soup exactly, which London pastry-cooks keep in their shops, ready for immediate use.

What an odd thing is custom! here is weather to fry one in, yet after exercise, and in a state of the most violent perspiration, no consequences follow the use of iced beverages, except the sense of pleasure resulting from them at the moment. Should a Bath belle indulge in such luxury, after dancing down forty couple at Mr. Tyson's ball, we should expect to hear next day of her surfeit at least, if not of her sudden death. Lying-in ladies take the same liberty with *their* constitutions, and *say* that no harm comes of it; and when I tell them how differently we manage in England, cry, " *mi pare che dev'essere schiavitù grande in quel paese della benedetta libertà**." Fine muslin linen nicely got up is however, say they, one of the things to be produced only in Great Britain, and much do our Italian ladies admire it, though they look very charmingly

---

* Methinks there seems to be much slavery required from those who inhabit your fine free country of England.

with much less trouble taken. I lent one lady at some place, I remember, my maid, to shew her, as she so much wished it, how the operation of clear-starching was performed; but as soon as it began, she laughed at the superfluous fatigue, as she called it; and her servants crossed themselves in every corner of the room, with wonder that such niceties should be required.—Well they might! for I caught a great tall fellow ironing his lady's best neck-handkerchief with the warming-pan here at Padua very quietly; and she was a woman of quality too, and looked as lovely, when the toilette was once performed, as if much more attention had been bestowed upon it.

PARMA.

WE passed through Mantua the 18th of June, where nothing much attracted my notice, except a female figure in the street, veiled from head to foot, and covered wholly in black; she walked backward and forward along the same portion of the same street, from one to three o'clock, in the heat of the burning sun; her hand held out; but when I, more from curiosity than any better motive put money in it, she threw it silently away, and the beggars picked it up, while she held her hand again as before. This conduct, in any town of England, would be deemed madness or mischief; the woman would be carried before a magistrate to give an account of herself, should the mob forbear to uncase her till they came; or some charitable person would seize and carry her home, fill her pockets with money, and coax her out of the anecdotes of her past life to put in the Magazine; her print would be published, and many engravers struggle for its profits; the name at bottom, *Annabella, or the Sable Matron;* while novels would be written without end, and the circulating libraries would lend them out all the live-long day. Things are differently carried on however at Mantua: I asked one shopkeeper, and she gravely replied, "*per divozione*," and took no further notice: another (to my inquiries, which appeared to him far odder than the woman's conduct) said, The lady was possibly doing a little penance; that he had not minded her till I spoke, but that perhaps it might be some woman of fashion, who having refused a poor

person

person roughly on some occasion, was condemned by her confessor to try for a couple of hours what begging *was*, and learn humanity from experience of evil. The idea charmed me; while the man coolly said, all this was only his conjecture; but that such things were done too often to attract attention; and hoped such virtue was not rare enough to excite wonder. My just applause of such sentiments was stopt by the *laquais de place* calling me to dinner; when he informed me, that he had asked about the person whose behaviour struck me so, and could now tell me all there was to be known: she was a lady of quality, he said, who had lost a dear friend on that day some years past, and that she wore black for two hours ever since upon its anniversary; but that she would now change her dress, and I should see her in the evening at the opera. My recollecting that if *this* were her case, I ought to have been keeping her company (as no one ever lost a friend so dear to them as was my incomparable mother, who likewise left me to mourn her loss on this day thirteen years), spoiled my appetite, and took from me all power of meeting the lady at the theatre.

We went again however to see Virgil's field, and recollected that *tenet nunc Parthenope*; congratulated the giants on their superiority over Pietro de Cortona's paltry creatures, in one of the Roman palaces; and drove forward to Parma, through bad roads enough.

This Mantua is a very disagreeable town; nor was Romeo wrong in lamenting his banishment to it; for though I will not say with him that—

There is no world without Verona's walls;

yet it must be allowed that few places do unite such various excellencies, and that the contrast is very striking between that city and this.

Parma exhibits an appearance somewhat different from all the rest; yet we should scarcely have visited it but for the sake of the four surprising pictures it contains: the *Madona della Scodella* is nature itself; and St. Girolamo exhibits such a proof of fancy and fervour, as are almost inconceivable; the general effect, and the difficulty one has to take one's eye off it, afford conviction of its superior

perior merit, and greatly compenfate for that tafte, character, and expreffion, which are found only in the Caraccis and their fchool. Corregio was perhaps one of the moft powerful geniuffes that has appeared on earth; deftitute of knowledge, or of the means of acquiring it, he has left glorious proofs of what uninftructed man may do, and is perhaps a greater honour to the human fpecies, than thofe who, from fermenting erudition of various kinds, produce performances of more complicated worth. The Fatal Curiofity, and Pilgrim's Progrefs, will live as long as the Prince of Abyffinia, or *Les Avantures de Telemaque*, perhaps: and who fhall dare fay, that Lillo, Bunyan, and Antonio Corregio, were not *naturally* equal to Johnfon, Michael Angelo, and the Archbifhop of Cambray?— Have I faid enough, or can enough be ever faid in praife of a painter, whofe works the great Annibale Caracci delighted to ftudy, to copy, and to praife?

Piacenza we found to offer us few objects of attention: an *improvifatore*, and not a very bad one, amufed that time which would otherwife have been paffed in lamenting our paucity

paucity of entertainment; while his artful praifes of England put me in good humour, fpite of the weather, which is too hot to bear. With all our lamentations about the heat however, here is no *cicala* on the trees, or *lucciola* in the hedges, as at Florence; the days are a little longer too, and the crepufcule lefs abrupt in its departure. How often, upon the *Ponte della Trinitá*, have I fecretly regretted the long-drawn evenings of an Englifh fummer; when the dewy night-fall refrefhes the air, and filent dufk brings on a train of meditations uninfpired by Italian fkies! In this decided country all that is not broad day is dark night; all that is not loud mirth, is penitence and grief; when the rain falls, it falls in a torrent; when the fun fhines, it glows like a burning-glafs; where the people are rich, they ftick gems in their very walls, and make their chimneys of amethyft; where they are poor, they clafp your knees in an agony of pinching want, and difplay difeafes which cannot be a day furvived!

Talking on about Italy in which there is no mediocrity, and of England in which there is nothing elfe, we arrived at Lodi; where I began

began to rejoice in hearing the people cry *no' cor' altr'* again, in reply to our commands; becaufe we were now once more returned to the diftrict and dialect of dear Milan, where we have cool apartments and warm friends; and where, after an abfence of fifteen months, we fhall again fee thofe acquaintance with whom we lived much before; a fenfation always delightfully foothing, even when one returns to lefs amiable fcenes, and lefs productive of innocent pleafure than thefe have been to me. The confcioufnefs of having, while at a diftance, feen few people more agreeable than thofe one left behind; the natural thankfulnefs of one's heart to God, for having preferved one's life fo as to fee them again, expands philanthropy; and gives unaffected comfort in the reftored fociety of companions long concealed from one by accident or diftance.

MILAN.

21st June 1786.

AFTER rejoicing over my house and my friends; after asking a hundred questions, and hearing a hundred stories of those long left; after reciprocating common civilities, and talking over common topics, we observed how much the general look of Milan was improved in these last fifteen months; how the town was become neater, the ordinary people smarter, the roads round their city mended, and the beggars cleared away from the streets. We did not find however that the people we talked to were at all charmed with these new advantages: their convents demolished, their processions put an end to, the number of their priests of course contracted, and their church plate carried by cart-loads to the mint; holidays forbidden, and every saint's name erased from the calendar, excepting only St. Peter and St. Paul; whilst those shopkeepers who worked for monasteries,

monasteries, and those musicians who sung or played in oratorios, are left to find employment how they can;—cloud the countenances of all, and justly; as such sudden and rough reforms shock the feelings of the multitude; offend the delicacy of the nobles; make a general stagnation of business and of pleasure, in a country where *both* depend upon religious functions; and terrify the clergy into no ill-grounded apprehensions of being found in a few years more wholly useless, and as such disinissied.—Well! whatever is done hastily, can scarcely be done quite well; and wherever much is done, a great part of it will doubtless be done wrong. A considerable portion of all this however will be confessed useful, and even necessary, when the hour of violence on one side, and prejudice on the other, is past away; as the fire of London has been found beneficial by those who live in the newly-restored town. Meantime I think the present precipitation indecent enough for my own part; a thousand little errors would burn out of themselves, were they suffered to die quietly away; and when the morning breaks in naturally, it is superfluous as awkward to put the stars out with one's fingers, like the

Hours

Hours in Guercino's Aurora*. Whoever therefore will be at the pains a little to pick their principles, not grasp them by the bunch, will find as many unripe at one end, I believe, as there are rotten at the other: for could we see these hasty innovators erecting public schools for the instruction of the poor, or public work-houses for their employment; did they unlock the treasure-house of true religion, by publishing the Bible in every dialect of their dominions, and oblige their clergy to read it with the souls committed to their charge;—I should have a better idea of their sincerity and disinterested zeal for God's glory, than they give by tearing down his statues, or those of his blessed Virgin Mother, which Carlo Borromæo set up.

The folly of hanging churches with red damask would surely fade away of itself, among people of good sense and good taste; who could not long be simple enough to suppose, that concealing Greek architecture with such transient finery, and giving to God's house the air of a tattered theatre, could in

---

* In the fine cieling of Palazzo Ludovigi at Rome, the Hours which surround Aurora's chariot are employed in extinguishing the Stars with their hands.

any

any wife promote his service, or their salvation. Many superstitious and many unmeaning ceremonies *do* die off every day, because unsupported by reason or religion: Doctor Carpanni, a learned lawyer, told me but to-day, that here in Lombardy they had a custom, no longer ago than in his father's time, of burying a great lord or possessor of lands, with a ceremony of killing on his grave the favourite horse, dog, &c. that he delighted in when alive; a usage borrowed from the Oriental Pagans, who burn even the widows of the deceased upon their funeral pile; and among our monuments in Westminster Abbey, set up in the days of darkness, I have minded now and then the hawk and greyhound of a nobleman lying in marble at his feet; some of our antiquarians should tell us if they killed them.

Another odd affinity strikes me. Half a century ago there was an annual procession at Shrewsbury, called by way of pre-eminence *Shrewsbury Show*; when a handsome young girl of about twelve years old rode round the town, and wished prosperity to every trade assembled at the fair: I forget what else made the amusement interesting; but have heard my mother tell of the particular beauty

of

of some wench, who was ever after called the *Queen*, because she had been carried in triumph as such on the day of *Shrewsbury Show*. Now if nobody gives a better derivation of that old custom, it may perhaps be found a dreg of the Romish superstition, which as many years ago, in various parts of Italy, prompted people to dress up a pretty girl, on the 25th of March, or other season dedicated to the Virgin, and carry her in procession about the streets, singing litanies to her, &c. and ending, in profaneness of admiration, a day begun in idleness and folly. At Rome however no such indecorous absurdities are encouraged: we saw a beautiful figure of the *Madonna*, dressed from a picture of Guido Rheni, borne about one day; but no human creature in the street offered to kneel, or gave one the slightest reason to say or suppose that she was worshipped: some sweet hymns were sung in her praise, as the procession moved slowly on; but no impropriety could I discern, who watched with great attention.

It is time to have done with all this though, and go see the Ambrosian library; which, as far as I can judge, is perfectly respectable. The Prefect's politeness kindly offered my curiosity any thing I was particularly anxious to see, and the learned Mr. Dugati was exceedingly obliging. The old Virgil preserved here with Petrarch's marginal notes in his own hand-writing, interest one much; this little narration, evidently written for his own fancy to feed on, of the day and hour he first felt the impression of Laura's charms, is the best proof of his genuine passion for that lady, as he certainly never meant for our inspection what he wrote down in his own Virgil. Here is likewise the valuable MS. of Flavius Josephus the Jewish historian, a curiosity deservedly admired and esteemed: it is kept with peculiar care I think, and is in high preservation: A Syriac bible too, very fine indeed, from which I understand they are now going to print off some copies. I have been taught by the scholars not to think a Syriac bible of the Samaritan text so very rare; but the Septuagint in that language is so exceedingly scarce, that many are persuaded this is the only one extant; and as our Lord, in his quotations from the old law, usually cites that version, it is justly preferred to all others. Leonardo da Vinci's famous folio preserved in this library, for which James I. of England offered three thousand ducats, an event recorded here over the cheft that contains it on a tablet of marble, deferves attention and reverence: nothing feems above, nothing below, the obfervation of that prodigious genius. He has in this, and other volumes of the fame curious work, apparently put down every painter's or mathematician's thought that croffed his imagination. It is a *Leonardiana**, the common-place book of a great and wife man; nor did our Britifh fovereign ever with more good fenfe evince his true love of learning, than by his princely offer of its purchafe.

Till now the looking at friends, and rarities, and telling old ftories, and feeing new fights, &c. has lulled my confcience afleep, nor fuffered me to recollect that, dazzled by the brightnefs of the Corregios at Parma, the account of their prefs, the fineft in Europe, and infinitely fuperior to our Bafkerville, efcaped me. They have a glorious collection too of bibles in their library; their illuminations are moft delicate, and their

---

* One volume of this Leonardiana is now in the private library of the king of England at the queen's houfe in the park, preferved from Charles or James the Firft's collection, and written with the left hand, or rather backwards, to be read only with the help of a mirror.

bind-

bindings pompous, but they poſſeſs a modern MS. of ſuch ſingular perfection, that none of thoſe finiſhed when chirography was more cultivated than it is now, can at all pretend to compare with it. The characters are all gilt, the leaves vellum, the miniatures finiſhed with a degree of nicety rarely found in union, as here, with the utmoſt elegance and taſte. No words I can uſe will give a juſt idea of this little MS.: whoever is a true fancier of ſuch things, would find his trouble well repaid, if he left London only to look at it. The book contains private devotions for the ducheſs with ſuitable ornaments—I will talk no more of it.

The fine coloſſal figure of the Virgin Mary in heaven crowned by her Son's hand, painted in the cieling of ſome church at Parma, has a bad light, and it is difficult to comprehend its ſublimity. One approaches nearer to underſtand the merits of that ſingular performance when one looks at Caracci's copy of it, kept in the Ambroſian library here at Milan. But how was I ſurpriſed to hear related as a fact happening to *him*, the old ſtory told to all who go to ſee St. Paul's cathedral in London, of our Sir James Thornhill, who, while he was intent on painting the cupola, walked backward to look at the effect, till, arriving at the very edge of the scaffold, he was in danger of dashing his brains out by falling from that horrible height upon the marble below, had not some bystander possessed readiness of mind to run suddenly forward, and throw a pencil daubed in white stuff which stood near him, at the figure Sir James's eyes were fixed on, which provoked the painter to follow him threatening, and so saved his life. Could such an accident have happened twice? and is it likely that to either of these persons it ever happened at all? Would such men as Annibal Caracci and Sir James Thornhill have exposed themselves upon an undefended scaffold, without railing it round to prevent their tumbling down, when engaged in a work that would take them many days, nay weeks, to finish it? Impossible! in every nation traditionary tales shake my belief exceedingly; and what astonishes one more than it disgusts, if possible, is to see the same story fitted to more nations than one.

It is now many years since a counsellor related at my house in Surrey the following narration, of which I had then no doubts, or idea of suspicion; for he said he was himself witness to the fact, and laid the scene at St. Edmondsbury, a town in our county of Suffolk: how a man accused of murder, with every corroborating circumstance, escaped by the steady resolution of one juryman, who could not, by any arguments or remonstrances of his companions, be prevailed on to pronounce the fellow guilty, though every possible circumstance combined to ascertain him as the person who took the deceased's life; and how, after all was over, the juryman confessed privately to the judge, that *he himself*, by such and such an accident, had killed the farmer, of whose death the other stood accused. This event, true or false, of which I have since found the rudiments in a French Recueil, was told me at Venice by a gentleman as having happened *there*, under the immediate inspection of a friend he named. Quere, whether any such thing ever happened at all in any time or place? but laxity of narration, and contempt of all exactness, at last extinguish one's best-founded confidence in the lips of mortal man. It is, however, clearly proved, that no duty is so difficult as to preserve truth in all our transactions, while no transaction is so trifling as to preclude

clude temptation of infringing it: for if there is no intereſt that prompts a liar, his vanity ſuffices; nor will we mention the ſuggeſtions of cowardice, malignity, or any ſpecies of vice, when, as in theſe laſt-mentioned ſtories, many fictions are invented by well-meaning people, who hope to prevent miſchief, inculcate the poſſibility of hanging innocence, &c. and violate truth out of regard to virtue.

Well, well! our good Italians here will not condeſcend to live or lie, if now and then they ſcruple not to tell one. No man in this country pretends either to tenderneſs or to indifference, when he feels no diſpoſition to be indifferent or tender; and ſo removed are they from all affectation of ſenſibility or of refinement, that when a conceited Engliſhman ſtarts back in pretended rapture from a Raphael he has perhaps little taſte for, it is difficult to perſuade theſe ſincerer people that his tranſports are poſſibly put on, only to deceive ſome of his countrymen who ſtand by, and who, if he took no notice of ſo fine a picture, would laugh, and ſay he had been throwing his time away, without making even the common and neceſſary improvements expected from every gentleman who travels through Italy; yet ſurely it is a choice delight to
live

live where the everlasting scourge held over London and Bath, of *what will they think?* and *what will they say?* has no existence; and to reflect that I have now sojourned near two years in Italy, and scarcely can name one conceited man, or one affected woman, with whom, in any rank of life, I have been in the least connected.

In Naples we see the works of nature displayed; at Rome and Florence we survey the performances of art; at every place in Italy there is much worthy one's esteem, said the Venetian Resident one day very elegantly; and at Milan there is the *Abate Boffi*. Should I forbear to add *my* testimony to such talents and such virtue, which, expanded by nature to the wide range of human benevolence, he knows how to concentre occasionally for the service of private friendship, how great would be my ingratitude and neglect, while no character ever so completely resembled his, as that of the famous *Hough* well known in England by the title of the *good* Bishop of Worcester. His ingenuity in composing and placing these words on the 13th of May 1775, is perhaps one of his least valuable jeux d'esprit; but pretty, when one knows that on that day the empress was born, on that day the archduke arrived at Milan on a visit to his brother, and on that day the duchess was delivered of a son. The words may be read our way or the Chinese:

Natalis	Adventus	Partus
Matris	Fratris	Conjugis
Felix	Optatus	Incolumis
Principem	Aulam	Urbem
	Lectificabant.	

What a foolish thing it is in princes to give pain in a place like this, where all are disposed to derive pleasure even from praising them! There is a natural loyalty among the Lombards, which oppression can scarcely extinguish, or tyranny destroy: and, as I have said a thousand times, they *pretend* to love no one; they *do* love their rulers; and, rather grieve than growl at the afflictions caused by their rapacity.

I was told that I should find few discriminations of character in Italy; but the contrary proves true, and I do not wonder at it. Among those people who, by being folded or driven all together in flocks as the French are, with one fashion to serve for the whole society, a man may easily contract a similarity of manners

ners by rubbing down each asperity of character against his nearest neighbour, no less plastic than himself; but here, where there is little apprehension of ridicule, and little spirit of imitation, monotonous tediousness is almost sure to be escaped. The very word *polite* comes from *polish* I suppose; and at Paris the place where you enjoy *le veritable vernis St. Martin* in perfection, the people can scarcely be termed *polished*, or even *varnished*: they are *glazed*; and every thing slides off the *exterieur* of course, leaving the heart untouched. It is the same thing with other productions of nature; in caverns we see petrifactions shooting out in angular and excentric forms, because in Castleton Hole dame Nature has fair play; while the broad beach at Brighthelmstone, evermore battered by the same ocean, exhibits only a heap of round pebbles, and those round pebbles all alike.

But we must cease reflections, and begin describing again. We have got a country house for the remaining part of the hot weather upon the confines of the Milanese dominions, where Switzerland first begins to bow her bleak head, and soften gradually in the sunshine of Italian fertility. From every walk

walk and villa round this delightful spot, one sees an assemblage of beauties rarely to be met with: and there is a resemblance in it to the Vale of Llwydd, which makes it still more interesting to *me*. But we have obtained leave to spend a week of our destined Villeggiatura at the Borromæan palace, situated in the middle of Lago Maggiore, on the island so truly termed Isola Bella; every step to which from our villa at Varese teems with new beauties, and only wants the sea to render it, in point of mere landscape, superior to any thing we have seen yet.

Our manner of living here is positively like nothing real, and the fanciful description of oriental magnificence, with Seged's retirement in the Rambler to his palace on the Lake Dambea, is all I ever read that could come in competition with it: for here is one barge full of friends from Milan, another carrying a complete band of thirteen of the best musicians in Italy, to amuse ourselves and them with concerts every evening upon the water by moonlight, while the inhabitants of these elysian regions who live upon the banks, come down in crowds to the shores glad to receive additional

additional delight, where satiety of pleasure seems the sole evil to be dreaded.

It is well known that the wild mountains of Savoy, the rich plains of Lombardy, the verdant pastures of Piedmont, and the pointed Alps of Switzerland, form the limits of Lago Maggiore: where, upon a naked rock, torn I trust from some surrounding hill, or happily thrown up in the middle of the water by a subterranean volcano, the Count Borromæo, in the year 1613, began to carry earth; and lay out a pretty garden, which from that day has been perpetually improving, till an appearance of eastern grandeur which it now wears, is rendered still more charming by all the studied elegance of art, and the conveniencies of common life. The palace is constructed as if to realise Johnson's ideas in his Prince of Abyssinia: the garden consists of ten terraces; the walls of which are completely covered with orange, lemon, and cedrati trees, whose glowing colours and whose fragrant scent are easily discerned at a considerable distance, and the perfume particularly often reaches as far as to the opposite shore: nor are standards of the same plants wanting. I measured one not the largest in the grove, which had been planted

one hundred and five years; it was a full yard and a quarter round. There were forty-six of them set near each other, and formed a delightful shade. The cedrati fruit grows as large as a late romana melon with us in England; and every thing one sees, and every thing one hears, and every thing one tastes, brings to one's mind the fortunate islands and the golden age. Walks, woods, and terraces *within* the island, and a prospect of unequalled variety *without*, make this a kind of fairy habitation, so like something one has seen represented on theatres, that my female companion cried out as we approached the place, " If we go any nearer now, I am sure it will all vanish into air." There is solidity enough however: a little village consisting of eighteen fishermen's houses, and a pretty church, with a dozen of well-grown poplars before it, together with the palace and garden, compose the territory, which commodiously contains two hundred and fifty souls, as the circuit is somewhat more than a measured mile and a half, but not two miles in all: and we have cannons to guard our Calypso-like dominion, for which Count Borromæo pays tribute to the king of Sardinia; but has
himself

himself the right of raising men upon the main land, and of coining money at *Macau*, a little town amid the hollows of these rocks, which present their irregular fronts to the lake in a manner surprisingly beautiful. He has three other islets on the same water, for change of amusement; of which that named la Superiore is covered with a hamlet, and l'Isola Madre with a wood full of game, guinea fowl, and common poultry; a summer-house beside furnished with chintz, and containing so many apartments, that I am told the uncle of the present possessor, having quarrelled with his wife, and resolving in a pet to leave the world, shut himself up on that little spot of earth, and never touched the continent, as I may call it, for the last seventeen years of his life. Let me add, that he had there his church and his chaplain, three musical professors in constant pay, and a pretty yatcht to row or sail, and fetch in friends, physicians, &c. from the main land. His nephew has not the same taste at all, seldom spending more than a week, and that only once a-year, among his islands, which are kept however quite in a princely style: the family crest, a unicorn, made in white marble,

ble, and of coloſſal greatneſs, proudly overlooking ten broad terraces which riſe in a pyramidal form from the water: each wall richly covered with orange and lemon trees, and every parapet concealed under thickly-flowering ſhrubs of inceſſant variety, as if every climate had been culled, to adorn this tiny ſpot. More than a hundred beds are made in the palace, which has likewiſe a grotto floor of infinite ingenuity, and beautiful from being happily contraſted againſt the general ſplendour of the houſe itſelf. I have ſeen no ſuch effort of what we call taſte ſince I left England, as theſe apartments on á level with the lake exhibit, being all roofed and wainſcotted with well-diſpoſed ſhellwork, and decorated with fountains in a lively and pleaſing manner. The library up ſtairs had many curious books in it—a Camden's Britannia particularly, tranſlated into Spaniſh; an Arabic Bible worthy of the Bodleian collection, and well-choſen volumes of natural hiſtory to a very ſerious degree of expence. Painting is not the firſt or ſecond boaſt of Count Borromæo, but there are ſome tolerable landſcapes by Tempeſta, and three famous pictures of Luca Giordano, well known in London

don by the general diffusion of their prints, reprefenting the Rape of the Sabines, the Judgment of Paris, and the Triumph of Galatea. Thefe large hiftory pieces adorn the walls of the vaft room we dine in; where, though we never fit down fewer than twenty or twenty-five people to table, all feem loft from the greatnefs of its fize, till the concert fills it in the evening.

It is the garden however more than the palace which deferves defcription. He who has the care of it was born upon the ifland, and never ftrayed further than four miles, he tells me, from the borders of his mafter's lake. Sure he muft think the fall of man a fable: *he* lives in Eden ftill. How much muft fuch a fellow be confounded, could he be carried blind-folded in the midft of winter to London or to Paris! and fet down in Fleet-ftreet or Rue St. Honoré! That he underftands his bufinefs fo as to need no tuition from the inhabitants of either city, may be feen by a fig-tree which I found here ingrafted on a lemon; both bear fruit at the fame moment, whilft a vine curls up the ftem of the lemon-tree, dangling her grapes in that delicious company with apparent fatisfaction to herfelf.

Another

Another inoculation of a moſs-roſe upon an orange, and a third of a carnation upon a cedrati tree, gave me new knowledge of what the gardener's art, aided by a happy climate, could perform. But when rowing round the lake with our band of muſic yeſterday, we touched at a country ſeat upon the ſide which joins the Milaneſe dominion, and I found myſelf preſented with currants and gooſeberries by a kind family, who having made their fortune in Amſterdam, had imbibed ſome Dutch ideas; my mind immediately felt her elaſtic force, and willingly confeſſed that liberty, ſecurity, and opulence alone give the true reliſh to productions either of art or nature; that freedom can make the currants of Holland and golden pippins of Great Britain ſweeter than all the grapes of Italy; while to every manly underſtanding ſome ſhare of the government in a well-regulated ſtate, with the every-day comforts of common life made durable and certain by the laws of a proſperous country, are at laſt far preferable to ſplendid luxuries precariouſly enjoyed under the conſciouſneſs of their poſſible privation when leaſt expected by the hand of deſpotic power.

St.

St. Carlo Borromæo's coloſſal ſtatue in bronze fixed up at the place of his nativity by the ſide of this beautiful water, fifteen miles from l'Iſola Bella, was our next object of curioſity. It is wonderfully well proportioned for its prodigious magnitude, which, though often meaſured and well known, will never ceaſe to aſtoniſh travellers, while twelve men can be eaſily contained in his head only, as ſome of our company had the curioſity to prove; but repented their frolic, as the metal heated by ſuch a ſun became inſupportable. Abate Bianconi bid me remark that it was juſt the height of twelve men, each ſix feet high; that it is but juſt once and a half leſs than that erected by Nero, which gives name to the Roman Coloſſeo; that it is to be ſeen clearly at the diſtance of twelve miles, though placed to no advantage, as ſituation has been ſacrificed to the greater propriety of ſetting it up upon the place where he was actually born, whoſe memory they hold, and juſtly, in ſuch perfect veneration. I returned home perſuaded that the cardinal's dreſs, though an unfavourable one to pictures, is very happily adapted to a coloſſal ſtatue, as the three cloaks or petti-

petticoats made a sort of step-ladder drapery which takes off exceedingly from the offence that is given by too long lines to the eye.

We returned to our enchanted palace with music playing by our side: I never saw a party of pleasure carried on so happily. The weather was singularly bright and clear, the moon at full, the French-horns breaking the silence of the night, invited echo to answer them. The nine days (and we enjoyed seventeen or eighteen hours out of every twenty-four) seemed nine minutes. When we came home to our country-house in the Varesotto, verses and sonnets saluted our arrival, and congratulated our wedding-day.

The Madonna del Monte was the next show which called us abroad; it is within a few miles of our present sweet habitation, is celebrated for its prospect, and is indeed a very astonishing spot of ground, exhibiting at one view the three cities of Turin, Milan, and Genoa; and leading the eye still forward into the South of France. The lakes, which to those who go o'pleasuring upon them, seem like seas, and very like the mouth of our river Dart, where she disgorges her elegantly-ornamented stream into the harbour at Kingsweare,

weare, here afford too little water, in proportion, though five in number, and the largeſt fifty miles round. I ſcarcely ever ſaw ſo much land within the eye from any place. That the road ſhould be adorned with chapels up the mountain is leſs ſtrange: there is a church dedicated to the Virgin at top. We have one here in Italy in every diſtrict almoſt, as the rage of *worſhipping on high places,* ſo expreſsly and repeatedly forbidden in ſcripture, has laſted ſurpriſingly in the world. Every reſting-place is marked, and decorated with ſtatues cut in wood, and painted to imitate human life with very extraordinary ſkill. They are capital performances of their kind, and moſt reſemble, but I think excel, Mrs. Wright's fineſt figures in wax. A convent of nuns, ſituated on the ſummit of the hill, where theſe chapels end in an exceeding pretty church, entertained our large party with the moſt hoſpitable kindneſs: gave us a handſome dinner and delicious deſſert. We diverted the ladies with a little concert in return, and paſſed a truly delightful day.

All the environs of this *Vareſotto* are very charmingly varied with mountains, lakes, and cultivated life; the only fault in our proſpect is is the want of water. Had I told my companions of yesterday perhaps, that the view from *Madonna del Monte* reminded me of Chirk Castle Hill in North Wales, they would have laughed; yet from that extraordinary spot are to be distinctly seen several fertile counties, with many great, and many small towns, and a most extensive landscape, watered by the large and navigable rivers Severn and Dee, roughened by the mountains of Merionethshire, and bounded by the Irish sea: I think that view has scarce its equal any where; and, if any where, it is here in the vicinity of Varese, where many gay villas interspersed contribute to variegate and enliven a scene highly finished by the hand of Nature, and wanting little addition from her attendant *Art*.

Of the noblemen's seats in the neighbourhood it may indeed be remarked, that however spacious the house, and however splendid the furniture may prove upon examination, however pompous the garden may be to the first glance, and the terraces however magnificent,—spiders are seldom excluded from the mansion, or weeds from the pleasure-ground of the possessor. A climate so warm would

afford

afford some excuse for this nastiness, could one observe the inhabitants were discomposed at such an effect from a good cause, or if one could flatter one's self that they themselves were hurt at it; but when they gravely display an embroidered bed or counterpane worthy of Arachne's fingers before her metamorphosis, covered over by her present labours, who can forbear laughing?—The gardener in two minutes arriving to assist you up slopes, all flourishing with cat's-tail and poppy; while your friends cry,—" *Here, this is nature! is it not?* pure nature!—*Tutto naturale sì, secondo l'uso Inglese* *."

Well! we have really passed a prodigiously gay *villegiatura* here in this charming country, where the snowy cap of the *gros* St. Bernard cools the air, though at so great a distance; and we have the pleasure of seeing Switzerland, without the pain of feeling its cold, or the fatigue of climbing its *glacieres:* the Alps of the Grisons rise up like a fortification behind us; the sun glows hot in our rich and fertile valleys, and throws up every vegetable production with all the poignant

* All so natural and pretty,—quite in the English style.

flavour that Summer can beſtow; nor is ſhade wanting from the walnut and large cheſnut trees, under which we often dine, and ſing, and play at *tarocco*, and hear the horns and clarinets, while ſipping our ice or ſwallowing our lemonade. The *cicala* now feels the genial influence of that heat ſhe requires, but her voice here is weak, compared to the powers ſhe diſplayed ſo much to our diſturbance in Tuſcany; and the *lucciola* has loſt much of her ſcintillant beauty, but ſhe darts up and down the hedges now and then. Here is an emerald-coloured butterfly, whoſe name I know not, plays over the lakes and ſtanding pools, in a very pleaſing abundance; the moſt exquiſitely-tinted æphemera frolic before one all day long; and Antiope flutters in every parterre, and ſhares the garden ſweets with a pale primroſe-coloured creature of her own kind, whoſe wings are edged with brown, and, if I can remember right, bears the name of *hyale*. But we are not yet paſt the reſidence of ſcorpions, which certainly do commit ſuicide when provoked beyond all endurance; a ſtory I had always heard, but never gave much credit to.

But

But I am disturbed from writing my book by the good-humoured gaiety of our cheerful friends, with whom we never sit down fewer than fourteen or fifteen to table I think, and surely never rise from it without many a genuine burst of honest merriment undisguised by affectation, unfettered by restraint. Our gentlemen make *improviso* rhymes, and cut comical faces; go out to the field after dinner, and play at a sort of blindman's buff, which they call breaking the pan; nor do the low ones in company arrange their minds as I see in compliment to the high ones, but tell their opinions with a freedom I little expected to find: mixed society is very rare among them, almost unknown it seems; but when they *do* mix at a country place like this, the great are kind, to do them justice, and the little not servile. They are wise indeed in making society easy to them, for no human being suffers solitude so ill as does an Italian. An English lady once made me observe, that a cat never purs when she is alone, let her have what meat and warmth she will; I think these social-spirited Milanese are like *her*, for they can hardly believe that there is existing a person, who would

would not willingly prefer any company to none: when we were at the islands three weeks ago,—" A charming place," says one of our companions,—" *Cio é con un mondo d'amici cosi* *."— "But with one's own family, methinks," said I, " and a good library of books, and this sweet lake to bathe in :"— " O!" cried they all at once, " *Dio ne liberi* †." —This is national character.

Why there are no birds of the watery kind, coots, wild ducks, cargeese, upon these lakes, nobody informs me: I have been often told that of Geneva swarms with them, and it is but a very few miles off: our people though have little care to ascertain such matters, and no desire at all to investigate effects and causes; those who study among them, study classic authors and learn rhetoric; poetry too is by no means uncultivated at Milan, where the Abate Parini's satires are admirable, and so esteemed by those who themselves know very well how to write, and how to judge: common philosophy *(la physique,* as the French call it), geography, astronomy, chymistry, are

* That is, with a heap of friends about one in this manner.

† Oh! God keep one from that.

oddly

oddly left behind fomehow; and it is to their ignorance of thefe matters that I am apt to impute Italian credulity, to which every wonder is welcome.

We have now paffed one day in Switzerland however, rowing to the little town Lugano over its pretty lake. The mountains at the end are a neat miniature of Vefuvius, Somma, &c.; and the fituation altogether looks as a picture of Naples would look, if painted by Brughuel; but not fo full of figures. A fanciful traveller too might be tempted to think he could difcern fome ftreaks of liberty in the manners of the people, if it were but in the inn-keeper at whofe houfe we dined; this may however be merely my own prejudice, and fomebody told me it was fo.

We were fhewn on one fide the water as we went acrofs, a fmall place called Campioni, which is *feudo Imperiale*, and governed by the Padre Abate of a neighbouring convent, who has power even over the lives of his fubjects for fix years; at the expiration of which term another defpot of the day is chofen—appointed I fhould have faid; and the laft returns to his original ftate, amenable however for any *very* fhocking thing he may have done during the
courfe

course of his dictatorship; and no complaint has been ever made yet of any such governor so circumstanced and appointed, whose conduct is commonly but too mild and clement. This I thought worth remarking, as consolatory to one's feelings.

Lugano meantime scorns absolute authority: our Cicerone there, in reply to the question asked in Italy three times a-day I believe—*Che Principe fà qui la sua residenza**?—replied, that they were plagued with no Principi at all, while the thirteen Cantons protected all their subjects; and though, as the man expressed it, only half of them were *Christians*, and the other half *Protestants;* no church or convent had ever wanted respect; while their town regularly received a monthly governor from every canton, and was perfectly contented with this ambulatory dominion. Here was the first gallows I have seen these two years. They have a pretty commerce too at Lugano for the size of the place, and the shopkeepers shew that officiousness and attention seldom observed in arbitrary states, where

. Content, the bane of industry,

---

* What prince makes his residence here?

soon

soon leads people to neglect the trouble of getting, for the pleasure of spending their money. One therefore sees the inhabitants of Italian cities for the most part merry and cheerful, or else pious and penitent; little attentive to their shops, but easily disposed to loiter under their mistress's window with a guitar, or rove about the streets at night with a pretty girl under their arm, singing as they go, or squeaking with a droll accent, if it is the time for masquerades. Fraud, avarice, ambition, are the vices of republican states and a cold climate; idleness, sensuality, and revenge, are the weeds of a warm country and monarchical governments. If these people are not good, they at least wish they were better; they do not applaud their own conduct when their passions carry them too far; nor rejoice, like old Moneytrap or Sir Giles Overreach, in their successful sins: but rather say with Racine's hero, translated by Philips, that

> Pyrrhus will ne'er approve his own injustice,
> Or form excuses while his heart condemns him.

They beat their bosoms at the feet of a crucifix in the street, with no more hypocrisy than they beat a tam-a tambourine there; perhaps with no more effect neither, if no alteration of behaviour succeeds their contrition: yet when an Englishman (who is probably more ashamed of repenting than of sinning) accuses them of false pretensions to pious fervour, he wrongs them, and would do well to repent himself.

But a natural curiosity seen at Milan this 16th day of August 1786, leads my mind into another channel. I went to wait upon and thank the lady, or the relations of the lady, who lent us her house at Varese, and make our proper acknowledgments; and at that visit saw something very uncommon surely: though I remember Doctor Johnson once said, that nobody had ever seen a very strange thing; and challenged the company (about seventeen people, myself among them) to produce a strange thing;—but I had not then seen Avvocato B—, a la wyerhere at Milan, and a man respected in his profession, who actually chews the cud like an ox; which he did at my request, and in my presence: he is apparently much like another tall stout man, but has many extraordinary properties, being eminent for strength, and possessing a set of ribs and sternum very surprising, and worthy the attention of anatomists: his body, upon the slightest touch, even through all his clothes, throws out electric sparks; he can reject his meals from his stomach at pleasure, and did absolutely in the course of two hours, the only two I ever passed in his company, go through, to oblige me, the whole operation of eating, masticating, swallowing, and returning by the mouth, a large piece of bread and a peach. With all this conviction, nothing more was wanting; but I obtained beside, the confirmation of common friends, who were willing likewise to bear testimony of this strange accidental variety. What I hear of his character is, that he is a low-spirited, nervous man; and I suppose his *ruminating* moments are spent in lamenting the singularities of his frame:—be this how it will, we have now no time to think any more of them, as we are packing up for a trip to Bergamo, a city I have not yet seen.

BERGAMO

Is built up a steep hill, like Lansdown road at Bath; the buildings not so regular; the prospect not inferior, but of a different kind, resembling that one sees from Wrotham hill in Kent, but richer, and presenting a variety beyond credibility, when it is premised that scarce any water can be seen, and that the plains of Lombardy are low and flat: within the eye however one may count all the original blessings bestowed on humankind,—corn, wine, oil, and fruit;—the inclosures being small too, and the trees *touffu*, as the French call it. No parterre was ever more beautifuly disposed than are the fields surveyed from the summit of the hill, where stands the Marquis's palace elegantly sheltered by a still higher rising ground behind it, and commanding from every window of its stately front a view of prodigious extent and almost unmatched beauty: as the diversification of colouring reminds one of nothing

but

but the fine pavement at the Roman Pantheon, so curiously interfected are the patches of grass and grain, flax and vines, arable and tilth, in this happy disposition of earth and its most valuable products; while not a hedge fails to afford perfume that fills the very air with fragrance, from the sweet jessamine that, twisting through it, lends a weak support to the wild grapes, which, dangling in clusters, invite ten thousand birds of every European species I believe below the size of a pigeon. Nor is the taking of these creatures by the *roccolo* to be left out from among the amusements of Brescian and Bergamasc nobility; nor is the eating of them when taken to be despised: *beccaficos* and *ortolans* are here in high perfection; and it was from these northern districts of Italy I trust that Vitellius, and all the classic gluttons of antiquity, got their curious dishes of singing-bird pye, &c. The rich scent of melons at every cottage door is another delicious proof of the climate's fertility and opulence,—

Where every sense is lost in every joy,

as Hughes expresses it; and where, in the delightful villa of our highly accomplished acquaintance

quaintance the Marquis of Aracieli, we have paſſed ten days in all the pleaſures which wit could invent, money purchaſe, or friendſhip beſtow. The laſt nobleman who reſided here, father to the preſent lord, was *cavalier ſervente* to the immortal Clelia Borromæo, whoſe virtues and varieties of excellence would fill a volume; nor can there be a ſtronger proof of her uncommon, almoſt unequalled merit, than the long-continued eſteem of the famous Valliſnieri, whoſe writings on natural hiſtory, particularly inſects, are valued for their learning, as their author was reſpected for his birth and talents. Letters from him are ſtill preſerved in the family by Marcheſe Aracieli, and breathe admiration of the conduct, beauty, and extenſive knowledge poſſeſſed by this worthy deſcendant of the Borromæan houſe; to whoſe incomparable qualities his father's ſteady attachment bore the trueſt teſtimony, while the ſon ſtill ſpeaks of her death with tears, and delights in nothing more than in paying juſt tribute to her memory. He ſhewed me this pretty diſtich in her praiſe, made improviſo by the celebrated philoſopher Valliſnieri:

       Contemptrix

JOURNEY THROUGH ITALY. 241

Contemptrix sexus, omniscia Clelia sexum,
Illustrat studio, moribus, arte metro *.

The Italians are exceedingly happy in the power of making verses improviso, either in their *old* or their *new* language: we were speaking the other day of the famous epigram in Ausonius;

Infelix Dido, nulli bene nupta marito,
Hoc moriente fugis, hoc fugiente peris †.

Our equally noble and ingenious master of the house rendered it in Italian thus immediately:

Misera Dido! fra i nuziali ardori,
L'un muore e fuggi—l'altro fuggi e mori.

This is more compressed and clever than that of Guarini *himself* I think,

Oh fortunata Dido!
Mal fornita d'amante e di marito,
Ti fu quel traditor, l'altro tradito;
Mori l'uno e fuggisti,
Fuggi l'altro e moristi.

---

* Her studies, manners, arts, to all proclaim
Fair Clelia's glory, and her sex's shame.

† Two lords in vain unlucky Dido tries;
One dead, she flies the land; one fled—she dies.

Though this latter has been preserved with many deserved eulogiums from Crescembini, and likewise by Mr. de Chevreau.

Could I clear my head of prejudice for such talents as I find here, and my heart of partial regard, which is in reality but grateful friendship, justly due from me for so many favours received; could I forget that we are now once more in the state of Venice, where every thing assumes an air of cheerfulness unknown to other places, I might perhaps perceive that the fair at Bergamo differs little from a fair in England, except that these cattle are whiter and ours larger. *How a score of good ewes now?* as Master Shallow says; but I really did ask the price of a pair of good strong oxen for work, and heard it was ten zecchines; about half the price given at Blackwater, but ours are stouter, and capable of rougher service. It is strange to me where these creatures are kept all the rest of the year, for except at fair time one very seldom sees them, unless in actual employment of carting, ploughing, &c. Nothing is so little animated by the sight of living creatures as an Italian prospect. No sheep upon their hills, no cattle grazing in their meadows, no water-fowl, swans, ducks, &c.

upon

upon their lakes; and when you leave Lombardy, no birds flying in the air, save only from time to time betwixt Florence and Bologna, a solitary kite soaring over the surly Appenines, and breaking the immense void which fatigues the eye; a ragged lad or wench too now and then leading a lean cow to pick among the hedges, has a melancholy appearance, the more so as it is always fast held by a string, and struggles in vain to get loose. These however are only consequences of luxuriant plenty, for where the farmer makes four harvests of his grass, and every other speck of ground is profitably covered with grain, vines, &c. all possibility of open pasturage is precluded. Horses too, so ornamental in an English landscape, will never be seen loose in an Italian one, as they are all *chevaux entiers*, and cannot be trusted in troops together as ours are, even if there was ground uninclosed for them to graze on, like the common lands in Great Britain. A nobleman's park is another object never to be seen or expected in a country, where people would really be deserving much blame did they retain in their hands for mere amusement ten or twelve miles circuit of earth, capable to produce two or three thousand

pounds

pounds a-year profit to their families, beside making many tenants rich and happy in the mean time. I will confess, however, that the absence of all these *agrémens* gives a flatness and uniformity to the views which we cannot complain of in England; but when Italians consider the cause, they will have reason to be satisfied with the effect, especially while vegetable nature flourishes in full perfection, while every step crushes out perfume from the trodden herbs, and those in the hedges dispense with delightful liberality a fragrance that enchants one. Hops and pyracantha cover the sides of every cottage; and the scent of truffles attracts, and the odour of melons gratifies one's nerves, when driving among the habitations of fertile Lombardy.

The old church here of mingled Gothic and Grecian architecture pleased me exceedingly, it sends one back to old times so, and shews one the progress of *barbarism*, rapid and gigantic in its strides, to overturn, confound, and destroy what taste was left in the world at the moment of its *onset*. Here is a picture of the Israelites passing over the Red Sea, which Luca Giordano, contrary to his usual custom, seems to have taken pains with, a

rarity

rarity of courfe; and here are fome fingle figures of the prophets, heroes, and judges of the Old Teftament, painted with prodigious fpirit indeed, by Ciro Ferri. That which ftruck me as moft capital, was Gideon wringing the dew out of the fleece, full of character and glowing with expreffion.

The theatre has fallen down, but they are building it up again with a nicety of proportion that will enfure it from falling any more. Italians cannot live without a theatre; they have erected a temporary one to ferve during the fair time, and even that is beautiful. The Terzetto of charming Guglielmi was fung laft night; I liked it ftill better than when we heard it performed by fingers of more eftablifhed reputation at St. Carlo; but then I like every thing at Bergamo, till it comes to the thunder ftorms, which are far more innoxious here than at Naples or in Tufcany.

We could contemplate electricity from this fine hill yefterday with great compofure, being amufed with her caprices and not endangered by her anger. There has however been a fierce tempeft in the neighbourhood, which has greatly lowered the fpirits of the farmer; and we have been told another tale, that lowers mine

mine much more as an Englishwoman, because the people of this town complain of strange failure in their accustomed orders for silk from England, and the foreigners make disgraceful conjectures about our commerce, in consequence of that failure.

Here is a report prevailing too, of King George III. being assassinated, which, though we all know to be false, fails not to produce much unpleasing talk. Were the Londoners aware of the diffusion of their newspapers, and the strange ideas taken up by foreigners about things which pass by *us* like a day dream, I think more caution would be used, and characters less lightly hung up to infamy or ridicule, on which those very prints mean not to bestow so lasting or severe a punishment, as their ill word produces at a distance from home, whither the contradiction often misses though the report arrives, and mischief, originally little intended, becomes the fatal consequence of a joke. But it is time to return to

MILAN,

MILAN,

Whence I went for my very first airing to Casa Simonetti, in search of the echo so celebrated by my country-folks and fellow-travellers, but did not find all that has been said of it strictly true. It certainly does repeat a single sound more than seventy times, but has no power to give back by reverberation a whole sentence. I have met too with another petty mortification; having been taught by Cave to expect, that in our Ambrosian library here at Milan, there was a MS. of Boethius preserved relative to his condemnation, and confessing his design of subverting the Gothic government in Lombardy. I therefore prevailed on Canonico Palazzi, a learned old ecclesiastic, to go with me and beg a sight of it. The præfect politely promised indulgence, but referred me to a future day; and when we returned again at the time appointed, shewed me only Pere Mabillon's book, in which we read that it is to be found no where

where but at Florence, in the library of Lorenzo de Medicis. We were however ſhewn ſome curioſities to compenſate our trouble, particularly the ſkeleton of the lady mentioned by Dr. Moore and Lady Millar with ſome contempt. This is the copy of her inſcription:

ÆGROTANTIUM
SANITATI
MORTUORUM
INSPECTIONE
VIVENTES
PROSPICERE
POSSINT
HUNC
ΣΚΕΛΕΤΟΝ
P.

A MS. of the Conſolations of Philoſophy, very finely written in the tenth century, and kept in elegant preſervation;—a private common-place of Leonardo da Vinci never ſhewn, full of private memoirs, caricaturas, hints for pictures, ſketches, remarks, &c.; it is invaluable. But there is another treaſure in this town, the præfect tells me, by the ſame inimitable maſter, no other than an alphabet, pater noſter, &c. written out by himſelf for the uſe of his own little babies, and ornamented ed with vignettes, &c. to tempt them to study it. I shall not see it however, as Conte Trivulci is out of town, to whom it belongs. I have not neglected to go see the monument erected to one of his family, with the famous inscription,

Hic quiescit qui nunquam quievit;

preserved by father Bouhours. The same day shewed me the remains of a temple to Hercules, with many of the fine old pillars still standing. They are soon to be taken down we hear for the purpose of widening the street, as Carfax was at Oxford.

My hunger after a journey to Pavia is much abated; since professor Villa, whose erudition is well known, and whose works do him so much honour, informed me that the inscription said by Pere Mabillon still to subsist in praise of Boethius, is long since perished by time; nor do they now shew the brick tower in which it is said he was confined while he wrote his Consolations of Philosophy: for the tower is fallen to the ground, and so is the report, every body being now persuaded that they were composed in a strong place then standing upon the spot called Calventianus Ager,

Ager, from the name of a noble houſe to which it had belonged for ages, and which I am told Cicero mentions as a family half Placentian, half Milaneze. The field ſtill goes by the name of *Il Campo Calvenziano*; but, as it now belongs to people careleſs of remote events, however intereſting to literature, is not adorned by any obeliſk, or other mark, to denote its paſt importance, in having been once the ſcene of ſufferings glorioufly endured by the moſt zealous chriſtian, the moſt ſteady patriot, and the moſt refined philoſopher of the age in which he lived.

I have ſeen a fine MS. of the Conſolations copied in the tenth century, not only legible but beautiful; and I have been aſſured that the hymns written by his firſt wife Elpis, who, though ſhe brought him no children, as Bertius ſays, was yet *fida curarum, et ſtudiorum ſocia* *, are ſtill ſung in the Romiſh churches at Breſcia and Bergamo, ſomewhat altered from the ſtate we find them in at the end of Cominus's edition of the Conſolations.

Tradition too, I find, agrees with Procopius in telling that this widow of Boethius,

* Faithful to his cares, and companionable in his ſtudies.

Ruſticiana,

Rusticiana, daughter of Symmachus, spent all the little money she had left in hiring people to throw down in the night all the statues set up in Rome to the honour of Theodoric, who had sentenced her husband to a death so dreadful, that it gave occasion to many fabulous tales reported by Martin Rota as miraculous truths. His bones, gathered up as relics by Otho III. were placed in a chapel dedicated to St. Austin in St. Peter's church at Pavia four hundred and seventy-two years after his death, with an epitaph preserved by Pere Mabillon, but now no longer legible.

We are now cutting hay here for the last time this season, and all the environs smell like spring on this 15th September 1786. The autumnal tint, however, falls fast upon the trees, which are already rich with a deep yellow hue. A wintery feel upon the atmosphere early in a morning, heavy fogs about noon, and a hollow wind towards the approach of night, make it look like the very last week of October in England, and warn us that summer is going. The same circumstances prompt me, who am about to forsake this her favourite region, to provide furs, flannels, &c. for the passing of those Alps

which

which look so formidable when covered with snow even at their present distance. Our swallows are calling their clamorous council round me while I write; but the butterflies still flutter about in the middle of the day, and grapes are growing more wholesome as with us when the mornings begin to be frosty. Our deserts, however, do not remind us of Tuscany: the cherries here are not particularly fine, and the peaches all part from the stone—miserable things! an English gardener would not send them to table: the figs too were infinitely finer at Leghorn, and nectarines have I never seen at all.

Well, here is the opera begun again; some merry wag, Abate Casti I think, has accommodated and adapted the old story of king Theodore to put in ridicule the present king of Sweden, who is hated of the emperor for some political reasons I forget what, and he of course patronises the jester. Our honest Lombards, however, take no delight in mimicry, and feel more disgust than pleasure when simplicity is insulted, or distress made more corrosive by the bitterness of a scoffing spirit. I have tried to see whether they would laugh at any oddity in their neigh-

neighbour's manner, but never could catch any, except perhaps now and then a fly Roman who had a liking for it. " I fee nothing abfurd about the man," fays one gentleman; " every body may have fome peculiarity, and moft people have; but fuch things make me no fport: let us, when we have a mind to laugh, go and laugh at Punchinello."—From fuch critics, therefore, the king of Sweden is fafe enough, as they have not yet acquired the tafte of hunting down royalty, and crowing with infantine malice, when poffeffed of the mean hope that they are able to pinch a noble heart. This old-fafhioned country, which detefts the fight of fuffering majefty, hiffes off its theatre a performance calculated to divert them at the expence of a fovereign prince, whofe character is clear from blame, and whofe perfonal weakneffes are protected by his birth and merit; while it is to his open, free, and politely generous behaviour alone, they owe the knowledge that he *has* fuch foibles. Paifiello, therefore, cannot drive it down by his beft mufic, though the poor king of Sweden is a Lutheran too, and if any thing would make them hate him, *that* would.

One

One vice, however, sometimes prevents the commission of another, and that same prevailing idea which prompts these prejudiced Romanists to conclude him doomed to lasting torments who dares differ from them, though in points of no real importance, inspires them at the same time with such compassion for his supposed state of predestinated punishment, that they rather incline to defend him from further misery, and kindly forbear to heap ridicule in this world upon a person who is sure to suffer eternal damnation in the other.

How melancholy that people who possess such hearts should have the head thus perversely turned! I can attribute it but to one cause; their strange neglect and forbearance to read and study God's holy word: for not a very few of them have I found who seem to disbelieve the Old Testament entirely, yet remain steadily and strenuously attached to the precedence their church claims over every other; and who shall wonder if such a combination of bigotry with scepticism should produce an evaporation of what little is left of popery from the world, as emetics triturated with opium are said to produce a sudorific powder which no earthly constitution can resist?

But

But the Spanish grandee, who not only entertained but astonished us all one night with his conversation at Quirini's Casino at Venice, is arrived here at Milan, and plays upon the violin. He challenged acquaintance with us in the street, half invited himself to our private concert last night, and did us the honour to perform there, with the skill of a professor, the eager desire of a dilletante, and the tediousness of a solitary student; he continued to amaze, delight, and fatigue us for four long hours together. He is a man of prodigious talents, and replete with variety of knowledge. A new dance has been tried at here too, but was not well received, though it represents the terrible story which, under Madame de Genlis' pen, had such uncommon success among the reading world, and is called *La sepolta viva*; but as the duchess Girafalco, whose misfortune it commemorates, is still alive, the pantomime will probably be suppressed: for she has relations at Milan it seems, and one lady distinguished for elegance of form, and charms of voice and manner, told me yesterday with equal sweetness, spirit, and propriety, that though the king of Naples sent his soldiers to free her aunt from that horrible

horrible dungeon where she had been nine years confined, yet if her miseries were to become the subject of stage representation, she could hardly be pronounced happy, or even at ease. Truth is, I would be loath to see the spirit of producing every one's private affairs, true or false, before the public eye, spread into *this* country: No! let that humour be confined to Great Britain, where the thousand real advantages resulting from living in a free state, richly compensate for the violations of delicacy annexed to it; and where the laws do protect, though the individuals insult one: but *here*, why the people would be miserable indeed, if to the oppression which may any hour be exercised over them by their prince, were likewise to be added the liberties taken perpetually in London by one's next door neighbour, of tearing forth every transaction, and publishing even every conjecture to one's disadvantage.

With these reflections, and many others, excited by gratitude to private friends, and general admiration of a country so justly esteemed, we shall soon take our leave of Milan, famed for her truly hospitable disposition; a temper of mind sometimes abused by travellers

travellers perhaps, whofe birth and pretenfions are feldom or ever inquired into, whilft no people are more careful of keeping their rank inviolate by never converfing on equal terms with a countryman or woman of their own, who cannot produce a proper length of anceftry.

I will not leave them though, without another word or two about their language, which, though it founded ftrangely coarfe and broad to be fure, as we returned home from Florence, Rome, and Venice, I felt fincerely glad to hear again; and have fome notion by their way of pronouncing *bicchiere*, a word ufed here to exprefs every thing that holds water, that our *pitcher* was probably derived from it; and the Abate Divecchio, a polite fcholar, and an uncommonly agreeable companion, feemed to think fo too. His knowledge of the English language, joined to the fingular power he has over his own elegant Tufcan tongue, made me torment him with a variety of inquiries about thefe confufing dialects, which leave me at laft little chance to underftand any, whilft a child is called *bambino* at Florence, *putto* at Venice, *fchiatto* at Bergamo, and *creatura* at Rome;

Vol. II.   S   and

and at Milan they call a wench *tofa:* an apron is *grembiule* at Florence I think, *traverfa* at Venice, *bigarrol* at Brefcia and fome other parts of Lombardy, *fenale* at Rome, and at Milan *fcozzà*. A foreigner may well be diftracted by varieties fo ftriking; but the turn and idiom differ ten times more ftill, and I love to hear our Milanefe call an oak *robur* rather than *quercia* fomehow, and tell a lady when dreffed in white, that fhe is *tutto in albedine.*

On Friday the 22d of September then we left Milan, and I dropt a tear or two in remembrance of the many civilities fhewn by our kind and partial companions. The Abate Bianconi made me wild to go to Drefden, and enjoy the Correggios now moved from Modena to that gallery. I find he thinks the old Romans pronounced Cicero and Cæfar as the moderns do, and many Englifh fcholars are of the fame mind; but here are coins dug up now out of the Veronefe mountain with the word Carolus, fpelt *Karrulus,* upon them quite plain; and Chriftus was fpelt *Kriftus* in Vefpafian's time it is certain, becaufe of the player's monument at Rome.— Dr. Johnfon, I remember, was always fteady to that opinion; but it is time to leave all this, and rejoice in my third arrival at gay, cheerful, charming

VERONA,

Whither some sweet leave-taking verses have followed us, written by the facetious Abate Ravaſi, a native of Rome, but for many years an inhabitant of Milan. His agreeable ſonnet, every line ending with *tutto*, being upon a ſubject of general importance, would ſerve as a better ſpecimen of his abilities than lines dictated only by partial friendſhip;—but I hear *that* is already circulated about the world, and printed in one of our magazines; to them let him truſt his fame, they will pay my juſt debts.

We have now ſeen this enchanting ſpot in ſpring, ſummer, and autumn; nor could winter's ſelf render it undelightful, while uniting every charm, and gratifying every ſenſe. Greek and Roman antiquities ſalute one at the gates; Gothic remains render each place of worſhip venerable: Nature in her holiday dreſs decks the environs, and ſociety animates with intellectual fire the amiable inhabitants. Oh! were I to live here long, I ſhould not only excuſe, but applaud the Scaligers for ſtraining probability, and neglecting higher praiſe, only to claim kindred with the Scalas of Verona. Improviſation at this place pleaſes me far better than it did in Tuſcany. Our truly-learned Abate Lorenzi aſtoniſhes all who hear him, by *repeating*, not *ſinging*, a ſeries of admirably juſt and well-digeſted thoughts, which he, and he alone, poſſeſſes the power of arranging ſuddenly as if by magic, and methodically as if by ſtudy, to rhymes the moſt melodious, and moſt varied; while the Abbé Bertola, of the univerſity at Pavia, gives one pleaſure by the ſame talent in a manner totally different, ſinging his unpremeditated ſtrains to the accompaniment of a harpſichord, round which ſtand a little chorus of friends, who interpolate from time to time two lines of a well-known ſong, to which he pleaſingly adapts his compoſitions, and goes on gracing the barren ſubject, and adorning it with every poſſible decoration of wit, and every deſirable elegance of ſentiment. Nothing can ſurely ſurpaſs the happy promptitude

titude of his expression, unless it is the brilliancy of his genius.

We were in a large company last night, where a beautiful woman of quality came in dressed according to the present taste, with a gauze head-dress, adjusted turbanwise, and a heron's feather; the neck wholly bare. Abate Bertola bid me look at her, and, recollecting himself a moment, made this Epigram improviso:

> Volto e Crin hai di Sultana,
>   Perchè mai mi vien disdetto,
> Sodducente Mussulmana
>   Di gittarti il *Fazzoletto?*

of which I can give no better imitation than the following:

> While turban'd head and plumage high
>   A Sultaness proclaims my Cloe;
> Thus tempted, tho' no Turk, I'll try
>   The handkerchief you scorn—to throw ye.

This is however a weak specimen of his powers, whose charming fables have so completely, in my mind, surpassed all that has ever been written in that way since La Fontaine. I am strongly tempted to give one little story out of his pretty book.

Una lucertoletta
Diceva al cocodrillo,
Oh quanto mi diletta
Di veder finalmente
Un della mia famiglia
Si grande e si potente!
Ho fatto mille miglia
Per venirvi a vedere,
Mentre tra noi si serba
Di voi memoria viva;
Benche fuggiam tra l'erba
E il sassoso sentiero;
In sen però non langue
L'onor del prisco sangue.
L'anfibio rè dormiva
A questi complimenti,
Pur sugli ultimi accenti
Dal sonno se riscosse
E dimandò chi fosse?
La parentela antica,
Il viaggio, la fatica,
Quella torno a dire,
Ed ei torne a dormire.

Lascia i grandi ed i potenti,
A sognar per parenti;
Puoi cortesi stimarli
Se dormon mentre parli.

Walking full many a weary mile
The lizard met the crocodile;

And

And thus began—how fat, how fair,
How finely guarded, Sir, you are!
'Tis really charming thus to see
One's kindred in prosperity.
I've travell'd far to find your coast,
But sure the labour was not lost:
For you must think we don't forget
Our loving cousin now so great;
And tho' our humble habitations
Are such as suit our slender stations,
The honour of the lizard blood
Was never better understood.

Th' amphibious prince, who slept content,
Ne'er listening to her compliment,
At this expression rais'd his head,
And—Pray who are you? cooly said;
The little creature now renew'd
Her history of toils subdu'd,
Her zeal to see her cousin's face,
The glory of her ancient race;
But looking nearer, found my lord
Was fast asleep again—and snor'd.

Ne'er press upon a rich relation
Rais'd to the ranks of higher station;
Or if you will disturb your coz,
Be happy that he does but doze.

But I will not be seduced by the pleasure of praising my sweet friends at Verona, to lengthen this chapter with further panegyrics upon a place I leave with the truest tenderness, and with the sincerest regret; while the correspondence I hope long to maintain with the charming Contessa Mosconi, must compensate all it can for the loss of her agreeable Coterie, where my most delightful evenings have been spent; where so many topics of English literature have been discussed; where Lorenzi read Tasso to us of an afternoon, Bertola made verses, and the cavalier Pindemonte conversed; where the three Graces, as they are called, joined their sweet voices to sing when satiety of pleasure made us change our mode of being happy, and kept one from wishing ever to hear any thing else; while countess Carminati sung Bianchi's duets with the only tenor fit to accompany a voice so touching, and a taste so refined. *Verona! qui te viderit, et non amarit,* says some old writer, I forget who, *protinus amor perditissimo; is credo se ipsum non amat**. Indeed I never saw people live so pleasingly together as these do; the women apparently delighting in each other's company, without mean rivalry,

---

* Whoever sees thee without being smitten with extraordinary passion, must, I think, be incapable of loving even himself.

or envy of thofe accomplifhments which are commonly beftowed by heaven with diverfity enough for all to have their fhare. The world furely affords room for every body's talents, would every body that poffeffed them but think fo; and were malice and affectation once completely banifhed from cultivated fo-ciety, *Verona* might be found in many places perhaps; fhe is now confined, I think, to the fweet ftate of *Venice.*

JOURNEY

THROUGH

TRENT, INSPRUCK, MUNICK, AND SALTZSBURG, TO VIENNA.

THE Tyrolese Alps are not as beautiful as those of Savoy, though the river that runs between them is wider too; but that very circumstance takes from the horror which constitutes beauty in a rocky country, while a navigable stream and the passage of large floats convey ideas of commerce and social life, leaving little room for the solitary fancies produced, and the strokes of sublimity indelibly impressed, by the mountains of La Haute Morienne. The sight of a town where

all.

all the theological learning of Europe was once concentred, affords however much ground of mental amusement; while the sight of two nations, not naturally congenial, living happily together, as the Germans and Italians here do, is pleasing to all.

We saw the apartments of the Prince Bishop, but found few things worth remarking, except that in the pictures of Carlo Loti there is a shade of the Flemish school to be discerned, which was pretty as we are now hard upon the confines. Our sovereign here keeps his little menagerie in a mighty elegant style: the animals possess an insulated rock, surrounded by the Adige, and planted with every thing that can please them best; the wild, or more properly the predatory creatures, are confined, but in very spacious apartments; with each a handsome outlet for amusement: while such as are granivorous rove at pleasure over their domain, to which their master often comes in summer to eat ice at a banquetting house erected for him in the middle, whence a prospect of a peculiar nature is enjoyed; great beauty, much variety, and a very limited horizon, like some of the views about Bath.

At

At the death of one prince another is chosen, and government carried on as at Rome in miniature. We staid here two nights and one day, thought perpetually of Matlock and Ivy Bridge, and saw some rarities belonging to a man who shewed us a picture of our Saviour's circumcision, and told us it was *San Simeone*, a baby who having gone through many strange operations and torments among some Jews who stole him from his parents, as the story goes here at Trent, they murdered him at last, and he became a saint and a martyr, to whom much devotion is paid at this place, though I fancy he was never heard of any where else.

The river soon after we left Trent contracted to a rapid and narrow torrent, such as dashes at the foot of the Alps in Savoy; the rocks grew more pointed, and the prospects gained in sublimity at every step; though the neatness of the culture, and quantity of vines, with the variegated colouring of the woods, continued to excite images more soft than formidable, less solemn than lovely. The barberry bushes bind every mountain round the middle as with a scarlet sash, and when

we

we looked down upon them from a house situated as if in the place which the Frenchman seemed to have a notion of, when he thought the aerian travellers were gone *au lieu ou les vents se forment*, they looked wonderfully pretty. The cleanliness and comfort with which we are now lodged at every inn, evince our distance from France however, and even from Italy, where low cielings, clean windows, and warm rooms, are deemed pernicious to health, and destructive of true delight. Here however we find ourselves cruelly distressed for want of language, and must therefore depend on our eyes only, not our ears, for information concerning the golden house, or more properly the golden roof, long known to subsist at Inspruck. The story, as well as I can gather it, is this: That some man was reproached with spending more than he could afford, till some of his neighbours cried out, " Why he'll roof his house with gold soon, but who shall pay the expence?"—" *I* will;" quoth the piqued German, and actually did gild his tiles. My heart tells me however, though my memory will not call up the particulars, that I have heard a tale very like this before now; but one is always listening to the same

same stories I think: At Rome, when they shew a fine head lightly sketched by Michael Angelo, they inform you how he left it on Raphael's wall, after the manner of Apelles and Protogenes; it is called Testa di Ciambellaro, because he came disguised as a seller of *ciambelle,* or little biscuits, while Raphael's scholars were painting at the Farnesini. At Milan, when they point out to you the extraordinary architecture of the church *detto il Giardino,* the roof of which is supported by geometrical dependance of one part upon another, without columns or piers, they tell how the architect ran away the moment it was finished, for fear its sudden fall might disgrace him. This tale was very familiar to me, I had heard it long ago related of a Welch bridge; but it is better only say what is true.

This is a sweetly situated town, and a rapid stream runs through it as at Trent; and it is no small comfort to find one's self once more waited on by clean looking females, who make your bed, sweep your room, &c. while the pewters in the little neat kitchens, as one passes through, amaze me with their brightness,

ness, that I feel as if in a new world, it is *so* long since I have seen any metal but gold unencrusted by nastiness, and gold *will* not be dirty.

The clumsy churches here are more violently crowded with ornaments than I have found them yet; and for one crucifix or Madonna to be met with on Italian roads, here are at least forty; an ill carved and worse painted figure of a bleeding Saviour, large as life, meets one at every turn; and I feel glad when the odd devotion of the inhabitants hangs a clean shirt or laced waistcoat over it, or both. Another custom they have wholly new to me, that of keeping the real skeletons of their old nobles, or saints, or any one for whom they have peculiar veneration, male or female, in a large clean glass box or crystal case, placed horizontally, and dressed in fine scarlet and gold robes, the poor naked skull crowned with a coronet, and the feet peeping out below the petticoats. These melancholy objects adorn all their places of worship, being set on brackets by the wall inside, and remind me strangely of our old ballad of Death and the Lady;

Fair lady, lay your costly robes aside, &c.

No

No body ever mentions that Infpruck is fubject to fires, and I wonder at it, as the roofs are all wood cut tile-ways, and heavily penfile, like our barns in England, for the fnow to roll off the eafier.

Well! we are far removed indeed from Italian architecture, Italian fculpture, and Italian manners; but here are twenty-eight old kings, or keyfers, as our German friends call them, large as life, and of good folid bronze, curioufly worked to imitate lace, embroidery, &c. ftanding in two rows, very extraordinarily, up one of their churches. I have not feen more frowning vifages or finer dreffes for a long time; and here is a warm feel as one paffes by the houfes, even in the ftreet, from the heat of the ftoves, which moft ingenioufly conceal from one's view that moft cheerful of all fights in cold weather, a good fire. This feems a very unneceffary device, and the heated porcelain is apt to make one's head ache befide; all for the fake of this cunning contrivance, to make one enjoy the effect of fire without feeing the caufe.

The women that run about the town, mean time, take the neareft way to be warm, wrapping

ping themselves up in cloth clothes, like so many fishermen at the mouth of the Humber, and wear a sort of rug cap grossly unbecoming. But too great an attention to convenience disgusts as surely as too little; and while a Venetian wench apparently seeks only to captivate the contrary sex, these German girls as plainly proclaim their resolution not to sacrifice a grain of personal comfort for the pleasure of pleasing all the men alive.

How truly hateful are extremes of every thing each day's experience convinces; from superstition and infidelity, down to the Fribble and the Brute, one's heart abhors the folly of reversing wrong to look for right, which lives only in the middle way; and Solomon, the wisest man of any age or nation, places the sovereign good in mediocrity of every thing, moral, political, and religious.

With this good axiom of *nequid nimis* * in our mouths and minds, we should not perhaps have driven so very hard; but a less effort would have detained us longer from the finest object I almost ever saw; the sun rising between six and seven o'clock upon the plains of Munich, and discovering to our soothed

* Nothing too much.

sight a lovely champain country, such as might be called a flat I fear, by those who were not like us accustomed to a hilly one; but after four-and-twenty hours passed among the Alps, I feel sincerely rejoiced to quit the clouds and get upon a level with human creatures, leaving the goats and chamois to delight as they do in bounding from rock to rock, with an agility that amazes one.

Our weather continuing particularly fine, it was curious to watch one picturesque beauty changing for another as we drove along; for no sooner were the rich vineyards and small inclosures left behind, than large pasture lands filled with feeding or reposing cattle, cows, oxen, horses, fifty in a field perhaps, presented to our eyes an object they had not contemplated for two years before, and revived ideas of England, which had long lain buried under Italian fertility.

Instead of lying down to rest, having heard we had friends at the same inn, we ran with them to see the picture gallery, more for the sake of doing again what we had once done before at Paris with the same agreeable company, than with any hope of entertainment, which

which however upon trial was found by no means deficient. Had there been no more than the glow of colouring which refults from the fight of fo many Flemifh pictures at once, it muft have ftruck one forcibly; but the murder of the Innocents by Rubens, a great performance, gave me an opportunity of obferving the different ways by which that great mafter, Guido Rheni, and Le Brun, lay hold of the human heart. The difference does not however appear to me infpired at all by what we term national character; for the inhabitants of Germany are reckoned flow to anger, and of phlegmatic difpofitions, while a Frenchman is accounted light and airy in his ideas, an Italian fiery and revengeful. Yet Rubens's principal figure follows the ruffian who has feized her child, and with a countenance at once exciting and expreffive of horror, endeavours, and almoft arrives at tearing both his eyes out. One actually fees the fellow ftruggling between his efforts to hold the infant faft, and yet rid himfelf of the mother, while blood and anguifh apparently follow the impreffion her nails are making in the tendereft parts of his face. Guido, on the contrary, in one of the churches at Bologna, ex-

hibits

hibits a beautiful young creature of no mean rank, elegant in her affliction, and lovely in her diſtreſs, ſitting with folded arms upon the fore-ground, contemplating the cold corpſe of her murdered baby; his nurſe wringing her hands beſide them, while crowds of diſtracted parents fill the perſpective, and the executioners themſelves appear to pay unwilling obedience to their inhuman king, who is ſeen animating them himſelf from the top of a diſtant tower.—Le Brun mean time, with more imagination and ſublimity than either, makes even brute animals ſeem ſenſible, and ſhudder at a ſcene ſo dreadful; while the very horſes who ſhould bear the cruel prince over the theatre of his crimes, ſnort and tremble, and turning away with uncontrollable fury, refuſe by trampling in their blood to violate ſuch injured innocence!—Enough of this.

The patient German is ſeen in all they ſhew us, from the painting of Brughuel to the muſic of Haydn. A friend here who ſpeaks good Italian ſhewed us a collection of rarities, among which was a picture formed of butterflies wings; and a ſet of boxes one within another, till my eyes were tired with trying to diſcern, and the patience of my companions was

was wearied with counting them, when the number paffed feventy-three: this amufement has at leaft the grace of novelty to recommend it. I had not formed to myfelf an idea of fuch unmeaning, fuch taftelefs, yet truly elaborate nicety of workmanfhip, as may be found in the Elector's chapel, where every relic repofes in fome frame, enamelled and adorned with a minutenefs of attention and delicacy of manual operation that aftonifhes. The prodigious quantity of thefe gold or ivory figures, finifhed fo as to require a man's whole life to each of them, are of immenfe value in their way at leaft, and fill one's mind with a fort of petty and frivolous wonder totally unexperienced till now, bringing to one's recollection every hour Pope's famous line—

Lo! what huge heaps of littlenefs around!

The contraft between this chapel and Cappella Borghefe never left my fancy for a moment: but if the coft of thefe curious trifles caufed my continued furprife, how was that furprife increafed by obferving the bedchamber of the Elector; where they told us that no lefs than one hundred thoufand pounds

pounds sterling were buried under loads of gold tissue, red velvet, and old-fashioned carved work, without the merit even of an attempt towards elegance or taste?

Nimphenbourg palace and gardens reminded me of English gardening forty years ago, while—

> Grove nods at grove, each alley has a brother,
> And half the platform just reflects the other.

I do think I can recollect going with my parents and friends to see Lord Royston's seat at Wrest, when we lived in Hertfordshire, in the year 1750; and it was just such a place as Nimphenbourg is at this day. Now for some just praise: every thing is kept so neat here, so clean, so sweet, so comfortably nice, that it is a real pleasure somehow either to go out in this town or stay at home: the public baths are delicious; the private rooms with boarded floors, all swept, and brushed, and dusted, that not a cobweb can be seen in Munich, except one kept for a rarity, with the Virgin and Child worked in it, and wrought to such an unrivalled pitch of delicate fineness, that till we held it up to the light no naked eye

eye could difcern the figures it contained, till a microfcope foon difcovered the fkill and patience requifite to its production;—great pains indeed, and little effect! We have left the country where things were exactly the reverfe,—great effect, and little pains! But it is the fame in every thing.

The women's fcrupulous attention to keep their perfons clear from dirt, makes their faces look doubly fair; their complexions have quite a luftre upon them, like fome of our wenches in the Weft of England, whofe tranfparent fkins fhew, by the motion of the blood beneath, an illuminated countenance that ftands in the place of eye-language, and betrays the fentiments of the innocent heart with uncontrolable fincerity. Thefe girls however will not be found to attract or retain lovers, like an Italian, whofe black eyes and white teeth (though their poffeffor thinks no more of cleaning the laft-named beauty than the firft) tell her mind clearly, and with little pains again produce certain and ftrong effect. Our ftiff gold-ftuff cap here too, as round, as hard, and as heavy as an old Japan China bafon, and not very unlike one, is by no means

means favourable to the face, as it is clapped clofe round the head, the hair combed all fmooth out of fight, and a plaited border of lace to it made firm with double-fprigged wire; giving its wearer all the hardnefs and prim look of a Quaker, without that idea of fimplicity which in their drefs compenfates for the abfence of every ornament.

The gentlemen's *maniere de s'ajufter* is to me equally ftriking: an old nobleman who takes delight in fhewing us the glories of his little court (where I have a notion he himfelf holds fome honourable office) came to dine with us yefterday in a dreffed coat of fine, clean, white broad-cloth, laced all down with gold, and lined with crimfon fattin, of which likewife the waiftcoat was made, and laced about with a narrower lace, but pretty broad too; fo that I thought I faw the very coat my father went in to the old king's birth-day five and thirty years ago. There is more ftatelinefs too and ceremonious manners in the converfation of this gentleman, and the friends he introduced us to, than I have of late been accuftomed to; and they fatigue one with long, dry, uninterefting narratives. The inn-keepers

keepers are honest, but inflexible; the servants silent and sullen; the postillions slow and inattentive; and every thing exhibits the reverse of what we have left behind.

The treasures of this little Elector are prodigious, his jewels superb; the Electress's pearls are superior in size and regularity to those at Loretto, but that distinguished by the name of the " Pearl of the Palatinate" is surely incomparable, and, as such, always carried to the election of a new Emperor, when each brings his finest possession in his hand, like the Princess of Babylon's wooers,—which was perhaps meant by Voltaire as a joke upon the custom. This pearl is about the bigness and shape of a very fine filberd, the upper part or cap of it jet black, smooth and perfectly beautiful; *it is unique in the known world.*

Our Prince's dinner here is announced by the sound of drums and trumpets, and he has always a concert playing while he dines: pomp is at this place indeed so artfully substituted instead of general consequence, that while one remains here one scarcely feels aware how little any one but his own courtiers can be thinking about the Elector of Bavaria;

Bavaria; but ceremony is of moſt uſe where there is leaſt importance, and glitter beſt hides the want of ſolidity.

From Munich to Saltzbourg nothing can exceed the beauties of the country; whole woods, and we may ſay foreſts, of evergreen timber, keep all idea of winter kindly at a diſtance: the road lies through theſe elegantly-varied thickets, which ſometimes are formed of cedars, often of foxtailed pines, while a pale larch ſometimes, and gloomy cypreſs, hinder the verdure from being too monotonous; here are likewiſe mingled among them ſome oak and beech of a majeſtic ſize. Nor do our proſpects want that dignity which mountains alone can beſtow; thoſe which ſeparate Bavaria from Hungary are high, and of conſiderable extent; a long range they are of bulky fortifications, behind which I am informed the country is far coarſer than here.

The cathedral at Saltzbourg is modern, built upon the model of St. Peter's at Rome, but on a ſmall ſcale: one now ſees how few the defects are of that aſtoniſhing pile, though brought cloſe to one's eye, by being ſtript of the

the awful magnitude that kept examination at a diſtance. The muſical bells remind me of thoſe at Bath, and every thing here ſeems, as at Bath, the work of this preſent century; but there is a Benedictine convent ſeated on the top of a hill above the town, of exceeding antiquity, founded before the conqueſt of England by William the Norman; under which lie its founder and protectors, the old Dukes of Bavaria; which they are happy to ſhew travellers, with the regiſtered account of their young Prince *Adam*, who came over to our iſland with William, and gained a ſettlement: they were pleaſed when I proved to them, that his blood was not yet wholly extinct among us.

A fever hindered us here from looking at the ſalt-works, from which the city takes its name: but the water-works at Heelbrun pleaſed us for a moment; and I never ſaw beavers live ſo happily as with the Archbiſhop of Saltzbourg, who ſuffers, and even encourages, his tame ones to dig, and build, and amuſe themſelves their own way: he has fiſh too which eat out of his hand, and are not carp, but I do not know what they are;

my

my want of language diſtracts me. Theſe German ſtreams appear to us particularly pellucid, and, by what I can gather from the people, this water never freezes. The taſte of gardening ſeems juſt what ours was in England before Stowe was planned, and they divert you now with puppets moved by concealed machinery, as I recollect their doing at places round London, called the Spaniard at Hampſtead and Don Saltero's at Chelſea.

The Prince Archbiſhop's income is from three to four hundred thouſand a year I underſtand, and he ſpends it among his ſubjects, who half adore him. His chief delight is in brute animals they tell me, particularly horſes, which engroſs ſo much of his attention that he keeps one hundred and ſeventeen for his own private and perſonal uſe, of various merits, beauties, and pedigrees; never ſurely was ſo elegant, ſo capital a ſtud! And he is ſingularly fond of a breed of fine ſilky-haired Engliſh ſetting-dogs, red and white, and very high upon their legs.

The country which carried us forward to Vienna is eminently fine, and fine in a way that is now once more grown new to me; no hedges here, no ſmall incloſures at all; but rich

rich land, lying like as in Dorfetſhire, divided into arable and paſture grounds, clumped about with woods of evergreen. Such is the genius of this ſovereign for Engliſh manners and Engliſh agriculture, that no converſation is ſaid to be more welcome at his court than what relates to the ſports or profits of the field in Britain; to which accounts he liſtens with good-humoured earneſtneſs, and talks of a fine ſcenting day with the true taſte of an Engliſh country gentleman.

On this day I firſt ſaw the Danube at Lintz, where, though but juſt burſt from the ſpring, it is already ſo deep and ſtrong that ſcarcely any wooden bridge is capable to reſiſt it, and accordingly it did a few months ago overwhelm many cottages and fields, among which we paſſed. The inhabitants here call it *Donaw* from its ſwiftneſs; and it deſerves beſide, any name expreſſive of that ſingular purity which diſtinguiſhes the German torrents.

The rivers of France, Italy, and England, give one no idea of that elemental perfection found in the fluids here; not a pebble, not a fiſh in theſe tranſlucent ſtreams, but may be diſcerned to a depth of twelve feet. As the water in Germany, so is the atmosphere in Italy, a medium so little obstructed by vapour I remember, that Vesuvius looked as near to Naples, from our window, as does lord Lisburne's park from the little town of Exmouth opposite, a distance of about five miles I believe, and the other is near ten. Let me add, that this peculiarity brings every object forward with a certain degree of hardness not wholly pleasing to the eye. The prospects round Naples have another fault, resulting from too great perfection: the sky's brilliant uniformity, and utter cloudlessness for many months together, takes away those broad masses of light and shade, with the volant shadows that cross our British hills, relieving the sight, and discriminating the landscape.

The scenery round Conway Castle in North Wales, with a thunder-storm rolling over the mountain; the sea strongly illuminated on one side, with the sun shining bright upon the verdure on the other; the lights dropping in patches about one; exhibits a variety, the which to equal will be very difficult, let us travel as far as we please.

Magnificence of a far different kind however claims our present attention—a convent

and

and church shewn us at Molcke upon our way, the residence of eighteen friars who inhabit a stately palace it is confessed, while three immense courts precede your entrance to a splendid structure of enormous size, on which the finery bestowed amazed even me, who came from Rome; nor had entertained an idea of seeing such gilding, and carving, and profusion of expence, lavished on a place of religious retirement in our road to

VIENNA.

We entered the capital by night; but I fancied, perhaps from having been told so, that I saw something like a look of London round me. Apartments furnished wholly in the Paris taste take off that look a little; so do the public walks and drives which are formed etoile-wise, and moving slowly up and down the avenues, you see large stags, wild boars, &c. grazing at liberty: this is grander than our park, and graver than the Corso. Whenever they lay out a piece of water in this country, it is covered as in ours with swans, who have completely quitted the odoriferous Po for the clear and rapid Danube.

Vienna was not likely to ſtrike one with its churches; yet the old cathedral is majeſtic, and by no means ſtript of thoſe ornaments which, while one ſect of Chriſtians think it parlicularly pleaſing in the ſight of God to retain, is hardly warrantable in another ſect, though wiſer, to be over-haſty in tearing away. Here are however many devotional figures and chapels left in the ſtreets I ſee, which, from the tales told in Auſtrian Lombardy, one had little reaſon to expect; but the emperor is tender even to the foibles of his Vienneſe ſubjects, while he ſhews little feeling to Italian miſery. Men drawing carts along the roads and ſtreet afford, indeed, ſomewhat an awkward proof the government's lenity when human creatures are levelled with the beaſts of burden, and called *ſtott eiſel*, or *ſtout aſſes*, as I underſtand, who by this information have learned that the frame which ſupports a picture is for the ſame reaſon called an *eiſel*, as we call a thing to hang clothes on a *horſe*. It is the genius of the German language to degrade all our Engliſh words ſomehow:

how: they call a coach a *waggon*, and afk a lady if fhe will buy pomatum to *fmear* her hair with. Such is however the refemblance between their tongue and ours, that the Italians proteft they cannot feparate either the ideas or the words.

I muft mention our going to the poft-office with a Venetian friend to look for letters, where, after receiving fome furly replies from the people who attended there, our laquais de place reminded my male companions that they fhould ftand *uncovered*. Finding them however fomewhat dilatory in their obedience, a rough fellow fnatched the hat from one of their heads, faying, " *Don't you know, Sir, that you are ftanding before the emperor's officers ?*"—" *I know*," replied the prompt Italian, " *that we are come to a country where people wear their hats in the church, fo need not wonder we are bid to take them off in the poft-office.*" Well, where rulers are faid or fuppofed to be tyrannical, it is rational that good provifion fhould be made for arms; otherwife defpotifm dwindles into nugatory pompoufnefs and airy fhow; Profpero's empire in the enchanted ifland of Shakefpeare is not more fhadowy than the fight of princedom united with impotence of power:—such have I seen, but such is not the character of Keysar's dominion. The arsenal here is the finest thing in the world I suppose; it grieved me to feel the ideas of London and Venice fade before it so; but the enormous size and solidity of the quadrangle, the quantity and disposition of the cannon, bombs, and mortars, filled my mind with enforced respect, and shook my nerves with the thought of what might follow such dreadful preparation.

Nothing can in fact be grander than the sight of the Austrian eagle, all made out in arms, eight ancient heroes sternly frowning round it. The choice has fallen on Cæsar, Pompey, Alexander, Scipio, Hannibal, Fabius Maximus, Cyrus, and Themistocles. I should have thought Pyrrhus worthier the company of all the rest than this last-named hero; but petty criticisms are much less worthy a place in Vienna's arsenal, which impresses one with a very majestic idea of Imperial greatness.

On the first of November we tried at an excursion into Hungary, where we meant to have surveyed the Danube in all its dignity at Presburgh, and have heard Hayden at Estherhazie.

hazie. But my being unluckily taken ill, prevented us from profecuting our journey further than a wretched village, where I was laid up with a fever, and difappointed my company of much hoped-for entertainment. It was curious however to find one's felf within a few pofts of the places one had read fo much of; and the words *Route de Belgrade* upon a finger-poft gave me fenfations of diftance never felt before. The comfortable fight of a proteftant chapel near me made much amends however. The officiating priefts were of the Moravian fect it feems, and dear Mr. Hutton's image rufhed upon my mind. A burial paffing by my windows, ftruck me as very extraordinary: not one follower or even bearer being dreffed in black, but all with green robes trimmed with dark brown furs, not robes neither; but like long coats down to the men's heels, cut in fkirts, and trimmed up thofe fkirts as well as round the bottom with fur.

It was a melancholy country that we paffed through, very bleak and difmal, and I truft would not have mended upon us had we gone further. The few people one fees are all ignorant, and can all fpeak Latin—fuch as it is—

is—very fluently. I have lived with many very knowing people who never could fpeak it with any fluency at all. Such is life!—and fuch is learning! I long to talk about the fheep and fwine: they feem very worthy of obfervation; the latter large and finely fhaped, of the old favage race; one fancies them like thofe Eumæus tended, and perhaps they are fo; with tufks of fingular beauty and whitenefs, which the uniformly brown colour of the creature fhews off to much advantage; amidft his dark curls, waving all over his high back and long fides, in the manner of a curl-pated baby in England, only that the laft is commonly fair and blonde.

The fheep are fpotted like our pigs, but prettier; black and yellow like a tortoife-fhell cat, with horns as long as thofe of any he-goat I ever faw, but very different; thefe animals carrying them ftraight upright like an antelope, and they are of a fpiral fhape. Our mutton meantime is deteftable; but here are incomparable fifh, carp large as fmall Severn falmon, and they bring them to table cut in pounds, and the joul for a handfome difh. I only wonder one has never heard of any ancient or any modern gluttons driving away to Prefburg

Prefburg or Buda, for the fake of eating a fine Danube carp.

With regard to men and women in Hungary, they are not thickly fcattered, but their lamentations are loud; the emperor having refumed all the privileges granted them by Maria Therefa in the year 1740, or thereabouts, when diftrefs drove her to fhelter in that country, and has prohibited the importtion of falt herrings which ufed to come duty free from Amfterdam, fo that their fafts are rendered incommodious from the afperity of the foil, which produces very little vegetable food.

Ground fquirrels are frequent in the forefts here; but without Pennant's Synopfis I never remember the Linnæan names of quadrupeds, fo can get no information of the animal called a glutton in Englifh, whofe fkin I fee in every fur-fhop, and who, I fancy, inhabits our Hungarian woods.

The Imperial collection of pictures here is really a magnificent repofitory of Italian tafte, Flemifh colouring, and Dutch exactnefs: in which the Baptift, by Giulio Romano, the crucifixion by Vandyke, and the phyfician holding up a bottle to the light by Gerard Douw, are great examples.

One does not in these countries look out particularly for the works of Roman or Bolognese masters; but I remember a wonderful Caracci at Munich, worthy a first place even in the Zampieri palace; the subject, Venus sitting under a great tree diverting herself with seeing a scuffle between the two boys Cupid and Anteros.

In the gallery here at Vienna, many of the pictures have been handled a good deal; one is dazzled with the brilliancy of these powerful colourists: and here is a David Teniers surprisingly natural, of Abraham offering up Isaac; a glorious Pordenone representing Santa Justina, reminded me of her fine church at Padua, and *his* centurion at Cremona, which I know not who could excel; and here is Furino's Sigismunda to be seen, the same or a duplicate of that sold at Sir Luke Schaub's sale in London about thirty years ago, and called Correggio. I have seen it at Merriworth too, if not greatly mistaken. The price it went for in Langford's auction-room I cannot surely forget, it was three thousand pounds, *or they said so*.

I will

I will only add a word of a Dutch girl reprefenting Herodias, and fo lively in its colouring, that I think the king would have denied her who refembled it nothing, had he been a native of Amfterdam. A Mount Calvary painted by the fame hand is very ftriking, with a crowd of people gathered about the crofs, and men felling cakes to the mob, as if at a fair or horfe-race: two young peafants at fifty-cuffs upon the fore ground quarrelling, as it fhould feem, about the propriety of our Saviour's execution.

But I have this day heard fo many and fuch interefting particulars concerning the emperor, that I fhould not forgive myfelf if I failed to record and relate them, the lefs becaufe my authority was particularly good, and the anecdotes fingular and pleafing.

He rifes then at five o'clock every morning, even at this fharp feafon, writes in private till nine, takes fome refrefhment then, and immediately after calls his minifters, and employs the time till one profeffedly in ftate affairs, rides out till three, returns and ftudies alone, letting the people bring his dinner at the appointed hour, chufes out of all the things they bring him one difh, and fets it on the ftove to keep hot, eating it when nature calls for food, but never detaining a fervant in the room to wait; at five he goes to the Corridor juft near his own apartment, where poor and rich, fmall and great, have accefs to his perfon at pleafure, and often get him to arbitrate their law-fuits, and decide their domeftic differences, as nothing is more agreeable to him than finding himfelf confidered by his people as their father, and difpenfer of juftice over all his extenfive dominions. His attention to the duties he has impofed upon himfelf is fo great, that, in order to maintain a pure impartiality in his mind towards every claimant, he fuffers no man or woman to have any influence over him, and forbears even the flight gratification of fondling a dog, left it fhould take up too much of his time. The emperor is a ftranger upon principle to the joys of confidence and friendfhip, but cultivates the acquaintance of many ladies and gentlemen, at whofe houfes (when they fee company) he drops in, and fpends the evening cheerfully in cards or converfation, putting no man under the leaft reftraint; and if he fees a new comer in look difconcerted, goes up to him and fays kindly, " Divert

vert yourself your own way, good Sir; and do not let me disturb you." His coach is like the commonest gentleman's of Vienna; his servants distinguished only by the plainness of their liveries; and, lest their insolence might make his company troublesome to the houses where he visits, he leaves the carriage in the street, and will not even be driven into the court-yard, where other equipages and footmen wait. A large dish of hot chocolate thickened with bread and cream is a common afternoon's regale here, and the emperor often takes one, observing to the mistress of the house how acceptable such a meal is to him after so wretched a dinner.

A few mornings ago showed his character in a strong light. Some poor women were coming down the Danube on a float, the planks separated, and they were in danger of drowning; as it was very early in the day, and no one awake upon the shore except a sawyer that was cutting wood; who, not being able to obtain from his phlegmatic neighbours that assistance their case immediately required, ran directly to call the emperor who he knew would be stirring, and who came flying to give that help which from some happy accident was no longer

longer wanted: but Joseph lost no good humour on the occasion; on the contrary, he congratulated the women on their deliverance, praising at the same time and rewarding the fellow for having disturbed him.

My informer told me likewise, that if two men dispute about any matter till mischief is expected, the wife of one of them will often cry out, "Come, have done, have done directly, or I'll call our master, and he'll make you have done." Now is it fair not to do every thing but adore a sovereign like this? when we know that if such tales were told us of Marcus Aurelius, or Titus Vespasian, it would be our delight to repeat, our favourite learning to read of them. Such conduct would serve succeeding princes for models, nor could the weight of a dozen centuries smother their still rising fame. Yet is not my heart persuaded that the reputation of Joseph the Second will be consigned immaculate from age to age, like that of these immortal worthies, though dearly purchased by the loss of ease and pleasure; while neither the mitred prelate nor the blameless puritan pursue with blessings a heart unawed by splendour, unsoftened by simplicity; a hand stretched forth rather to dispense justice, than opening spontaneously to distribute charity.

To

To speak less solemnly, if men were nearer than they are to perfect creatures, absolute monarchy would be the most perfect form of government, for the will of the prince could never deviate from propriety; but if one king can see all with his own eyes, and hear all with his own ears, no successor will ever be able to do the same; and it is like giving Harrison 10,000 l. for finding the longitude, to commend a person for having hit on the right way of governing a great nation, while his science is incommunicable, and his powers of execution must end with his life.

The society here is charming; Sherlock says, that he who does not like Vienna is his own satirist; I shall leave others to be mine. The ladies here seem very highly accomplished, and speak a great variety of languages with facility, studying to adorn the conversation with every ornament that literature can bestow; nor do they appear terrified as in London, lest pedantry should be imputed to them, for venturing sometimes to use in company that knowledge they have acquired in private by diligent application. Here also are to be seen young unmarried women once again: misses, who wink at each other, and
titter

titter in corners at what is passing in the rooms, public or private: I had lived so long away from *them*, that I had half forgotten their existence.

The horses here are trimmed at the heels, and led about in body clothes like ours in England; but their drawing is ill managed, no shafts somehow but a pole, which, when there is one horse only, looks awkward and badly contrived. Beasts of various kinds plowing together has a strange look, and the ox harnessed up like a hunter in a phaeton cuts a comical figure enough. One need no longer say, *Optat ephippia bos piger* *; but it is very silly, as no use can be thus made of that strength which lies only in his head and horns. Plenty of wood makes the Germans profusely elegant in their pales, hurdles, &c. which give an air of comfort and opulence, and make the best compensation a cold climate can make for the hedges of jessamine and medlar flowers, which I shall see no more.

Our architecture here can hardly be expected to please an eye made fastidious from the contemplation of Michael Angelo's works at Rome, or Palladio's at Venice; nor will Ger-

* The lazy ox for trappings sighs.

man music much delight those who have been long accustomed to more simple melody, though intrinsic merit and complicated excellence will always deserve the highest note of praise. Whoever takes upon him to under-rate that which no one can obtain without infinite labour and study, will ever be censured, and justly, for refusing the reward due to deep research; but if a man's taste leads him to like *Cyprus* wine, let him drink *that*, and content himself with commending the *old bock*.

Apropos, we hear that *Sacchini*, the Metastasio of musical composers, is dead; but nobody at Vienna cares about his compositions. Our Italian friends are more candid; they are always talking in favour of Bach and Brughuel, Handel and Rubens.

The cabinet of natural history is exceedingly fine, and the rooms singularly well disposed. There are more cameos at Bologna, and one superior specimen of native gold: every thing else I believe is better here, and such opals did I never see before, no not at Loretto: the petrified lemon and artichoke have no equals, and a brown diamond was new to me to-day. A specimen of seasalt filled with air bubbles like the rings one buys

buys at Vicenza, is worth going a long way to look at; but the gentleman at Munich, who shewed us the Virgin Mary in a cobweb, had a piece of red silver shot out into a ruby like crystal, more extraordinary than any mineral production I have seen. Our attention was caught by Maria Theresa's bouquet, but one cannot forget the pearls belonging to the electress of Bavaria.

What seemed, however, most to charm the people who shewed the cabinet, was a snuff-box consisting of various gems, none bigger than a barley-corn, each of prodigious value, and the workmanship of more, every square being inlaid so neatly, and no precious stone repeated, though the number is no less than one hundred and eighty-three; a false bottom besides of gold, opening with a spring touch, and discovering a written catalogue of the jewels in the finest hand-writing, and the smallest possible. This was to me a real curiosity, afforded a new and singular proof of that astonishing power of eye, and delicacy of manual operation, seconded by a patient and persevering attention to things frivolous in themselves, which will be for ever alike neglected

glected by the fire of Italian genius, and difdained by the dignity of British science.

We have seen other sort of things to-day however. The Hungarian and Bohemian robes pleased me best, and the wild unset jewels in the diadem of Transylvania impressed me with a valuable idea of Gothic greatness. The service of gold plate too is very grand from its old-fashioned solidity. I liked it better than I did the snuff-box; and here is a dish in ivory puts one in mind of nothing but Achilles's shield, so worked is its broad margin with miniature representations of battles, landscapes, &c. three dozen different stories round the dish, one might have looked at it with microscopes for a week together. The porcelane plates have been painted to ridicule Raphael's pots at Loretto I fancy; Julio Romano's manner is comically parodied upon one of them.

Prince Lichtenstein's pictures are charming; a Salmacis in the water by Albano is the best work of that master I ever saw, not diffused as his works commonly are, but all collected somehow, and fine in a way I cannot express for want of more knowledge; *very, very* fine it is however, and full of expression and character. The Caracci school again;

again.—Here is the whole history of Decius by Rubens too, wonderfully learned; and an assumption of the Virgin so like Mrs. Pritchard our famous actress, no portrait ever represented her so well. A St. Sebastian divinely beautiful, by Vandyke; and a girl playing on the guitar, which you may run round almost, by the coarse but natural hand of Caravagio.

The library is new and splendid, and they buy books for it very liberally. The learned and amiable Abbé Denys shewed me a thousand unmerited civilities, was charmed with the character of Dr. Johnson, and delighted with the story of his conversation at Rouen with Monsf. l'Abbé Roffette. This gentleman seems to love England very much, and English literature; spoke of Humphry Prideaux with respect, and has his head full of Ossian's poetry, of which he can repeat whole pages. He shewed me a fragment of Livy written in the fifth century, a psalter and creed beautifully illuminated of the year nine hundred, and a large portion of St. Mark's gospel on blue paper of the year three hundred and seven. A Bibbia de Poveri too, as the Italians call it, curious enough; the figures all engraved on wood, and only a text at bottom to explain them.

Winces-

Winceslaus marked every book he ever possessed, it seems, with the five vowels on the back; and almost every one with some little miniature made by himself, recording his escape from confinement at Prague in Bohemia, where the washer-woman having assisted him to get out of prison under pretence of bathing, he has been very studious to register the event; so much so that even on the margins of his bible he has been tempted to paint past scenes that had better have been blotted from his memory.

The Livy which learned men have hoped to find safe in the seraglio of Constantinople, was burned by their late sultan Amurath, our Abbé Denys tells me; the motive sprung from mistaken piety, but the effect is to be lamented. He shewed me an Alcoran in extremely small characters, surprisingly so indeed, taken out of a Turkish officer's pocket when John Sobiesky raised the siege of this city in the year 1590, and a preacher took for his text the Sunday after, "*There was a man sent from God whose name was* John." I was much amused with a sight of the Mexican MSS and Peruvian quipos; nor are the Turkish figures of Adam and Eve, our Saviour and his mother, lefs remarkable; but Mahomet furrounded by a glory about his head, a veil concealing his face as too bright for infpection, exceeded all the reft.

Here are many ladies of fafhion in this town very eminent for their mufical abilities, particularly Mefdemoifelles de Martinas, one of whom is member of the Academies of Berlin and Bologna: the celebrated Metaftafio died in their houfe, after having lived with the family fixty-five years more or lefs. They fet his poetry and fing it very finely, appearing to recollect his converfation and friendfhip, with infinite tendernefs and delight. He was to have been prefented to the Pope the very day he died, I underftand, and in the delirium which immediately preceded diffolution he raved much of the fuppofed interview. Unwilling to hear of death, no one was ever permitted even to mention it before him; and nothing put him fo certainly out of humour, as finding that rule tranfgreffed even by his neareft friends. Even the fmall-pox was not to be named in his prefence, and whoever *did* name that diforder, though unconfcious of the offence he had

had given, Metaſtaſio would ſee him no more. The other peculiarities I could gather from Miſs Martinas were theſe: That he had contentedly lived half a century at Vienna, without ever even wiſhing to learn its language; that he had never given more than five guineas Engliſh money in all that time to the poor; that he always ſat in the ſame ſeat at church, but never paid for it, and that nobody dared aſk him for the trifling ſum; that he was grateful and beneficent to the friends who began by being his protectors, but ended much his debtors, for ſolid benefits as well as for elegant preſents, which it was his delight to be perpetually making them, leaving to them at laſt all he had ever gained without the charge even of a ſingle legacy; obſerving in his will that it was to them he owed it, and other conduct would in him have been injuſtice. Such were the ſentiments, and ſuch the conduct of this great poet, of whom it is of little conſequence to tell, that he never changed the faſhion of his wig, the cut or colour of his coat, ſo that his portrait taken not very long ago looks like thoſe of Boileau or Moliere at the head of their works. His life was arranged with ſuch methodical exactneſs, that he rose, studied, chatted, slept, and dined at the same hours for fifty years together, enjoying uninterrupted health, which probably gave him that happy sweetness of temper, or habitual gentleness of manners, which never suffered itself to be ruffled, but when his sole injunction was forgotten, and the death of any person whatever was unwittingly mentioned before him. No solicitation had ever prevailed on him to dine from home, nor had his nearest intimates ever seen him *eat* more than a biscuit with his lemonade, every meal being performed with even mysterious privacy to the last. When his end approached by steps so very rapid, he did not in the least suspect that it was coming; and Mademoiselle Martinas has scarcely yet done rejoicing in the thought that he escaped the preparations he so dreaded. His early passion for a celebrated singer is well known upon the continent; since that affair finished, all his pleasures have been confined to music and conversation. He had the satisfaction of seeing the seventieth edition of his works I think they said, but am ashamed to copy out the number from my own notes, it seems so *very* strange; and the delight he took in hearing the lady he lived with sing his songs, was visible to every one. An Italian Abate here said, comically enough, " Oh! he looked like a man in the state of beatification always when Mademoiselle de Martinas accompanied his verses with her fine voice and brilliant finger. The father of Metastasio was a goldsmith at Rome, but his son had so devoted himself to the family he lived with, that he refused to hear, and took pains not to know, whether he had in his latter days any one relation left in the world. On a character so singular I leave my readers to make their own *observations and reflections.*

Au reste, as the French say; I have no notion that Vienna, *sempre ventoso o velenoso* *, can be a very wholesome place to live in; the double windows, double feather-beds, &c. in a room without a chimney, is surely ill contrived; and sleeping smothered up in down so, like a hydrophobous patient in some parts of Ireland, is not *particularly* agreeable, though I begin to like it better than I did. All external air is shut out in such a manner that I am frighted lest, after a certain time, the room should become like an exhausted receiver,

* Ever stormy or venemous.

while the wind whirls one about the ſtreet in ſuch a manner that it is diſpleaſing to put out one's head; and a phyſician from Raguſa ſettled here told me, that wounded lungs are a common conſequence of the triturated ſtone blown about here; and in fact aſthmas and conſumptions are their reigning diſeaſes.

Apropos, the plague is now raging in Tranſylvania; how little ſafe ſhould we think ourſelves at London, were a diſorder ſo contagious known to be no farther diſtant than Derby? The diſtance is ſcarcely greater now from Vienna to the place of diſtreſs; yet I will not ſay we are in much danger to be ſure, for that perpetual connection kept up between all the towns and counties of Great Britain is unknown in other nations, and we ſhould be as many days going to Tranſylvania from here perhaps, as we ſhould be *hours* running from Toddenham-court road to Derby.

Sheenburn is pretty, but it is no ſeaſon for ſeeing pretty places. The ſtreets of Vienna are not pretty at all, God knows; ſo narrow, ſo ill built, ſo crowded, many wares placed upon the ground where there is a little opening, ſeems a ſtrange awkward diſpoſition of things for ſale; and the people cutting wood in the ſtreet makes one

half

half wild when walking; it is hardly poſſible to paſs another ſtrange cuſtom, borrowed from Italy I truſt, of ſhutting up their ſhops in the middle of the day; it muſt tend, one would think, but little to the promotion of that commerce which the ſovereign profeſſes to encourage, and I ſee no excuſe for it *here* which can be made from heat, gaiety, or devotion. Many families living in the ſame houſe, and at the entrance of the apartments belonging to each, a ſtrong iron gate to ſeparate the reſidence of one ſet from that of another, has likewiſe an odd melancholy look, like that of a priſon or a nunnery. Nunneries, however, here are none; and if the old women turned out of thoſe they have long dwelt in, are not provided with decent penſions, it muſt ſurely diſtreſs even the Emperor's cold heart to ſee age driven from the refuges of diſappointment, and forced to wander through the world with inexperience for its guide, while youth is no longer *led*, but *thruſt* into temptation by ſuch a ſudden tranſition from utter retirement to open and buſy life.

We have been this morning to look over his academy of painting, &c. His exhibition-room is neatly kept, and I dare ſay will proſper:

sper: the students are zealous and laborious, and earnestly desire the promulgation of science: their collection of models is meagre, but it will mend by degrees. Perhaps Joseph the IId. is the first European sovereign who, establishing a school for painting and sculpture, has insisted on the artists never exercising their skill upon any subject which could hurt any person's delicacy;—an example well worthy honest praise and speedy imitation.

The very few charitable foundations established at Vienna by Imperial munificence are well managed; their paucity is accounted for by the recollection of many abuses consequent on the late Empress's bounty; her son therefore took all the annuities away, which he thought her tenderness had been duped out of; but let it be remembered that when he rides or walks in a morning, he always takes with him a hundred ducats, out of which he never brings any home, but gives in private donations what he knows to be well bestowed, without the ostentation of affected generosity: it is not in rewards for past services perhaps, nor in public and stately institutions, as I am told here, that this prince's liberalities are to be looked for; yet—

In

> In Mis'ry's darkeſt caverns known,
>   His uſeful care is ever nigh;
> Where hopeleſs Anguiſh pours her groan,
>   And lonely Want retires to die.

Tomorrow (23d of November) we venture to leave Vienna and proceed northwards, as I long to ſee the Dreſden gallery. Here every thing appears to me a caricatura of London; the language like ours, but coarſer; the plays like ours, but duller; the ſtreets at night lighted up, not like ours now, but very like what they were thirty or forty years ago.

Among the people I have ſeen here, Mademoiſelle Paradies, the blind performer on the harpſichord, intereſted me very much;—and ſhe liked England ſo, and the King and Queen were ſo kind to her, and ſhe was *ſo* happy, ſhe ſaid!—While life and its vexations ſeem to oppreſs ſuch numbers of hearts, and cloud ſuch variety of otherwiſe agreeable faces, one muſt go to a blind girl to hear of happineſs, it ſeems! But ſhe has wonderful talents for languages as well as muſic, and has learned the Engliſh pronunciation moſt ſurpriſingly. It is a ſoothing ſight when one finds the mind compenſate for the body's defects:

fects: I took great delight in the converfation of Mademoifelle Paradies.

The collection of rarities, particularly an Alexander's head worthy of Capo di Monte, now in the poffeffion of Madame de Heffe, became daily more my ftudy, as I received more and more civilities from the charming family at whofe houfe it refides: there are fome very fine cameos in it, and a great variety of mifcellaneous curiofities.

So different are the cuftoms here and at Venice, that the German ladies offer you chocolate on the fame falver with coffee, of an evening, and fill up both with milk; faying that you may have the latter quite black if you chufe it—" *Tout noir, Monfieur, à la Venetienne;*"—adding their beft advice not to rifque a practice fo unwholefome. While their care upon that account reminds me chiefly of a friend, who lives upon the Grand Canal, that in reply to a long panegyric upon Englifh delicacy, faid fhe would tell a ftory that would prove them to be nafty enough, at leaft in fome things; for that fhe had actually feen a handfome young nobleman, who came from London *(and ought to have known better),* fouce fome thick cream into the fine clear coffee

coffee she presented him with; which every body must confess to be *vera porcheria!* a very *piggish trick!*—So necessary and so pleasing is conformity, and so absurd and perverse is it ever to forbear such assimilation of manners, when not inconsistent with the virtue, honour, or necessary interest:—let us eat sour-crout in Germany, frittura at Milan, macaroni at Naples, and beef-steaks in England, if one wishes to please the inhabitants of either country; and all are very good, so it is a slight compliance. Poor Dr. Goldsmith said once—" I would advise every young fellow setting out in life *to love gravy;*"—and added, that he had formerly seen a glutton's eldest nephew disinherited, because his uncle never could persuade him to say he liked gravy.

PRAGUE.

The inns between Vienna and this place are very bad; but we arrived here safe the 24th of November, when I looked for little comfort but much diverfion; things turned out however exactly the reverfe, and *aux bains de Prague* in Bohemia we found beds more elegant, dinners neater dreffed, apartments cleaner and with a lefs foreign afpect, than almoft any where elfe. Such is not mean time the general appearance of the town out of doors, which is favage enough; and the celebrated bridge fingularly ugly I think, crowded with vaft groupes of ill-made ftatues, and heavy to excefs, though not incommodious to drive over, and of a furprifing extent. Thefe German rivers are magnificent, and our Mulda here (which is but a branch of the Elbe neither) is refpectable for its volume of water, ufeful for the fifh contained in it, and lovely in the windings of its courfe.

Bohemia seems no badly-cultivated country; the ground undulates like many parts of Hertfordshire, and the property seems divided much in the same manner as about Dunstable; my head ran upon Lilly-hoo, when they shewed me the plains of Kolin.

Doctor Johnson was very angry with a gentleman at our house once, I well remember, for not being better company; and urged that he had travelled into Bohemia, and seen Prague :—" Surely," added he, " the man who has seen Prague might tell us something new and something strange, and not sit silent for want of matter to put his lips in motion !" *Horresco referens;*—I have now been at Prague as well as Doctor Fitzpatrick, but have brought away nothing very interesting I fear; unless that the floor of the opera-stage there is inlaid, which so far as I have observed is a *new* thing; the cathedral I am sure is an *old* thing, and charged with heavy and ill-chosen ornaments, worthy of the age in which it was fabricated!—One would be loth to see any alteration take place, or any picture drive old Frank's Three Kings, divided into three compartments, from its station over the high altar.

St.

St. John Neppomucene has an altar here all of solid silver, very bright and clean; his having been flung into the river Mulda in the persecuting days, holding fast his crucifix and his religion, gives him a rational title to veneration among the martyrs, and he is considered as the tutelar saint here, where his statue meets one at the entrance of every town.

This truly Gothic edifice was very near being destroyed by the King of Prussia, who bombarded the city thirty-five years ago; I saw the mark made by one ball just at the cathedral door, and heard with horror of the dreadful siege, when an egg was sold for a florin, and other eatables in proportion: the whole town has, in consequence of that long blockade, a ragged and half-ruined melancholy aspect; and the roads round it, then broken up, have scarcely been mended since.

The ladies too looked more like masquerading figures than any thing else, as they sat in their boxes at the opera, with rich embroidered caps, or bright pink and blue sattin head-dresses, with ermine or sable fronts, a heavy gold tassel hanging low down from the left

left ear, and no powder; which gives a girlish look, and reminded me of a fashion our lower tradesmen in London had about fifteen or eighteen years ago, of dressing their daughters, from nine to twelve years old, in puffed black sattin caps, with a long ear hanging down on one side. It is a becoming mode enough as the women wear it here, but gives no idea of cleanliness; and I suppose that whilst finery retains its power of striking, delicacy keeps her distance, nor attempts to come in play till the other has failed of its effect. Ladies dress here very richly, as indeed I expected to find them, and coloured silk stockings are worn as they were in England till the days of the Spectator:—" *Thrift, thrift, Horatio;*" as Hamlet observes; for our expences in Great Britain are infinitely increased by our advancement from splendor to neatness.

Here every thing seems at least five centuries behind-hand, and religion has not purified itself the least in the world since the days of its early struggle; for here Huss preached, and here Jerome, known by the name of Jerome of Prague, first began to project the scheme of a future reformation.

The

The Bohemians had indeed been long before that time indulged by the Popes with permiſſion to receive the cup in the ſacrament, a favour granted no one elſe; and of that no notice was ever taken, till further ſteps were made for the obtaining many alterations that have crept in ſince that time in other nations, not ſo haſty to do by violence what will one day be done of themſelves without any violence at all.

I aſked to ſee ſome Proteſtant meeting-houſes, and was introduced to a very pleaſing-mannered Livorneſe, who ſpoke ſweet Italian, and was miniſter to a little place of worſhip which could not have contained two hundred people at the moſt; in fact his flock were all ſoldiers, he ſaid. Not a perſon who could keep a ſhop was to be found of *our* perſuaſion, nor was Lutheraniſm half ſo much deteſted even in Italy, he ſaid. Though I remember the boys hooting us at Tivoli too, and calling our Engliſh Gentlemen, *Monſieur Dannato.*

The library does not ſeem ancient, but the grave perſon who ſhewed it ſpoke very indifferent French, ſo that I could better truſt my eyes than my ears; this want of language is terrible!—A celeſtial globe moving by clock-
work

work concealed within, and shewing the sun's place upon the ecliptic very exactly, detained our attention agreeably; and I observed a polyglot bible printed at London in Cromwell's time, with a compliment to him in the preface, which they have expunged in succeeding editions. A missal too was curious enough from its being decorated with some singular illuminations upon one leaf; at the top of the page a figure of Wickliffe is seen, striking the flint and steel; under him, in another small compartment, Jerome of Prague blowing tinder to make his torch kindle; below him again down the same side, Martin Luther, the flambeau well lighted and blazing in his hand; at the bottom of the page poor John Hufs, betrayed by the Emperor who promised him protection, and burning alive at a stake, to the apparent satisfaction of the charitable fathers assembled at the council of Constance. Another curiosity should be remembered; the manuscript letter from Zisca, the famous Protestant general who headed the revolters in 1420; I was amazed to see in how elegant an Italian hand it was written; the librarian said comically enough—" *Ay, ay, it begins all about the fear of God, &c.; those fellows,"* continued he, *" you know, are always sure to be canters!"*

The reigning sovereign has made few changes in church matters here, except that which was become almost indispensable, the resolution to have mass said only at one altar, instead of many at a time; the contrary practice does certainly disturb devotion, and produce unavoidable indecorums, as no one can tell what he turns his back upon, while the bell rings in so many places of a large church at once, and so many different functions are going forward, that people's attention must almost necessarily be distracted.

The eating here is incomparable; I never saw such poultry even at London or Bath, and there is a plenty of game that amazes one; no inn so wretched but you have a pheasant for your supper, and often partridge soup. The fish is carried about the streets in so elegant a style it tempts one; a very large round bathing-tub, as we should call it, set barrow-wise on two not very low wheels, is easily pushed along by one man, though full of the most pellucid water, in which the carp, tench,

tench, and eels, are all leaping alive, to a fize and perfection I am afhamed to relate; but the tench of four and five pounds weight have a richnefs and flavour one had no notion of till we arrived at Vienna, and they are the fame here.

How trade ftands or moves in thefe countries I cannot tell; there is great rigour fhewn at the cuftom-houfe; but till the fhopkeepers learn to keep their doors open at leaft for the whole of the fhort days, not fhut them up fo and go to fleep at one or two o'clock for a couple of hours, I think they do not deferve to be difturbed by cuftomers who bring ready money. To-morrow (30th November 1786) we fet out, wrapped in good furs and flannels, for

DRESDEN;

WHITHER we arrive safe this 4th of December,—

———A wond'rous token
Of Heav'n's kind care, with bones unbroken!

As the ingenious Soame Jenyns says of a less hazardous drive in a less barbarous country I hope: but really to English passengers in English carriages, the road from Prague hither is too bad to think on; while nothing literally impels one forward except the impossibility of going back. Lady Mary Wortley says, her husband and postillions slept upon the precipices between Lowositz and Aussig; but surely the way must have been much better then, as all the opium in both would scarce have stupefied their apprehensions now, when a fall into the Elbe must either have interrupted or finished their nap; because our coach was held up every step of the journey

by

by men's hands, while we walked at the bottom about seven miles by the river's side, suffering nothing but a little fatigue, and enjoying the most cloudless beautiful weather ever seen. The Elbe is here as wide I think as the Severn at Gloucester, and rolls through the most varied and elegant landscape possible, not inferior to that which adorns the sides of the little Dart in Devonshire, but on a greater scale; every hill crowned with some wood, or ornamented by some castle.

As soon as we arrived, tired and hungry, at Aussig, we put our shattered coach on board a bark, and floated her down to Dresden; whither we drove forward in the little carts of the country, called chaises, but very rough and with no springs, as our very old-fashioned curricles were about the year 1750. The brightness of the weather made even such a drive delightful though, and the millions of geese on and off the river gave animation to the views, and accounted for the frequency of those soft downy feather-beds, which sooth our cares and relieve our fatigue so comfortably every night. Hares will scarce move from near the carriage wheels, so little apprehensive are they of offence; and the partridges run before one so, it is quite amusing to look at them. The trout in these great rivers are neither large nor red: I have never seen trout worth catching since I left England; the river at Rickmansworth produces (one should like to know why) that fish in far higher perfection than it can be found in any other stream perhaps in Europe.

The being served at every inn, since we came into Saxony, upon Dresden china, gives one an odd feel somehow; but here at the Hôtel de Pologne there is every thing one can wish, and served in so grand a style, that I question whether any English inn or tavern can compare with it; so elegantly fine is the linen, so beautiful the porcelaine of which every the meanest utensil is made; and if the waiter did not appear before one dressed like Abel Drugger with a green cloth apron, and did not his entrance always fill the room with a strong scent of tobacco, I should think myself at home again almost. This really does seem a very charming town; the streets well built and spacious; the shops full of goods, and the people willing to shew them; and if they *do* cut all their wood before their own doors, why there is room to pass here without brawling

brawling and bones-breaking, which difgufts one fo at Vienna; it feems lighter too here than there; I cannot tell why, but every thing looks clean and comfortable, and one feels *fo much at home.* I hate prejudice; nothing is fo ftupid, nothing fo fure a mark of a narrow mind: yet who can be fure that the fight of a Lutheran town does not afford in itfelf an honeft pleafure to one who has lived fo long, though very happily, under my Lord Peter's protection?

Here Brother Martin has all precedence paid *him;* for though the court are Romanifts, their fplendid church here is *called* only a chapel, and they are not permitted to ring the bell, a privilege the Lutherans feem much attached to, for nothing can equal the noife of *our* bells on a Sunday morning at Drefden.

The architecture is truly hideous, but no ornaments are fpared; and the church of Notre Dame here is very magnificent. The china fteeples all over the country are the oddeft things in the world; fpires of blue or green porcelaine tiles glittering in the fun have a ftrange effect. But nothing can afford a ftronger proof that crucifixes, Madonnas, and faints, need not be driven out of churches for fear they fhould be worfhipped, than the Lutherans admiffion of them into *theirs*; for no people can be further removed from idolatry, or better inftructed in the Chriftian religion, than the common people of this town; where a decent obfervation of the fabbath ftruck me with moft confolatory feelings, after living at Paris, Rome, and Florence, where it is confidered as a *merry*, not a *holy* day at all! and though there feems nothing inconfiftent or offenfive in our rejoicing on the day of our Lord's refurrection, yet if people are encouraged to *play*, they will foon find out that they may *work* too, the fhops will fcarcely be fhut, and all appearance of regard to the fourth commandment will be done away. The Lutherans really feem to obferve the golden mean; they frequent their churches all morning with a rigorous folemnity, no carts or bufinefs of any fort goes forward in the ftreets, public and private devotion takes up the whole forenoon; but they do not forbear to meet and dance after fix o'clock in the evening, or play a fober game for fmall fums at a friend's houfe.

The

The fociety is to me very delightful; more women than men though, and the women moſt agreeable; exceedingly fenſible, well informed, and willing to talk on every ſubject of general importance, but religion or politics feem the favourite themes, and are I believe moſt ſtudied here;—no wonder, the court and city being of different ſects, each ſteadily and irrevocably fixed in a firm perſuaſion that their own is beſt, cauſes an inveſtigation that comes not in the head of people of other countries; and it is wonderful to ſee even the low Romaniſts ſkilled in controverſial points to a degree that would aſtoniſh the people neareſt the Pope's perſon, I am well perſuaded.

The Saxons are exceſſively loyal however, and have the fenſe to love and honour their fovereign no leſs for his difference of opinion from theirs, than if all were of one mind; yet knowing his principles, they watch with a jealous eye againſt encroachments, while the amiable elector and electreſs uſe every tender method to induce their ſubjects to embrace *their* tenets, and weary heaven with prayers for their converſion, as if the people were heathens.

heathens. One great advantage results from this odd mixture of what so steadily resists uniting; it is the earnest desire each has to justify and recommend their notions by their practice, so that the inhabitants of Dresden are among the most moral, decent, thinking people I have seen in my travels, or indeed in my life. The general air and manner both of place and people, puts one in mind of the pretty clean parts of our London, about Queen Square, Ormond Street, Lincoln's-Inn-Fields, and Southampton Row.

The bridge is beautiful, more elegant than showy; the light iron railing is better in some respects than a stone balustrade, and I do not dislike the rule they make to themselves of going on *one* side the way always, and returning the other, to avoid a crowd and confusion.

But it is time to talk about the picture gallery, where, cold as our weather is, I contrive to pass three hours every day, my feet well defended by *perlaches*, a sort of cloth clogs, very useful and commodious. And now I have seen the *Notte di Corregio*, from which almost all pictures of *effect* have taken their

JOURNEY THROUGH GERMANY.

their original idea; and here are three other Corregios inimitable, invaluable, incomparable. Surely this *Notte* might stand side by side with Raphael's Transfiguration; and as Sherlock says that Shakespear and Corneille would look only on the Vesuvius side of the prospect at Naples, while Pope and Racine would turn their heads towards Posilippo; so probably, while the two first would fasten all their attention upon the Demoniac, the two last would console their eyes with the sweetness of Corregio's Nativity. His little Magdalen too set round with jewels, itself more precious than any or than all of them, possesses wonderful powers of attraction; it is an hour before one can recollect that there are some glorious Titians in the same façade; but Caracci, who depends not on his colouring for applause, loses little by their vicinity, and Poussin is always equally respectable. The Rembrandts are beyond credibility perfect of their kind, and produce a most powerful effect. His portrait of his own daughter has neither equal nor price, I believe; though the girl has little dignity to be sure, and less grace about her; but if to represent nature as she *is* suffices, this is the first single figure in Europe

as

as painting a *live woman*.—The Jupiter and Ganymede is very droll indeed, and done with very *un*-Italian notions; but the eagle looks as if one might pluck his feathers; it is very life itself.—A candle-light Rubens here is shewn as a prodigious rarity; a Ruysdael as much resembling nature in *his* country, I do believe, as Claude Lorraine ever painted in *his*.—The crayons Cupid of Mengs which dazzles, and the portrait of old Parr by Vandycke which interests one, are pictures which call one to look at them again and again; and the little Vanderwerfs kept in glass cases, smooth as ivory, and finished to perfection, are all alike to be sure; one would wonder that a man should never be weary of painting single figures so, and constantly repeating the same idea; his eyes must have had peculiar strength too, to endure such trials, mine have been pained enough this morning with only looking at his labours, and those of the indefatigable Denny. Let me refresh them with a Parnassus of Giacomo Tintoret, who puts all the colourists to flight except Corregio.

But here are two pictures which display prodigious genius, by a master of whom I never

never heard any one speak, Ferdinand Bol, who unites grace and dignity to the clear obscure of Rembrandt, whose scholar he was. Jacob blessing Pharoah, painted by him, is delightful; and Joseph's expressions while he presents his father, full of affectionate partiality and fond regard for the old man, heightens his personal beauty; while the king's character is happily managed too, and gives one the highest idea of the artist's skill. A Madonna reposing in her flight to Egypt with a fatigued look, her head supported by her hand, is elegant, and worthy of the Roman or Bolognese schools; the landscape is like Rembrant. This gallery boasts an Egyptian Mary by Spagnolet, too terrifying to look long at; and a small picture by Lodovico Carracci of the Virgin clasping her Son, who lies asleep in her lap, while a vision of his future crucifixion shewn her by angels in the sky, agitates every charming feature of her face, and causes a shrinking in her figure which no power of art can exceed.

As I suffered so much for the sake of seeing this collection, I have indulged myself too long in talking of it perhaps; but Garrick is dead, and Siddons at a distance, and some compensation

sation must be had; can any thing afford it except the statues of Rome, and the pictures of Bologna? here are a vast many from thence in this magnificent gallery.

We had a concert made on purpose for us last night by some amiable friends: it was a very good one. What I liked best though, was Mr. Tricklir's new invention of keeping a harpsichord always in tune; and it seems to answer. I am no good mechanic, nor particularly fond of multiplying combinations; but the device of adding a thermometer to shew how much heat the strings will bear without relaxation seems ingenious enough: we had a vast many experiments made, and nobody could put the strings out of tune, or even break them, when his method was adopted; and it does not take up two minutes in the operation.

We have seen the Elector's treasures; and, as a Frenchman would express it, *C'est icy qu'on voit des beaux diamants**! The yellow brilliant ring is *unique* it seems, and valued at an enormous sum; the green one is larger, and set transparent; it is not green like an emerald, but pale and bright, and beyond

---

* Here's the place to see fine diamonds.

conception beautiful: hyacinths were new to me here, their glorious colour dazzles one; and here is a white diamond from the Great Mogul's empire, of unequalled perfection; besides an onyx large as a common dinner plate, well known to be first in the universe. What majestic treasures are these!—The sapphires and rubies beat those of Bavaria, but the Electress's pearls at Munich are unrivalled yet. Saxony is a very rich country in her own bosom it seems; the agates and jaspers produced here are excellent, nor are good amethysts wanting; the topazes are pale and sickly.

Nothing can be finer, or in its way more tasteful, than a chimney-piece made for the Elector, entirely from the manufacture and produce of his own dominions; that part which we should form of marble is white porcelane, with an exquisite bas-relief in the middle copied from the antique; its sides are set with Saxon gems, cameowise; and such carnelions much amaze one in so northern a latitude; the workmanship is beyond praise. —I asked the gentleman who shewed us the cabinet of natural history, why such richly-coloured minerals, and even precious stones, were found in these climates; while every

animal

animal product grows paler as it approaches the pole?—" Where phlogiston is frequent," replied he, " there is no danger of the tint being too lightly bestowed: our quantity of iron here in Saxony, gives purple to the amethysts you admire; and see here if the rainbow-stone of Labrador yields in glowing hue to the productions of Mexico or Malabar."—The specimens here however were not as valuable as the conversation of him who has the care of them; but a *plica Polonica* took much of my attention; the size and weight of it was enormous, its length four yards and a half; the person who was killed by its growth was a Polish lady of quality well known in King Augustus's court; it is a very strange and a very shocking thing!

Our library here is new and not eminently well stocked; but it is too cold weather now to stand long looking at rarities. The first Reformation bible published by Luther himself, with a portrait of the first Protestant Elector, is however too curious and interesting to be neglected; in frost and snow such sights might warm a heart well disposed to see the word of God disseminated, which had lain too long locked up by ignorance and interest tereft united. Here is a book too, which how it efcaped Pinelli I know not, a Venetian tranflation of the holy fcriptures *a Brucioli*, the date 1592. King Auguftus's maps pleafe one from their coftlinefs; the Elector has twelve volumes of them; every letter is gold, every city painted in miniature at the corners, while arms, trophies, &c. adorn the whole, to an incredible expence: they were engraved on purpofe for his ufe; and that no other Prince might ever have fuch again, he ordered the plates to be broke.

Sunday, December 17. I am juft now returned home from the Lutheran church of Nôtre Dame; where, though the communicants do not kneel down like us, it is odd to fay I never faw the facrament adminiftered with fuch folemnity and pomp. Four priefts ornamented with a large crofs on the back, a multitude of lighted tapers blazing round them, a uniformity in the drefs of all who received, and mufic played in a flat third fomehow very impreffively, as they moved round in a fort of proceffion, making a profound reverence to the altar when they paffed it, ftruck me extremely, who have been lately accuſtomed to ſee very little ceremony uſed on *ſuch* occaſions; and I well remember at Piſa in particular, that while we were looking about the church for curioſity, one poor woman knelt down juſt by us, and a prieſt coming out adminiſtered the ſacrament to her alone, the whole finiſhing in leſs than five minutes I am perſuaded. I ſaid to Mr. Seydelman, when we had returned home today, that the Saxons ſeemed to follow the firſt manner in reformation, our Anglicans the ſecond, and the Calviniſts the third: he underſtood my alluſion to the cant of connoiſſeurſhip.

The ſedan chairs here give the town a ſort of homeiſh look; I had not been carried in one ſince I left Genoa, and it is ſo comfortable this cold clear weather! A regular market too, though not a fine one, has an Engliſh air; and a ſaddle of mutton, or more properly a chine, was a ſight I had not contemplated for two years and a half. The Italians do call a cook *teologo*, out of ſport; but I think he would be the propereſt theologian in good earneſt, to tell why Catholics and Proteſtants ſhould not cut their meat alike at leaſt, if they cannot agree in other points.

This

This is the firſt town I have ſeen however, where the butchers divided their beaſts as we do.

The arſenal we have walked over delighted us but little: Saxons ſhould ſay to their ſwords, like Benvolio in the play, " *God ſend me no need of thee!*"—for the Emperor is on one ſide of them, and the King of Pruſſia on the other. This laſt is always mentioned as a pacific prince though; and the firſt has ſo much to do and to think of, I hope he will forget Dreſden, and ſuffer them to poſſeſs their fine territory and gems in perfect peace and quietneſs. One thing however was odd and pretty, and worth remarking, That at Rome there was an arſenal in the church—I mean belonging to it; and here there is a church in the arſenal.

The bombardment of this pretty town by their active neighbour Frederic; the ſweet Electreſs's death in conſequence of the perſonal mortifications ſhe received during that dreadful ſiege; the embarkation of the treaſures to ſend them ſafe away by water; and the various diſtreſſes ſuffered by this city in the time of that great war;—make much of our converſation, and that converſation is intereſt-ing.

ing. I only wonder they have so quickly recovered a blow struck so hard.

The gaiety and good-humour of the court are much desired by the Saxons, who have a most lofty notion of princes, and repeat all they say, and all that is said of them, with a most venerating affection. I see no national partiality to England however, as in many other parts of Europe, though our religions are so nearly allied: and here is a spirit of subordination beyond what I have yet been witness to—an aunt kissing the hand of her own niece (a baby not six years old), and calling her " *ma chere comtesse !*"—carried it as high I think as it can be carried.

The environs of Dresden are happily disposed, for though it is deep winter we have had scarcely any snow, and the horizon is very clear, so that one may be a tolerable judge of the prospects. Our river Elbe is truly majestic, and the great islands of ice floating down it have a fine appearance.

They do not double their sash-windows as at Vienna, but there is less wind to keep out. In every place people have a trick of lamenting, and there are two themes of lamentation universal for aught I see—the weather and the poor. I see no beggars here, and feel no rain,—but hear heavy complaints of both. Crying the hour in the night as at London pleased me much; why the ceremony is accompanied by the sound of a horn, nobody seems able to tell. The march of soldiers morning and night to music through the streets is likewise agreeable, and gives ideas of security; but driving great heavy waggons up and down, with two horses a-breast, like a chaise in England, and a postillion upon one of them, is very droll to look at. Ordinary fellows too in the Elector's livery (blue and yellow) would seem strange, but that as soon as Dover is left behind every man seems to belong to some other man, and no man to himself. The Emperor's livery is very handsome, but I do not admire *this*. A custom of fifteen or twenty grave-looking men, dressed like counsellors in Westminster Hall, with half a dozen boys in their company for *sopranos*, singing counterpoint under one's window, has an odd effect; they are confraternities of people I am told, who live in a sort of community together, are maintained by contributing friends, and taught mufic at their expence; fo in order to accomplifh themfelves, and fhew how well they are accomplifhed, this curious contrivance is adopted. Every Sunday we hear them again in the church belonging to the parifh that maintains them. A proceffion of bakers too is a droll oddity, but fhews that where there is much leifure for the common people, fome cheap amufement muft be found: two of thefe bakers fight at the corner of every ftreet for precedence, which by this means often changes hands; yet does not the conquered baker fhew any figns of fhame or depreffion, nor does the conteft laft long, or prove interefting. I fuppofe they have fettled all the battles beforehand: no meaning feemed to be annexed either by performers or fpectators to the fhow; we could make little diverfion out of it, but have no doubt of its being an old fuperftition.

On Chriftmas eve I went to Santa Sophia's church, and heard a famous preacher; his manner was energetic, and he kept an hourglafs by him, finifhing with ftrange abruptnefs the moment it was expired. This was in ufe use among our distant provinces as late as Gay's time; he mentions it in a line of his pastorals, and says—

He preach'd the hour-glass in her praise quite out; speaking of dead Blouzelind as I recollect. It now seems a strange *grossiereté*, but refinement follows hard upon the heels of reformation.

There is an agreeable fancy here, which one has always heard of, but never seen perhaps; the notion of calling together a dozen pretty children to receive presents upon Christmas eve. The custom is exceedingly amiable in itself, and gives beside a pleasing pretext for parents and relations to meet, and while away the time till supper in reciprocating caresses with their babies, and rejoicing in that species of happiness (the purest of all perhaps) which childhood alone can either receive or bestow. I was invited to an exhibition of this sort, and for some time saw little preparation for pleasure, except the sight of fourteen or fifteen well-dressed little creatures, all under the age of twelve I think, and more girls than boys: the company consisted of three or four and twenty people; all spoke French,

French, and I was directed to obferve how the young ones watched for the opening of a particular door; which however remained fhut fo long, that I forgot it again, and had begun to intereft myfelf in chat with my neareft neighbour (no mother of courfe), when the door flew wide, and the mafter of the houfe announced the hour of felicity, fhewing us an apartment gaily illuminated with coloured lamps; a fort of tree in grotto-work adorned the middle, and the prefents were arranged all round; dolls innumerable, varioufly adjufted; fine new clothes, fans, trinkets, work-bafkets, little efcritoires, purfes, pocket-books, toys, dancing-fhoes,—every thing. The children fkipped about, and capered with exultation;—" My own mama! my dear aunt! my fweet kind grandpapa!"—refounded wherever we turned our heads; I think it was the lovelieft little fhow imaginable, and am forry to know how defcription muft necefſarily wrong it: *les etrennes de Drefde* fhall however remain indelibly fixed in my memory. When the pretty dears had appropriated and arranged their prefents, cake and lemonade were brought to quiet their agitated

tated spirits, and all went home happy to bed. Their sparkling eyes and rosy cheeks served for our theme till supper-time; and I sat trying, but in vain, to find a reason why paternal affection appears so much warmer always in Protestant countries, and filial piety in those which remain firm to the church of Rome.

We returned home to our inn exceedingly well amused; the supper had been magnificent, and the preceding fast gave it additional relish. I now tremble with apprehension however lest the show of yesterday was too splendid: for if the mothers begin once to vie with each other whose gifts shall be grandest, or if once the friend at whose house the treat is prepared produces a more costly entertainment than his neighbours have hitherto contented themselves with giving, this innocent and even praiseworthy pastime will soon swell into expensive luxury, and burst from having been poisoned by the corroding touch of malice and of envy.

Our Saxons however seemed well-bred, airy, and agreeable in last night's hour of festivity; and could I have fancied their gaiety quite natural like that of Venice or Verona, I might

might perhaps have caught the sweet infection, and felt disposed to merriment myself; but much of this was studied mirth one saw, and pleasure upon principle, as in our own island; which, though more elegant, is less attractive. It is difficult to catch the contagion of artificial hilarity, and a celebrated surgeon once told me, that one might live with safety at Sutton-house among the inoculated patients, without ever taking the disorder, unless the operation were regularly performed upon one's self.

Well! we must shortly quit this very comfortable resting-place, and leave a town more like our own than any I have yet seen; where, however, the dresses, of ordinary women I mean, are extraordinary enough, each when she is made up for show wearing a rich old-fashioned brocade cloke lined with green lutestring, and edged round with narrow fur. This is universal. Her neat black love-hood however is not so ugly as the man's bright yellow brass comb, stuck regularly in all their heads of long straight hair who are not people of fashion; and no powder is ever used among the Lutherans here in Saxony I see, except by gentlemen and ladies, who often

take

take all *theirs* out when they go to church, from fome odd principle of devotion. It is very pretty though to fee the little clean-faced lads and wenches running to fchool fo in a morning at every proteftant town, with the grammar and teftament under their arm, while every the meaneft houfe has a folio bible in it, and all the people of the loweft ranks can read it.

On this 1ft of January 1787, I may boaft of having vifited lord Peter, Jack, and Martin, all in the courfe of one day. Hearing Monf. Dumarre preach to the French Huguenots in the morning, attending the eftablifhed church at Notre Dame at noon, and going to the Elector's truly-magnificent place of worfhip at night, where Haffe's Te Deum was fung, and executed with prodigious regularity and pomp, over againft an altar decorated with well-employed fplendour, exhibiting zeal for God's houfe, animated by elegant tafte, and encouraged by royal prefence;

> While from the cenfer clouds of fragrance roll,
> And fwelling organs lift the rifing foul.

I studied then to keep my mind, I hope I kept it free from narrow and from vulgar prejudice, desirous only of seeing the three principal sects of Christians adoring their Redeemer, each in the way they think most likely to please him; nor will I mention which method had the most immediate effect on *me*; but this I saw, that beneath

> Such plain roofs as piety could raise,
> Made vocal only by our maker's praise,

Monsieur Dumarre produced from his peaceful auditors more tears of gratitude and tenderness in true remembrance of the sacred season, than were shed at either of the other churches. Indeed the sublime and pathetic simplicity of the place, the truly-touching rhetoric of the preacher, his story a sad one; while his persecuted family were forced to fly their native country, driven thence by the rigour of Romish severity, and his life exactly corresponding to the purity of that doctrine he teaches: his tones of voice, his tranquillity of manners,

> His plainness moves men more than eloquence,
> And to his flock, joy be the consequence!

The

The eſtabliſhed ſect here—*Lutheraniſm*, keeps almoſt the exact medium between the other two, though their places of worſhip ſtrike me as ſomething more theatrical than one could wiſh; very ſtately they are certainly, and very impoſing. As few people however are fond of a middle ſtate, as here is prodigious encouragement given by the court to Romaniſts, and full toleration from the ſtate to the diſciples of John Calvin, I wonder more members of the national church do not quit her communion for that of one of theſe chapels, which however owe their very exiſtence in Saxony to that truly chriſtian and catholick ſpirit of toleration, poſſeſſed by Martin alone.

We have recovered ourſelves now from all fatigues; our coach and our ſpirits are once more repaired, and ready to ſet out for

BERLIN.

BERLIN.

The road hither is all a heavy sand, cut through vast forests of ever-green timber, but not beautiful like those of Bavaria, rather tedious, flat, and tristful: to encrease which sensations, and make them more grievous to us, our servants complained bitterly of the last long frosty night, which we spent wholly in the carriage till it brought us here, where the man of the house, a bad one enough indeed, speaks as good English as I do, and has lived long in London. I am not much enchanted with this place however. Dean Swift said, that a good style was only proper words in proper places; and if a good city is to be judged of in the same way, perhaps Berlin may obtain the first place, which one would not on an immediate glance think it likely to deserve; as a mere residence however, it will be difficult to find a finer.

He who sighs for the happy union of situation, climate, fertility, and grandeur, will
think

think *Genoa* transcends all that even a warm imagination can wish. If with a very, very little less degree of positive beauty, he feels himself chiefly affected by a number of Nature's most interesting features, finely, and even philosophically arranged; *Naples* is the town that can afford him most matter both of solemn and pleasing speculation.

If ruins of pristine splendour, solid proofs of universal dominion, *once*, nay *twice* enjoyed: with the view of temporal power crushed by its own weight, solicits his curiosity.—It will be amply gratified at *Rome*; where all that modern magnificence can perform, is added to all that ancient empire has left behind. Romantic ideas of Armida's palace, fancied scenes of perennial pleasure, and magical images of ever varying delight, will be best realized at smiling *Venice* of any place; but if a city may be called perfect in proportion to its external convenience, if making many houses to hold many people, keeping infection away by cleanliness, and ensuring security against fire by a nice separation of almost every building from almost every other; if uniformity of appearance can compensate for elegance

gance of architecture, and space make amends for beauty, *Berlin* certainly deserves to be seen, and he who planned it, to be highly commended. The whole looks at its worst now; all the churches are in mourning, so are the coaches: no theatre is open, and no music heard, except now and then a melancholy German organ droning its dull round of tunes under one's window, without even the London accompaniment of a hoarse voice crying *Woolflect oysters*. Come! Berlin can boast an arsenal capable of containing arms for two hundred and fifty thousand men. The contempt of decoration for a place destined to real use seemed respectable in itself, and characteristic of its founder. No columns of guns or capitals of pistols, neatly placed, are to be seen here. A vast, large, clean, cold-looking room, with swords and muskets laid up only that they may be taken down, is all one has to look at in Frederick's preparations for attack or defence.

In accumulation of ornaments one hopes to find elegance, and in rejection of superfluity there is dignity of sentiment; but nothing can excuse a sovereign prince for keeping as curiosities

riofities worthy a traveller's attention, a heap of trumpery fit to furnifh out the fhop of a Weftminfter pawnbroker. Our cabinet of rarities here is literally no better than twenty old country gentlemen's feats, fituated in the diftant provinces of England, fhew to the fervants of a neighbouring family upon a Chriftmas vifit, when the houfekeeper is in good humour, and, gently wiping the duft off my *late lady's mother's* amber-boxes, produces forth the wax figures of my lord John and my lord Robert when *babies*. For this pitiable exhibition, fhips cut in paper, and faints carved in wood, we paid half a guinea each; not gratuity to the perfon who has them in charge, but tax impofed by the government. Every houfe here is obliged to maintain fo many foldiers, excepting fuch and fuch only who have the word *free* written over their doors; here feem to be no people in the town almoft except foldiers though; fo they naturally command whatever is to be had. Moft nations begin and end with a *military* dominion, as red is commonly the firft and laft colour obtained by the chymift in his various experiments upon artificial tints. This ftate is

yet young, and many things in it not quite come to their full growth, so we must not be rigorous in our judgments. I have seen the library, in which we were for the first time shewn what is confidently *said* to be an Æthiopian manuscript, and such it certainly may be for aught I know. What interested me much more was our Tonson's *Cæsar*, a book remarkable for having been written by the first hero and general in the world perhaps, dedicated to the second, and possessed by the third. Here is an exceeding perfect collection of all Hogarth's prints.

This city appears to be a very wholesome one; the houses are not high to confine the air between them, or drive it forward in currents upon the principle of Paris or Vienna; the streets are few, but long, straight, and wide; ground has not been spared in its construction, which seems a most judicious one; and with this well-earned praise I am most willing to quit it. It is the first place of any consequence I have felt in a hurry to run away from; for till now there have been *some* attractions in every town; something that commanded veneration or invited fondness; something

thing pleasing in its society, or instructive in its history. It would however be sullen enough to feel no agreeable sensation in seeing this child of the present century come to age so: the tomb of its author is the object of our present curiosity, which will be gratified tomorrow.

>Ou sont ils donc, ces foudres de guerre,
>   Qui faisoient trembler l'univers?
>Ils ne sont plus qu'un peu de terre,
>   Restes, qu'ont epargnis les vers*.

---

* What are they after all their pains,
    These thunderbolts of war?
Mere caput mortuum that remains
    Which worms vouchsafe to spare.

POTZDAM.

AND now, if Berlin wants taſte and magnificence, here's Potzdam built on purpoſe, I believe, to ſhew that even with both a place may be very diſmal and very diſagreeable. The commoneſt buildings in this city look like the beſt ſide of Groſvenor-ſquare in London, or Queen's-ſquare at Bath. I have not ſeen a ſtreet ſo narrow as Oxford Road, but many here are much wider, with canals up the middle, and a row of trees planted on each ſide, a gravel walk near the water for foot paſſengers, inſtead of a *trottoir* by the ſide of the houſes. Every dwelling is ornamented to a degree of profuſion; but to one's queſtion of, " Who lives in theſe palaces?" one hears that they are all empty ſpace, or only occupied by goods never wanted, or corn there is nobody to feed with: this amazes one; and in fact here are no inhabitants of dignity at all proportioned to the reſidences provided for them; ſo that when one ſees the copies of antique

bas-

bas-reliefs, in no bad sculpture, decorating the doors whence dangle a shoulder of mutton, or a shoemaker's last, it either shocks one or makes one laugh, like the old Bartholomew trick of putting a baby's face upon an old man's shoulders, or sticking a king's crown upon a peasant's head.

The churches are very fine on the outside, but strangely plain within: that, however, where the royal body reposes looked solemn and stately in its mourning dress. Black velvet, with silver fringe and tassels very rich and heavy, hung over the pulpit, family seat, &c. and every thing struck one with an air of melancholy dignity. The king of Prussia's corpse, no longer animated by ambition, rests quietly in an unornamented solid silver coffin, placed in a sort of closet above ground, the door to which opens close to the pulpit's feet, and shews the narrow space which now holds his body, beside that of his father, and the great elector, as he is still justly called.

My sepulchral tour is now nearly finished: we have in the course of this journey seen the last remains of many a celebrated mortal. Virgil, Raphael, Ariosto, Scipio, Galileo, Petrarch, Carlo Borromeo, and the king of Prussia.

Pruffia. How different each from other in his life! How like each other now! But

> Tous ces morts ont vecu; toi qui lis—tu mourras:
> L'inftant fatal approche, et tu n'y penfe pas*.

I could have wifhed before my return to have paufed a moment on the tomb of Melancthon, who might be faid to have united in himfelf *their* feparate perfections. Courage, genius, moderation, piety! perfevering fteadinefs in the right way himfelf; candid acknowledgment of merit, even in his enemies, where he faw their intentions right, though he thought their tenets and their conduct wrong. But we are removed far from the dwelling of the *peacemaker*; let us at leaft look at the palace, now we have examined the coffin of him whofe ftudy and delight was *war*.

Sans Souci is furely an elegantly chofen fpot, its architecture excellent, its furniture rich yet delicate, the gardens very happily difpofed, the profpect from its windows agreeable, the pictures within an admirable collec-

---

* All thefe have liv'd; ye too who read muft die:
Hafte and be wife, the fateful minutes fly.

tion. A hall built in imitation of the Colonna gallery shews Frederick's taste at once and liberal spirit: the front seems borrowed from something at St. Peter's; all is beautiful; the gilding of his long-room makes a very sudden and strong effect, nor are marbles of immense value wanting; here is a specimen of every thing I think, and two agate tables of prodigious size and beauty. The Silesian chrysopaz, and Carolina marble of a bright scarlet colour, quite luminous like the feathers of a fighting cock, struck me with their singular and splendid appearance. Rubens's merit was not new to me, I hope; yet here is a resurrection of Lazarus, in which he has been lavish of it. The composition of this picture seems to have been intended to surpass every thing put together by other artists: its colouring glows like life.

The king's town-house, however, is finer far than this his villa was designed to be; but I grew very tired walking over it: when one has dragged through twenty-four rooms variously hung with pink and silver, green and gold, &c. one grows cruelly weary with repeating the same ideas by drawling through forty-eight more.

I wished

I wiſhed to ſee his own private living apartments, and to mind with what books and pictures he adorned the dreſſing-room he always ſate in: the firſt were chiefly works of Voltaire and Metaſtaſio—the laſt were ſmall landſcapes of Albano and Watteau. At our deſire they ſhewed us the little bed he ſlept, the chairs he ſate in familiarly. Suetonius in French and Italian was the laſt author he looked into; they have made a mark at the death of Auguſtus, where he was reading when the ſame viſitant called on him, quite unexpected by himſelf it ſeems, though all his attendants were well aware of his approach. As he expired he ſaid, *I give you a vaſt deal of trouble.* We ſaw the ſpot he ſate in at the moment; for Frederick no more died in his bed, than did the famous Flavius Veſpaſian; his ſervants wept as they repeated the particulars, careſſing while they ſpoke his favourite dogs, one of which, a terrier, could hardly be prevailed upon to quit the body. It uſed to amuſe the king to ſee them frighted when he would take them to a long room lined with French mirrors, which he did now and then to laugh at the effect.

Every

Every thing at Potzdam ſhews a man in haſte to enjoy what he had laboured ſo hard to procure; nor did he ever refuſe himſelf, they ſay, any gratification that could make age leſs weariſome, or illneſs leſs afflictive. He had much taſte of Engliſh ingenuity—combinations of convenience, and improvements in mechaniſm: his own writing-table, however, was contrived by himſelf; it ſtands on four legs, one pair longer than the other to make it ſlope; the covering is green velvet, with a ſquare hole for the ſtandiſh to drop in and not ſpill the ink: I liked the device exceedingly, but wondered he thought any device worth his preference. His converſation to his ſervants was affable and even gay; they loved his perſon, it is plain, and half adore his memory.

Such were the manners then, and ſuch the death, of the far-famed philoſopher of Sans Souci! And in truth, when he had ſo often ſet all preſent and future happineſs to hazard, it would have been inconſiſtent not to haſten the enjoyment: nobody comes to inhabit his fine town, however, which has much the look of buildings in a ſtage perſpective. Soldiers only, and ſuch as ſell wares neceſſary to ſoldiers,

diers, were all the human creatures I could see here; nor are families, or travellers of any sort indeed, better accommodated here than at inns of less pompous appearance on the outside.

For accommodations, however, I care but little; I have now walked over the oldest and the youngest cities in all Europe, and have left each with sincere admiration of their contents. Both are full of buildings and empty of inhabitants, nor am I desirous to add to the number in either. I was going to step forward into some room of the palace yesterday—" Madam, come back this instant," exclaimed our Cicerone; " if that chamber is entered, my head will be off my shoulders in three days time." Another well attested anecdote may be worth relating: A gentleman with whom we passed an agreeable evening at Berlin, whose lady invited to meet us whatever was most charming in the town, told the following story of a soldier who, being desirous of his body's dissolution, but fearful of his soul's rushing unprepared into eternity, caught and murdered a six months old baby; giving this strange account of his own feelings on the occasion, and adding, that he did not like

like to kill an adult, left his own impatience of life's infupportable torment might by that means precipitate his neighbour to perdition; but that a baptized infant would be fure of heaven, and he himfelf fhould gain time to prepare for following it—"And, Lord!" faid my informer, "what reafoners this world has in it!" The foldier was hanged fix weeks after the dreadful crime was committed; he made a very decent and penitential end.

On fuch facts what obfervations or reflections can refult? I made none, but gave God thanks that I was born a fubject of Great Britain.

POTZDAM TO HANOVER.

On the 13th of January 1787 then we quitted Potzdam, ftrongly impreffed by the beauties of a town apparently fabricated by a modern Cadmus, who, when all the foldiers that he could *raife* were fallen in *battle* for his amufement, retired with the five that were left, and built a fine city!

Branden-

Brandenbourg was our next refting place, and feemed to me to merit a longer ftay in it; I faw an old Runick figure in the ftreet, its fize coloffal, and its compofition feemed black bafalt; but of this I could obtain no account for want of language, our ftill recurring torment.—This place feems fuller of inhabitants than the laft; but it is *fo* melancholy to have no compenfation for the fatigues of a tedious journey! and in thefe countries information cannot be procured for travellers that do not mean to refide, prefent letters, &c.; which tafk we have at this feafon little tafte to renew.

Magdebourg makes a refpectable appearance at a diftance, from the loftinefs of its turrets; one fees them at leaft four long hours before the roads which lead to it permit one's approach; and the towers feem to retire before one, like Ulyffes's fictitious country raifed to deceive him. Never was I fo weary in my life as when we entered Magdebourg, where, inftead of going out to fee fights as ufual, I defired nothing fo fincerely as a hot fupper and foft bed, which the inns of Germany never fail to afford us in even elegant perfection.

Our

Our linen too, so beautifully, and I will add so unnecessarily fine! The king of Naples probably never saw such sheets and table-cloths as we have been comforted with here, not only at Dresden, but every post since.

Magdebourg seems to have almost all its streets united by bridges; the Elbe divides there into so many branches, and none of them small.

Helmstadt is a little place which affords few images to the mind, and Brunswick to mere passengers, as we were, seemed to yield none but sad ones. The houses all of wood, even to prince Ferdinand's palace, and painted of a dull olive colour with heavy pensile roofs, giving the town a melancholy look; but we met with young Englishmen who commended the society, and said no place could be gayer than Brunswick. This is among the reports one wishes to be true, and we are led the more willingly to believe them.

Another delight which I enjoyed at this city was, to find that every body in it, and every body passing through it, adored the duchess, whose partial fondness, and tender remembrance of her native country, justly

endears

endears her name to every subject of Great Britain. Her chapel is pretty; the garden, where they said she always walked two hours every day, put me in mind of Gray's-Inn walks twenty or thirty years ago; they were then very like it.

From these scenes of solitude without retirement, and of age without antiquity, I was willing enough to be gone; but they would shew me one curiosity they said, as I seemed to feel particular pleasure in speaking of their charming duchess. We followed, and were shewn *her coffin!* all in silver, finely carved, chased, engraved, what you will. " Before she is dead!" exclaimed I—" Before she was even married, madam," replied our Cicerone; " it is the very finest ever made in Brunswick; we had it ready for her against she came home to us, and you see the plate left vacant for her age." I was glad to drive forward now, and slept at Peina; which, though in itself a miserable place, exhibits one consolatory sight for a Christian—the sight of toleration. Here Romanists, Lutherans, and Calvinists, live all affectionately and quietly together, under the protection of the bishop of Paderborne; and here I first saw the king of England's

land's livery upon the king of England's servants since I left home—"And if they *are* ragged youngsters who wear it," said I, "they are my fellow-subjects, and glad am I to see them!"

The villages and churches hereabouts resemble those of Merionethshire, only that not a mountain rears its head at all—one vast, wide, barren flat, through which roads that no weather can render better than barely passable brought us at length to Hanover, which stands, as all these cities do in the north of Germany, upon an immense plain, with a thick wood of noble timber trees breaking from time to time the almost boundless void, and relieving the eye, which is fatigued by extent without any object to repose upon, in a manner I can with difficulty comprehend, much less explain; but the sight of a passing waggon, or distant spire, is a felicity seldom found, though continually sought by me, while travelling through these wide wasted countries, where no idea is afforded to the imagination, no image remitted to the mind, but that of two armies encountering each other, to dispute the plunder of some place already unable to feed its few inhabitants.

The

The horses however are exceedingly beautiful; we were offered a pair of very fine ones for only forty pounds. They would have run such hazards getting home! "There are two ways to chuse out of," said I; " if we purchase them, we shall repent on it every day till we arrive in London; if we do not, we shall repent on it every day after we get there." Such is life! we did not buy the cattle.

The cleanliness of the windows, the manner of paving and lighting the streets at Hanover, put us in mind a little of some country towns in the remoter provinces of England; and there seems to be likewise a little glimpse of British manners, dress, &c. breaking through the common and natural fashions of the country. This was very pleasing to us, but I wished the place grander; I do not very well know why, but we had long counted on comforts here as at home, and I had formed expectations of something much more magnificent than we found; though the Duke of York's residence does give the town an air of cheerfulness it scarce could shew without that advantage; and here are concerts and balls, and efforts at being gay, which may probably succeed sometime. How did all the

the talk however, and all the pamphlets, and all the lamentations made by old King George's new subjects, rush into my mind, when I recollected the loud, illiberal, and indecent clamours made from the year 1720 to the year 1750, at least till the alarm given by the Rebellion began to operate, and open people's eyes to the virtues of the reigning family! for till then, no topic had so completely engrossed both press and conversation, as the misfortunes accruing to *poor* old England, from their King's desire of enriching his Electoral dominions, and feeding his favourite Hanoverians with their good guineas, making fat the objects of his partial tenderness with their best treasures—in good time! Such groundless charges remind one of a story the famous French wit Monsieur de Menage tells of his mother and her maid, who, having wasted or sold a pound of butter, laid the theft upon the *cat*, persisting so violently that it had been all devoured by the rapacious favourite, that Madame de Menage said, " It's very well; we will weigh the cat, poor thing! and know the truth:" The scales were produced, but puss could be found to weigh only *three quarters*, after all her depredations.

From HANOVER to BRUSSELS.

TRAVELLING night and day through the most dismal country I ever yet beheld, brought us at length to Munster, where we had a good inn again, and talked English. Well may all our writers agree in celebrating the miseries of Westphalia! well may they, while the wretched inhabitants, uniting poverty with pride, live on their hogs, with their hogs, and like their hogs, in mud-walled cottages, a dozen of which together is called by courtesy a village, surrounded by black heaths, and wild uncultivated plains, over which the unresisted wind sweeps with a velocity I never yet was witness to, and now and then, exasperated perhaps by solitude, returns upon itself in eddies terrible to look on. Well, the woes of mortal man are chiefly his own fault; war and ambition have depopulated the country, which otherwise need not I believe be poor, as here is capability enough, and the weather,

though

though stormy, is not otherwise particularly disagreeable. January is no mild month any where; even Naples, so proverbially delicious, is noisy enough with thunder and lightning; and the torrents of rain which often fall at this season at Rome and Florence, make them unpleasing enough. Nor do I believe that the *very* few people one finds here are of a lazy disposition at all; but it is so seldom that one meets with the *human face divine* in this Western side of Germany, that one scarce knows what they are, but by report.

The town of Munster is catholic I see; their cathedral heavily and clumsily adorned, like the old Lutheran church called Santa Sophia at Dresden. One pair of their silver candlesticks however are eight feet high, and exhibit more solidity than elegance. They told us something about the *three kings*, who must have lost their way amazingly if ever they wandered into Westphalia, and deserved to lose their name of *wise men* too, I think. We were likewise shewn the sword worn by St. Paul, they told us, and a backgammon table preserved behind the high altar, I could not for my life find out why; at first our interpreter told us, that the man said it had belonged to *John the Baptist*, but on further enquiry we understood him that it was once used by some Anabaptists; as that seemed no less wild a reason for keeping it there, than the other seemed as an account of its original, we came away uninformed.

Of the reason why Hams are better here than in any other part of Europe, it was not so difficult to obtain the knowledge, and the inquiry was much more useful.

Poor people here burn a vast quantity of very fine old oak in their cottages, which, having no chimney, detain the smoke a long time before it makes its escape out at the door. This smoke gives the peculiar flavour to that bacon which hangs from the roof, already fat with the produce of the same tree growing about these districts in a plenty not to be believed. Indeed the sole decoration of this devasted country is the large quantity of majestic timber trees, almost all oak, living to such an age, and spreading their broad arms with such venerable dignity, that it is *they* who appear the ancient possessors of the land, who, in the true style of Gothic supremacy,

suck

suck all the nutriment of it to themselves, only shaking off a few acorns to content the immediate hunger of the animal race, which here seems in a state of great degeneracy indeed, compared to those haughty vegetables.

This day I saw a fryar; the first that has crossed my sight since we left the town of Munich in Bavaria. On the road to Dusseldorp one sees the country mend at every step; but even *I* can perceive the language harsher, the further one is removed from Hanover on either side: for Hanover, as Madame de Bianconi told me at Dresden, is the Florence of Germany; and the tongue spoken at that town is supposed, and justly, the criterion of perfect *Teutsch*.

The gallery of paintings here shall delay us but two or three days; I am so very weary of living on the high roads of *Teuchland* all winter long! Gerard Dow's delightful mountebank ought, however, to have two of those days devoted to him, and here is the most capital Teniers which the world has to show. Jaques Jordaens never painted any thing so well as the feast in this gallery, where there are likewise some wonderful Sckalkens;

besides

befides Rembrandt's portrait of himfelf much out of repair, and old Franck's Seven Acts of Mercy varnifhed up, as well as the martyrdoms reprefenting fome of the perfecutions in early times of Chriftianity; thefe might be called the Seven Acts of Cruelty—a duplicate of the picture may be feen at Vienna. When one has mentioned the Vanderwerfs, which are all fifters, and the demi-divine Carlo Dolce in the window, reprefenting the infant Jefus with flowers, full of fweetnefs and innocent expreffion, it will be time to talk of the General Judgment, painted with aftonifhing hardihood by Rubens, and which we ftopt here chiefly to fee. The fecond Perfon of the Trinity is truly fublime, and formed upon an idea more worthy of him, at leaft more correfpondent to the general ideas than that in Cappella Seftini; where a beholder is tempted to think on Julius Cæfar fomehow, inftead of Jefus Chrift—a Conqueror, more than a Saviour of mankind.

St. Michael's figure is incomparable; thofe of Mofes and St. Peter happily imagined; the fpirit of compofition, the manner of grouping and colouring, the general effect of the whole, prodigious! I know not why he has fo fallen
below

below himself in the Madonna's character; perhaps not imitating Tintoret's lovely Virgin in Paradife, he has done worfe for fear of being fervile. Tintoret's idea of her is fo *very* poetical! but thofe who fhewed it me at Venice faid the drawing was borrowed from Guariento, I remember.

Who however except Rubens would have thought fo juftly, fo liberally, fo wifely, about the Negro drawn up to heaven by the angels? who ftill retains the old terreftrial character, fo far as to fhew a difpofition to laugh at *their* fituation who on earth tormented him. When all is faid, every body knows very well that Michael Angelo's picture on this fubject is by far the fineft; and that neither Rubens nor Tintoret ever pretended, or even hoped to be thought as great artifts as he: but though Dante is a fublimer poet than Taffo, and Milton a writer of more eminence than Pope, *thefe* laft will have readers, reciters, and quoters, while the others muft fit down contented with filent veneration and acknowledged fuperiority.

This day we faw the Rhine—what rivers thefe are! and what enormous inhabitants they do contain! a brace of bream, and eels of a magnitude

nitude and flavour very uncommon except in Germany, were our fupper here. But the manners begin I fee to fade away upon the borders; our foft feather beds are left behind; men too, fometimes fad, nafty, ill-looked fellows, come in one's room to fweep, &c. and light the fire in the ftove, which is now always made of lead, and the fumes are very offenfive; no more tight maids to be feen: but we fhall get good roads; at Liege, down in a dirty coal pit, the bad ones end I think; and that town may be faid to finifh all our difficulties. After paffing through our laft difagreeable refting-place then, one finds the manners take a tint of France, and begins to fee again what one has often feen before. The forefts too are fairly left behind, but neat agriculture, and comfortable cottages more than fupply their lofs. Broom, juniper, every Englifh fhrub, announce our proximity to Great Britain, while pots of mazerion in flower at the windows fhew that we are arrived in a country where fpring is welcomed with ceremony, as well as received with delight. The forwardnefs of the feafon is indeed furprifing; though it freezes at night now and then, the general feel of the air is very mild; willows
already

already give figns of refufcitation, while flights of yellowhammers, a bird never obferved in Italy I think, enliven the fields, and look as if they expected food and felicity to be near.

Louvaine would have been a place well worth ftopping at, they tell me; but we were in hafte to finifh our journey and arrive at

BRUSSELS.

Every ftep towards this comfortable city lies through a country too well known to need defcription, and too beautiful to be ever defcribed as it deferves. *Les Vues de Flandres* are bought by the Englifh, admired by the Italians, and even efteemed by the French, who like few things out of their own nation; but thefe places once belonged to Louis Quatorze, and the language has taken fuch root it will never more be eradicated. Here are very fine pictures in many private hands; Mr. Danot's collection does not want me to celebrate its merits; and here is a lovely park, and

and a pleasing coterie of English, and a very gay carnival as can be, people running about the streets in crowds; but their theatre is a vile one: after Italy, it will doubtless be difficult to find masques that can amuse, or theatres that can strike one. But never did nation possess a family more charming than that of *La Duchesse D'Arenberg*, who, graced with every accomplishment of mind and person, devotes her time and thoughts wholly to the amusement of her amiable consort, calling round them all which has any power of alleviating his distressful condemnation to perpetual darkness, from an accident upon a shooting party that cost him his sight about six or seven years ago. Mean time her arm always guides, her elegant conversation always soothes him; and either from *gaieté de cœur*, philosophical resolution to bear what heaven ordains without repining, or a kind desire of corresponding with the Duchess's intentions, he appears to lose no pleasure himself, nor power of pleasing others, by his misfortune; but dances, plays at cards, chats with his English friends, and listens delightedly (as who does not?) when charming Countess Cleri sings to the harpsichord's accompaniment,

with

with all Italian taſte, and all German execution. By the Duke D'Aremberg we were introduced to Prince Albert of Saxony, and the Princeſſe Gouvernante, whoſe reſemblance to her Imperial brother is very ſtriking; her hand however, ſo eminently beautiful, is to be kiſſed no more; the abolition of that ceremony has taken place in all the Emperor's family. The palace belonging to theſe princes is ſo entirely in the Engliſh taſte, with pleaſure grounds, ſhrubbery, lawn, and laid out water, that I thought myſelf at home, not becauſe of the polite attentions received, for thoſe I have found *abroad*, where no merits of mine could poſſibly have deſerved, nor no ſervices have purchaſed them. Spontaneous kindneſs, and friendſhip reſulting merely from that innate worth that loves to energize its own affections on an object which ſome circumſtances had caſually rendered intereſting, are the laſting comforts I have derived from a journey which has ſhewn me much variety, and impreſſed me with an eſteem of many characters I have been both the happier and the wiſer for having known. Such were the friends I left with regret, when, croſſing the Tyroleſe Alps, I ſent my laſt kind wiſhes back

back to the dear state of Venice in a sigh: such too were my emotions, when we took leave last night at Lady Torrington's; and resolving to quit Brussels to-morrow for Antwerp, determined to exchange the brilliant conversation of a *Boyle*, for the glowing pencil of a *Rubens*.

ANTWERP.

This is a dismal heavy looking town—so melancholy! the Scheld shut up! the grass growing in the streets! those streets so empty of inhabitants! and it was so famous once. *Atuatum nobile Brabantiæ opidum in ripâ Schaldis flu. Europæ nationibus maximè frequentatum. Sumptuosis tam privatis quam publicis nitet ædificiis**, say the not very old books of geography when speaking of this once stately city;

But trade's proud empire sweeps to swift decay,
As ocean heaves the labour'd mole away.
Goldsmith.

---

* Antwerp is a noble town of Brabant, situated on the banks of the Scheld; frequented by most of the nations in Europe, and sumptuous in its buildings both public and private.

And

And surely if the empire of Rome is actually fled away into air like a dream, the opulence of Antwerp may well crumble to earth like a clod. What defies time is genius; and of that, many and glorious proofs are yet left behind in this place. The composition of a picture painted to adorn the altar under which lies buried that which was mortal of its artist, is beyond all meaner praise. The figure of St. George might stand by that of Corregio, and suffer no diminution of one's esteem. The descent from the cross too!—Well! if Daniel de Volterra's is more elegantly pathetic, Rubens has put *his* pathos in a properer place.— The blessed Virgin Mary ought to be but the second figure certainly in a scene which represents our almighty Saviour himself completing the redemption of all mankind. But here is another devotional piece, highly poetical, almost dramatic, representing Christ descending in anger to consume a guilty world. The globe at a distance low beneath his feet, his pious mother prostrate before him, covering part of it with her robe, and deprecating the divine wrath in a most touching manner. St. Sebastian shewing his wounds with an air of the tenderest supplication; Carlo Borromæo beseeching

beseeching in heaven for those fellow-creatures he ceased not loving or serving while on earth; and St. Francis in the groupe, but surely ill-chosen; as he who left the world, and planned only his own salvation by retirement from its cares and temptations, would be unlikely enough to intreat for its longer continuance: his dress however, so favourable to painters, was the reason he was pitched upon I trust, as it affords a particularly happy contrast to the cardinal's robes of St. Carlo.

I will finish my reflections upon painting here, and apologize for their frequency only by confessing my fondness for the art; and my conviction, that had I said nothing of that art in a journey through Italy and Germany, where so much of every traveller's attention is led to mention it, I should have been justly blamed for affectation; while being censured for impertinence disgusts me less of the two. What I have learned from the Italians is a maxim more valuable than all my stock of connoisseurship: *Che c'è in tutto il suo bene, e il suo male*—that *there is much of evil and of good in every thing:* and the life of a traveller evinces the truth of that position perhaps more than

than any other. So perſuaded, we made a bold endeavour to croſs the Scheld; but the wind was ſo outrageouſly high, no boat was willing to venture till towards night: at that hour "*Unus, et hic audax*,*" as Leander ſays, offered his ſervice to convey us; but the paſſage of the Rhine had been ſo rough before, that I felt by no means diſpoſed to face danger again juſt at the cloſe of the battle.

When we find a diſpoſition to talk over our adventures, the great ice iſlands driving down *Rhenus ferox*, as Seneca juſtly calls it, and threatening to run againſt and deſtroy our awkward ill-contrived boat, may divert care over a winter's fire, ſome evening in England, by recollection of paſt perils. I thought it a dreadful one at the time; and have no taſte to renew a like ſcene for the ſake of croſſing the Scheld, and arriving a very few moments ſooner than returning through Bruſſels will bring us—*a la Place de*

* One—and he a bold one.

LILLE;

LILLE;

WHERE every thing appears to me to be juſt like England, at leaſt juſt by it; and in fact four and twenty hours would carry us thither with a fair wind: and now it really does feel as if the journey were over; and even in that ſenſation, though there is ſome pleaſure, there is ſome pain too;—the time and the places are paſt;—and I have only left to wiſh, that my improvements of the one, and my accounts of the others, were better; for though Mr. Sherlock comforts his followers with the kind aſſertion, That if a hundred men of parts travelled over Italy, and each made a ſeparate book of what *he* ſaw and obſerved, a hundred excellent compoſitions might be made, of which no two ſhould be alike, yet all new, all reſembling the original, and all admirable of their kind.—One's conſtantly-recurring fear is, leſt the readers ſhould cry out, with Juliet—

Yea, but all this did I know before!

How

How truly might they say so, did I mention the oddity (for oddity it still is) in this town of Lille, to see dogs drawing in carts as beasts of burden, and lying down in the market-place when their work is done, to gnaw the bones thrown them by their drivers: they are of mastiff race seemingly, crossed by the bull-dog, yet not quarrelsome at all. This is a very awkward and barbarous practice however, and, as far as I know, confined to this city; for in all others, people seem to have found out, that horses, asses, and oxen are the proper creatures to draw wheel carriages—except indeed at Vienna, where the streets are so very narrow, that the men resolve rather to be harnessed than run over.

How fine I thought these churches thirteen years ago, comes now thirteen times a-day into my head; they are not fine at all; but it was the first time I had ever crossed the channel, and I thought every thing a wonder, and fancied we were arrived at the world's end almost; so differently do the self-same places appear to the self-same people surrounded by different circumstances! I now feel as if we were at Canterbury. Was one to go to Egypt,

Egypt, the fight of Naples on the return home would probably afford a like fenfation of proximity: and I recollect, one of the gentlemen who had been with Admiral Anfon round the world told us, that when he came back as near as our Eaft India fettlements, he confidered the voyage as finifhed, and all his toils at an end—fo is my little book; and (if Italy may be confidered, upon Sherlock's principle, as a fort of academy-figure fet up for us all to draw from) my defign of it may have a chance to go in the portfolio with the reft, after its exhibition-day is over.

With regard to the general effect travelling has upon the human mind, it is different with different people. Brydone has obferved, that the magnetic needle lofes her habits upon the heights of Ætna, nor ever more regains her partiality for the *north*, till again newly touched by the loadftone: it is fo with many men who have lived long from home; they find, like Imogen,

> That there's living out of Britain;

and if they return to it after an abfence of feveral years, bring back with them an alienated

ated mind—this is not well. Others there are, who, being accustomed to live a considerable time in places where they have not the smallest intention to fix for ever, but on the contrary firmly resolve to leave *sometime*, learn to treat the world as a man treats his mistress, whom he likes well enough, but has no design to marry, and of course never provides for—this is not well neither. A third set gain the love of hurrying perpetually from place to place; living familiarly with all, but intimately with none; till confounding their own ideas (still undisclosed) of right and wrong, they learn to think virtue and vice ambulatory, as Browne says; profess that climate and constitution regulate men's actions, till they try to persuade their companions into a belief most welcome to themselves, that the will of God in one place is by no means his will in another; and most resemble in their whirling fancies a boy's top I once saw shewn by a professor who read us a lecture upon opticks; it was painted in regular stripes round like a narrow ribbon, red, blue, green, and yellow; we set it a-spinning by direction of our philosopher, who, whipping it merrily about, obtained as a general effect the total privation of all the four colours, so distinct at the beginning of its *tour;* —*it resembled a dirty white!*

With these reflexions and recollections we drove forward to Calais, where I left the following lines at our inn:

>Over mountains, rivers, vallies,
>Here are we return'd to Calais;
>After all their taunts and malice,
>Ent'ring safe the gates of Calais;
>While, constrain'd, our captain dallies,
>Waiting for a wind at Calais,
>Muse! prepare some sprightly sallies
>To divert *ennui* at Calais.
>Turkish ships, Venetian gallies,
>Have we seen since last at Calais;
>But tho' Hogarth (rogue who rallies!)
>Ridicules the French at Calais,
>We, who've walk'd o'er many a palace,
>Quite well content return to Calais;
>For, striking honestly the tallies,
>There's little choice 'twixt them and Calais.

It would have been graceless not to give these lines a companion on the other side the water, like Dean Swift's distich before and after he climbed Penmanmaur: these verses were therefore written, and I believe still remain, in an apartment of the Ship inn:

He

He whom fair winds have wafted over,
First hails his native land at Dover,
And doubts not but he shall discover
Pleasure in ev'ry path round Dover;
Envies the happy crows which hover
About old Shakespeare's cliff at Dover;
Nor once reflects that each young rover
Feels just the same, return'd to Dover.
From this fond dream he'll soon recover
When debts shall drive him back to Dover,
Hoping, though poor, to live in clover,
Once safely past the straits of Dover.
But he alone's his country's lover,
Who, absent long, returns to Dover,
And can by fair experience prove her
The best he has found since last at Dover.

THE END.

BOOKS printed for T. CADELL,
in the Strand.

LETTERS to and from the late Samuel Johnson, LL. D. To which are added, some Poems never before printed. Published from the original MSS. in her Possession. By Hester Lynch Piozzi. Two Vols. 8vo. 12s. in boards.

Mrs. Piozzi's Anecdotes of the late Dr. Johnson during the last Twenty Years of his Life, 4th Edition, 4s. in boards.

A Tour through Sicily and Malta. In a Series of Letters to William Beckford, Esq; of Somerly in Suffolk, from P. Brydone, F. R. S. 2 Vols. Illustrated with a Map. 3d Edition. 12s.

A View of Society and Manners in France, Switzerland, and Germany, with Anecdotes relating to some eminent Characters. By John Moore, M. D. 2 Vols. 3d Edition. 12s.

A View of Society and Manners in Italy, with Anecdotes relating to some eminent Characters. By John Moore, M. D. 2 Vols. 14s.

ZELUCO: Various Views of Human Nature, taken from Life and Manners, foreign and domestic. 2 Vols. 8vo. 12s. boards.

A Tour through some of the Northern Parts of Europe, particularly Copenhagen, Stockholm, and Petersburgh, in a Series of Letters. By N. Wraxall, jun. 3d Edition. 6s.

A Journey

BOOKS printed for T. CADELL.

A Journey to the Western Isles of Scotland. By the Author of the Rambler. 6s.

A Journey from Gibraltar to Malaga, with a View of the Garrison and its Environs, &c. &c. Illustrated with a View of each Municipal Town, and a Chart, &c. By Francis Carter, Esq; 2 Vols. with a great number of Plates. 2d Edition. 18s. in boards.

The History of England, from the Invasion of Julius Cæsar to the Revolution. A new Edition, printed on fine Paper, with many Corrections and Additions; and a complete Index. By David Hume, Esq; 8 Vols. Royal Paper. 4to. 7l. 7s.

*** Another Edition on small Paper. 4l. 10s.

The History of Scotland, during the Reign of Queen Mary and of King James VI. till his Accession to the Crown of England; with a Review of the Scottish History previous to that Period; and an Appendix, containing Original Papers. 2 Vols. 4to. By William Robertson, D. D. 5th Edition, 1l. 10s.

*** Another Edition in 2 Vols. 8vo. 14s.

The History of the Reign of the Emperor Charles V. with a View of the Progress of Society in Europe, from the Subversion of the Roman Empire to the Beginning of the Sixteenth Century. By William Robertson, D. D. embellished with 4 Plates, elegantly engraved. 3 Vols. 3l. 3s.

*** Another Edition in 4 Vols. 8vo. 1l. 4s.

The History of America, Vols. I. and II. By William Robertson, D. D. Illustrated with Maps. 2l. 2s.

*** Another Edition in 3 Vols. 8vo. 18s.

The History of Ancient Greece, its Colonies and Conquests; from the earliest Accounts, till the Division of of the Macedonian Empire in the East; including the History of Literature, Philosophy, and the Fine Arts. Adorned with a Head of the Author, and Maps adapted to the Work. 4 Vols. 1l. 8s.

The History of the Reign of Philip the Second, King of Spain. By Robert Watson, LL. D. Professor of Philosophy and Rhetoric at the University of St. Andrews. 2d Edition; 2 Vols. 2l. 2s.

⁎ Another Edition in 3 Vols. 8vo. 18s.

The History of the Decline and Fall of the Roman Empire. By Edward Gibbon, Esq; 6 Vols. which complete the original Design of the Author, and comprise the entire Series of History from the Age of Trajan and the Antonines, to the taking of Constantinople by the Turks, and the Establishment at Rome of the Dominion of the Popes. Adorned with a Head of the Author, and Maps adapted to the Work. 6l. 6s. Boards.

⁎ The 4th, 5th, and 6th Vols. may be had separate, to complete Sets, 3l. 3s. Boards.

An Historical View of the English Government, from the Settlement of the Saxons in Britain, to the Accession of the House of Stewart. By John Millar, Esq; Professor of Law in the University of Glasgow. 1l. 1s.

Miscellaneous State Papers, from 1501 to 1726, in 2 Vols. 4to. Collected from the Museum, Hardwicke, and other valuable Collections, 2l. 2s.

Memoirs of Great Britain and Ireland, from the Dissolution of the last Parliament of Charles II. till the Capture of the French and Spanish Fleets at Vigo. By Sir John Dalrymple, Bart. 2d Edit. 3 Vols. 3l. 1s.

Memoirs of the Marshal Duke of Berwick, written by himself, with a summary Continuation, from the Year 1716

BOOKS PRINTED FOR T. CADELL.

1716 to his Death in 1734; with explanatory Notes, and Original Letters relative to the Campaign in Flanders in 1708. 2 Vols. 12s.

The History of England, from the earliest Accounts of Time to the Death of George the Second, adorned with Heads elegantly engraved. By Dr. Goldsmith. 4 Vols. 1l. 4s.

An Abridgment of the above Book, by Dr. Goldsmith, adorned with Cuts, for the Use of Schools. 3s. 6d.

The Parliamentary or Constitutional History of England, from the earliest Times to the Restoration of King Charles II. Collected from the Records, the Rolls of Parliament, the Journals of both Houses, the public Libraries, original Manuscripts, scarce Speeches and Tracts. All compared with the several cotemporary Writers, and connected throughout with the History of the Times. With a good Index, by several Hands. 24 Vols. 8vo. 7l. 7s.

Grey's Debates, being a Continuation of the above. In 10 Vols. 3l. 3s.

Memoirs of the Duke of Sully, Prime Minister of Henry the Great. Containing the History of the Life and Reign of that Monarch, and his own Administration under him. Translated from the French. To which is added, the Trial of Ravaillac, for the Murder of Henry the Great. A new Edition. In 5 Vols. 8vo. 1l. 10s.

⁎ Another Edition, in 6 Vols. 12mo. 18s.

A Biographical History of England, from Egbert the Great to the Revolution: Consisting of Characters disposed in different Classes, and adapted to a Methodical Catalogue of engraved British Heads; interspersed with

variety

BOOKS PRINTED FOR T. CADELL.

variety of Anecdotes and Memoirs of a great Number of Perfons, not to be found in any other Biographical Works. 4 Vols. 1l. 4s.

The Lives of the moſt eminent Engliſh Poets; with Critical Obſervations on their Works. By Samuel Johnſon. 4 Vols. 1l. 4s.

An Eccleſiaſtical Hiſtory, Ancient and Modern, from the Birth of Chriſt to the beginning of the preſent Century. In which the Riſe, Progreſs, and Variations of Church Power are conſidered, in their Connection with the State of Learning and Philoſophy, and the Political Hiſtory of Europe, during that Period. By the late learned John Lawrence Moſheim, D. D. Tranſlated, and accompanied with Notes and Chronological Tables, by Archibald Maclaine, D. D. A new Edition, corrected and improved. 5 Vols. 1l. 10s.

An Hiſtorical and Claſſical Dictionary, containing the Lives and Characters of the moſt eminent and learned Perſons in every Age and Nation, from the earlieſt Period to the preſent Time. By John Noorthouck. 2 Vols. 12s.

A Philoſophical and Political Hiſtory of the Settlements and Trade of the Europeans in the Eaſt and Weſt Indies. Tranſlated from the French of the Abbé Raynall, by J. Juſtamond, M. A. A new Edition carefully reviſed, in 8 Vols. 8vo. and illuſtrated with Maps. 2l. 8s.

Sketches of the Hiſtory of Man, by the Author of the Elements of Criticiſm. 4 vols. 1l. 8s. 3d Edition.

An Account of the Voyages undertaken by Order of his preſent Majeſty for making Diſcoveries in the Southern Hemiſphere, and ſucceſſively performed by Commodore Byron, Capt. Wallis, and Capt. Carteret, in the Dolphin,

BOOKS PRINTED FOR T. CADELL.

Dolphin, and Swallow, and the Endeavour; drawn up from the Journals which were kept by the several Commanders, and from the Papers of Joseph Banks, Esq; and Dr. Solander. By John Hawkesworth, LL. D. Illustrated with Cuts and a great Variety of Charts and Maps (in all 52 Plates) relative to the Countries now first discovered, or hitherto but imperfectly known. Price 3l. 12s. bound.

An Account of a Voyage towards the South Pole, and round the World, performed in his Majesty's Ships the Resolution and Adventure, in the Years 1772, 1773, 1774, and 1775. Written by James Cook, Commander of the Resolution. In which is included, Captain Furneaux's Narrative of his Proceedings in the Adventure, during the Separation of the Ships. Elegantly printed in two Vols. Royal 4to. Illustrated with Maps and Charts, and a Variety of Portraits of Persons, and Views of Places, drawn during the Voyage by Mr. Hodges, and engraved by the most eminent Masters. 2l. 12s.

Travels into Poland, Russia, Sweden, and Denmark, interspersed with historical Relations and political Inquiries, illustrated with Maps and Engravings. By William Coxe, A. M. F. R. S. &c. 4 Vols. 1l. 10s.

An Account of the Russian Discoveries between Asia and America; to which are added, the Conquest of Siberia, and the History of the Transactions and Commerce between Russia and China. By William Coxe, A. M. Fellow of King's College, Cambridge. Illustrated with Charts, and a View of a Chinese Town. 3d Edit. 7s. 6d.

www.ingramcontent.com/pod-product-compliance
Lightning Source LLC
Chambersburg PA
CBHW030428300426
44112CB00009B/903